Unresolved Legibility

Published by Applied Research and Design
Publishing, an imprint of ORO Editions.
Gordon Goff: Publisher

www.appliedresearchanddesign.com
info@appliedresearchanddesign.com

Written and Illustrated by Clark Thenhaus
Edited by Ryan Roark
Graphic Design by Sean Yendrys
Project Manager Jake Anderson

10 9 8 7 6 5 4 3 2 1 First Edition

ISBN: 978-1-943532-39-1

Color Separations and Printing: ORO Group Ltd.
Printed in China.

AR+D Publishing makes a continuous effort
to minimize the overall carbon footprint of its
publications. As part of this goal, AR+D, in
association with Global ReLeaf, arranges to plant
trees to replace those used in the manufacturing
of the paper produced for its books. Global ReLeaf
is an international campaign run by American
Forests, one of the world's oldest nonprofit
conservation organizations. Global ReLeaf is
American Forests' education and action program
that helps individuals, organizations, agencies,
and corporations improve the local and global
environment by planting and caring for trees.

Unresolved Legibility *in Residential Types*

Clark Thenhaus

अ
ऱ
+d

APPLIED
RESEARCH
+DESIGN
PUBLISHING

To Mom and Dad, Nikki and Olive,
and Brian, Allison, and Reagan.

When I was in fourth grade my teacher's husband brought her flowers during class for their anniversary. As curious kids we were filled with questions, one of which was "what does he do?" Mrs. Kathka replied, "He's an architect." I didn't know what that was. I didn't recall having even heard the word. My mother was also a teacher at the school, and most days my older brother and I would hang around and play after school until she was done with work and go home with her instead of taking the bus. Having no idea what an architect was, I returned to my teacher's classroom after school and asked, "What does an architect do?" She replied, "He draws houses." I was so surprised; I replied with the unabashed excitement of a fourth-grader, "What!? I live in one of those!" That same evening when I got home I immediately began drawing houses. As it turned out, the house I lived in was not designed by an architect, nor were the other nine on the three-mile-long dirt road I grew up on. But in fourth grade the idea that someone could have drawn the house I lived in was enough to capture my imagination.

Some years later I discovered that my last name, Thenhaus, was adapted from Zehnhaus when my great grandparents on my dad's side immigrated from Germany. Zehn, meaning ten, and haus, meaning house, effectively translates to ten house(s). Several more years later I learned that Clark means "clerk or scholar" in Middle English. So, Clark Thenhuas translates to "clerk or scholar of ten houses."

Many years later, the house still captures my imagination.

An Introduction to
Unresolved Legibility in Residential Types

Legibility in architecture requires both visual clarity of a building's appearance such that its formal, spatial, and material compositions can be comprehended, as well as a certain clarity of its social, cultural, and political histories. While the term *legibility* carries a connotation of conclusiveness or objective qualifications, legibility in the context of architecture is most often inconclusive and unresolved. Such unresolved legibility is particularly salient in residential types.

Perhaps no genre of architecture has been written about more than the house—by architects and non-architects alike. As long-standing subjects of architectural discourse, cultural reflection, and experimentation, houses represent a confluence of disciplinary and extra-disciplinary phenomena. The house is not only susceptible to, but in fact requires, renewal and re-imagination; as an architectural type it reflects shifting architectural and cultural values and the constant reconstruction of meaning that this shifting entails.

In this book I have concentrated on ten residential types in order to distill a particular set of analytical and projective conceptualizations. However, these ten types can also be understood as surrogates through which the conceptual content and methods of their evaluation can be applied, abstracted, ahistoricized, or re-conceptualized for projective possibilities beyond the specificity of these ten residential types.

The ten residential types in this book reveal a story of American residential architecture in which social, cultural, and political histories are inextricable from architectural legibility. They are not lifted from the canon of architecture but rather from the familiarity of everyday experiences that include 1—the cabin, 2—the mountain house, 3—the farmhouse, 4—the Queen Anne, 5—the American Foursquare, 6—the ranch house, 7—the Federal-style, 8—the shotgun house, 9—the row house, and 10—mixed-use. These ten residential types, which figure prominently in the history of the residential architecture in America, invite open-ended readings and serve here as examples of the prevalence and the productive possibilities of unresolved legibility in architecture. I contend that the ten residential types in this book often appear so commonplace and ubiquitous that they are an under-examined source for architectural re-imaginations, re-interpretations, and disciplinary reflection. A wealth of specific details and variation has been overlooked in favor of a handful of canonical precedents. Furthermore, architects in the 21st century rarely design through the lens of residential types, as myriad other conceptual supports offer compelling alternatives for shaping architectural discourse, speculation, pedagogy, criticism, and practice.[1] Yet the house remains a centralizing source for architectural imagination spanning conceptual, practical, and contextual considerations as a continued site for (re)constructing identities, contemporaneity, and cultural questions.

One of the difficulties in approaching this book was the selection of the ten types. Most types herein are in fact subtypes of a principal type. For example, Victorian is a principal type encompassing the subtypes of Italianate, Second Empire, Stick, Queen Anne, Shingle Style, and Richardsonian Romanesque. For the purposes of this book, Queen Anne was selected because it tends to exhibit characteristics most often associated with Victorian houses. The same can be said of the one-room cabin as a subtype of Folk; of the Federal-style as a subtype of Colonial; and of the ranch house and the American Foursquare as subtypes of Modern. Others, such as the mountain house and farmhouse, are neither principal types nor subtypes, but rather are characterized by contextual circumstances. Relatedly, the row house, shotgun house, and mixed-use are types that evolved from urban imperatives.

Nearly all subtypes have their own subtypes that have been modified in contemporary culture through stylization. For example, the ranch house, itself a subtype of the Modern house, has sub-subtypes called *styled ranch houses*, including ranch houses in a Colonial ranch style or a French ranch style, and so on. In this book, however, the general reveals the particular. Rather than delving into sub-sub-subtypes, I examine the shared qualities among general subtypes to reveal specific patterns of unresolved legibility; in other words, this is not a guide book.[2]

In fact, these classifications are a product of contemporaneity. Prior to 1840, most single-family houses in America were highly specific to particular places and local cultures, creating a singular dominant residential type that remained relatively unchanged for long periods of time, sometimes with only in-kind variations. In 1842, Andrew Jackson Downing published one of the first pattern books for residential architecture in America, titled *Cottage Residences, Rural Architecture and Landscape Gardening*, focusing on Gothic and Italianate architecture. Rather than follow the book's stylistic patterns, the public usually found the most appealing elements from it and combined them without much regard for their stylistic appropriateness.[3] Pattern books sparked a combinatory affair that led to catalog, or kit, homes that could be purchased in full. Though catalog homes declined after a few decades, this combinatory approach increased, accelerating after 1940 and even more since the 1980s, as the American single-family house became a medley of mixed elements, forms, materials, colors, and organizations willfully biopsied from any variety of architectural styles and individual preferences.

For example, from the 1950s through the 1970s, ranch, minimal traditional, and split-level houses became so easy to repeat and were so fast to build that they became increasingly affordable for a growing middle class. Over the course of a relatively short period of time, roof types, dormers, windows, porches, columns, chimneys, materials, and even paint color hybridized previously distinct types and subtypes into something of a residential American mutt. While it can be argued that the origins of American single-family houses trace back to one of five principal types—Ancient Classical, Renaissance Classical, Medieval-style, Spanish influence, or Modernist—most houses today are hybridized combinations.[4] In fact, one of the defining qualities of the American single-family house is the appropriation of styles, elements, forms, materials, and organizations. Even the presumption of a 'typical' farmhouse is "a mixture of ingredients from the Old World [whose] style is somewhat Georgian, the posts holding up the porch roof are Greek revival, the louvers on the shutters come from colonial experience in Africa and the Caribbean, and the glossy dark green paint work from the Dutch."[5] The history of the single-family house in America reveals combinations of elements, forms, materials, scalar juxtapositions, awkward (a)symmetries, and manipulations to familiar elements that are at all times eclectic, often to the point of being overlooked for their ubiquity and prosaicness. In some cases the American culture of stylistic appropriation and banal eclecticism has been compounded by the emergence of Federal subsidies and community privatization with aesthetic regulations enforced by homeowners associations, covenants, master planning, and preservation codes which unknowingly solidify recombinant composition and appropriation as the norm.

When examined for compositional qualities, the single-family American house represents an unexpected and unassuming source of Mannerist tendencies that have been executed largely by non-avant-garde, everyday consumers, developers, architects, parts manufacturers, pattern books, and builders. In an art historical sense, a work of Mannerist art is composed with subtly strange compositions, postures, perspectives, elongations, poses, or scalar juxtapositions. In the case of painting, for example, the painter uses her mastery of technique to introduce unnatural poses, subtle elongations to limbs and torsos, strange scalar discrepancies between foreground and background, or spatial juxtapositions of familiar elements or subjects, with the effect of eliciting delight or curiosity in the mind of the viewer. The legibility and familiarity of the elements and forms in the final painting play a critical role in shifting the arc of perception in order to enroll audiences in the painting's becoming rather than to pictorialize an ideal state of perfection. In the case of the American single-family house, many of these same qualities have arisen not through masterful technique, but rather through the genericism of architecturally irreverent developers and homeowners. The resulting houses appear regressively prosaic to the vanguard architectural community, yet broadly appealing to populations with little to no architectural knowledge.

An examination of the 'prosaic' qualities found in the forms, elements, and organizations of these commonplace single-family American houses reveals strong and often surprising relationships between their formal and spatial qualities and broader cultural, social, political, and economic histories. These received histories and contingencies are embedded in architectural forms and cannot be ignored in an evaluation of their contemporary status or in any meaningful architectural re-reading of them. Therefore, this book's intention is not to produce a survey of prosaic oddities or to champion exuberant claims for quotidian architecture. Rather, the aim is to revisit the single-family house in its everyday state in order to offer re-readings that foster alternative disciplinary and public imaginaries. I raise the issue of seemingly banal or prosaic hybridizations here only to underscore the fact that to continue the discussion about the single-family American house is to be immersed already in a history of formal manipulations, scalar contrasts, material juxtapositions, and compositional transgressions largely accrued through non-disciplinary techniques, economic imperatives, and the tastes of broader cultures, developers, bureaucracies, and contractors. There is a certain freedom that this acknowledgment affords within the projective diagrams and conceptualizations found in each chapter.

Despite the peculiar histories and relationships between appropriated parts, elements, and styles, certain features still make distinctions between types legible. The first step in reading these distinctions is to analyze massing, followed by the composition of elements such as windows, doors, chimneys, porches, and materiality. Though primarily comprehended by the overall external address, which includes shape, bulk, height, width, and the distribution of elements, massing further involves specific internal organizations, programmatic allocations, and spatial distributions. These qualities permit distinctions between residential types even if their elements are stylistically varied. For example, a Federal-style house is legible as such even if its elements are not in kind because of its multi-storied five-bay, symmetrical massing with a central door punctuated by chimneys at each end or at the center of the house. The American Foursquare can be identified by its two-and-a-half-story cubic form, its central dormer on a hipped roof, and its raised entry fronted by a wide porch. A ranch house is distinguished by its low-lying roof, broad width, low-to-the-ground posture, and inconspicuous location of the front door. The farmhouse, typically laid out by women who were responsible for the management and operations of the house, derives its traditional massing primarily from the relationship of the kitchen to the dining room and from a desire for visual connection between the kitchen and the fields outside. Elements such as windows and doors, as well as materiality, add nuance and idiosyncrasy: they modify the underlying type. Even porches, turrets, and dormers that contribute to the massing of a whole are susceptible to biopsy as individual parts that introduce formal, spatial, and historical peculiarities.

Whereas massing conveys legibility of the whole and offers a means for distinguishing between types, elements are defining parts within the whole that contribute significantly to the house's outward address and register the contextual relationships of residential types. These differences both inflect and reflect cultural shifts, social attitudes, construction advancements, and architectural expression as inter-related influences. A re-reading based firstly on massing and elements in these ten residential types both reveals unresolved legibility among these houses and provokes projective re-imaginations of them. Each type or subtype is subject to interpretations rooted in a re-examination of its defining features, massing, elements, spatial organizations, façade compositions, tectonics, or contextual circumstances.

12

In elucidating relationships between context, formal analysis, and received histories, these ten types both reveal and contribute to a contemporary architectural discourse which does not divorce concerns traditionally understood as strictly disciplinary or extra-disciplinary; discourse about form, order, composition, and expression in the 21st century is broadly cultural, historic, contextual, and projective. Each chapter borrows from disciplinary scholarship and extra-disciplinary circumstances in order to construct analyses and interpretations that are simultaneously specific to the given residential type and relevant to broader architectural discourse. Ruminations on *character, context, frontality, the corner, differentiated systems, physiognomy, symmetry, thresholds, walls,* and *stacks* are conceptual springboards for interpreting and projecting forward alternative expressions in the ten residential types through the lens of unresolved legibility. Underscored by these disciplinary ruminations that link legibility in architecture to social, cultural, and political circumstances, each chapter involves the evaluation of legibility in form, space, and order through the biopsy of architectural elements, such as the porch, chimney, stair, window, roof, turret, front door, or façade. Because these elements reappear across various types as modified instantiations, they enable terms for collective comparison as well as idiosyncratic particularities that expand the lexicon used when assessing legibility in architecture generally, and in the house specifically.

The single-family house has long been a source for architectural imagination. It remains so today, and will continue to be so tomorrow because the house is unforgivingly intertwined with cultural customs, social transformations, personal expressions, politicized regulations, habits of contemporaneity, and disciplinary theorization. The house oscillates between its reality as a physical object susceptible to the effects of time, use, and popular taste and its representation as a pregnant form conceived by questions and speculations about what it means to dwell, to reside, or to domesticate. Because of this oscillation, houses accommodate explorations on formal, spatial, material, and representational expressions while being programmatically forgiving enough to accept almost innumerable possibilities in the organization of residential forms without sacrificing legibility as houses. Precisely because of their inherent familiarity, complexities, subjectivities, histories, and contradictions, houses enable architectural theories in ways that other architectural typologies simply do not.

Notes on Representation

You will often encounter what I call—inaccurately—"as-built" drawings. These are drawings of houses I have photographed, or in some cases from photographs taken by others. This series of drawings has been going on for years, long before the idea for a book occurred. Of course, they are not actually as-built drawings, which are properly the labor of a contractor for the purposes of noting changes to the construction drawings through the course of construction. I have appropriated the term for the purposes of drawing found conditions of built houses in their current state, as opposed to their intended conditions found in the architect's drawings or in plans and elevations found in catalogs or online. It would have been easier simply to put photographs in the book, and in some cases I have. But I'm better at drawing than photography. More importantly, I find that the abstract space of a drawing reveals qualities and compositions that photography sometimes causes to recede in buildings. The drawings in this book are black and white line drawings—a convention, like the residential types themselves, that may appear commonplace, even prosaic, within the contemporary context of architectural representation. However, their sobriety is intended to sharpen attention and to distill general conditions of these ten residential types into particular moments of unresolved legibility. If you prefer color—solid fill, gradients, spot-colors, blurred hues, whatever—many of the line drawings are ideal substrates for use as a coloring book or may be easily appropriated through the application of color.

The diagrams found in each chapter are intended to be both analytical and projective; they distill particular qualities, conditions, organizations, and forms to an analytical interpretation while suggesting terms and techniques for manipulation, abstraction, and ahistorical perversion. I have also included some of my own amateur photographs taken with a Droid Moto phone; here I have chosen to document the houses or landscapes in the way they are most commonly captured in mass culture. For these few photographs, cars get in the way, power lines cross through the scene, lens correction is non-existent, the lighting is suboptimal, and sometimes even the glare of my car window can be seen. I have not made them intentionally bad, but simply as they appear in my documentary travels. In a few instances I have solicited images from architects and professional photographers.[6]

This book is not a monograph. Yet, at the end of each chapter are images of proposals from my office, Endemic Architecture. In seven of the ten chapters, the project preceded the writing of the book, stemming from commissions, competitions, favors, critique, or simple curiosity. I see these as something of an incomplete appendix; they are not conclusions, nor are they intended as illustrations of the various diagrams or content found within each chapter. Instead, they are intended as open and projective representations that fit within the book without explicit explanation. They show that from familiar, perhaps even provincial, types we might discover other sources for architectural attention—that by seeking alternative expressions for familiar types, architecture can abstract conventions and pervert elements as calls for otherness at the margins of the everyday that allow us to see known things differently.

Introductory Conclusion

The following chapters are constructed in order to provoke alternative formal, spatial, material, and contextual possibilities that are both specific to each residential type as well as meaningful to broader architectural possibilities. The book slips in an abundance of terms, techniques, and diagrams within the re-reading of the ten residential types in order to reveal potential alternative expressions made possible by unresolved legibility in architecture. Much of what you are about to read may be debatable, even disagreeable to you. But, it should be explicitly noted that the very phrase *Unresolved Legibility* suggests that the conceptualizations herein remain unresolved, open, and inconclusive. Each chapter does not resolve or conclude lingering concerns about the house or the conceptual content around it. Instead, the residential types are read, inconclusively, to attract new modes of attention and spur imaginations both within the discipline and outside of it. There are obvious precedents to this book, but bear in mind that *Unresolved Legibility* is not an advocacy project for the quotidian, the everyday, or a longing nostalgia for generic residential types across the American landscape. Rather, this book proposes that unresolved legibility in architecture and its affiliated terms offer a historical, analytical, and projective source for shifting the arc of cultural, social, and political attention that welcomes the proliferation of alternative conceptualizations in contemporary architecture.

1
In 2018, I contributed two projects and an essay to the book *Possible Mediums*, authored and edited by Kelly Bair, Kristy Balliet, Adam Fure, and Kyle Miller with Courtney Coffman. The book outlines 16 mediums, or conceptual supports, found in today's architectural culture and points to the probability of many more.

Kelly Bair, Kristy Balliet, Adam Fure, and Kyle Miller, *Possible Mediums* (New York City: Actar, 2018).

2
For a comprehensive guidebook with a wealth of information see Virginia Savage McAlester's *A Field Guide to American Houses.*

Virginia Savage McAlester. *A Field Guide to American Houses.* (New York: Alfred Knopf, 1984).

3
McAlester, *Field Guide*, 14.

4
McAlester, *Field Guide*, 5.

5
David Larkin, *The Farmhouse Book: Tradition, Style, Experience* (New York: Universe Publishing, 2005), 10.

6
Thank you Bart Prince and Herb Greene for generously sharing images of built work for publication in this book. A special thank you also to the families of architect Charles Deaton and photo journalist Bud Lee for giving permission to publish images held in their family archives. Thank you also to professional photographers Rob Stephenson, Randy Calderone, and Brian Vanden Brink for permission to use their photographs in re-drawing some of the AS BUILT drawings, and to Dylan Krueger for your photographs.

15

Hatch and linetype index for all drawings in
Unresolved Legibility in Residential Types.

Character & Contradiction in Cabin Architecture

CHARACTER

1

The mental and moral qualities distinctive to an individual.

2

An architectural condition evoking a plurality of associations through formal, spatial, material, and contextual effects and which may arise from the individual interests or experiences of the architect.

Introduced to America by Swedish settlers in the 1630s along the current-day Delaware and Maryland tidewater, this residential type is first officially referenced in a court document from 1662 which mentions a "loged hows."[1] By the late 1600s cabins had become so numerous in the area that now comprises New Jersey, Pennsylvania, Delaware, and Maryland that William Penn believed them to be the indigenous style. In the 1700s, immigrants of German descent settled the Hudson Valley and Mohawk Valley, a region between the Adirondack and Catskill Mountains in current-day New York, and began incorporating German elements such as central fireplaces. The same was true of Norwegian influence as the cabin type moved westward. This midland log cabin seems to be the simplest of all houses: a one-room house constructed of stacked logs or framed walls with steep-gabled roofs and deep eaves in a squat, low-to-the-ground posture. The one-room cabin typically has a side-loaded chimney, historically averages a 16'-6" square footprint, and may be either side-gabled or front-gabled.

In an attempt to define houses in relation to their cultural geography, biological structuralist Edna Scofield remarked in 1936 that the one-room cabin represents the origin of a species, as there are species of houses, and that the one-room cabin was the point of origin for all other [American] houses in that it gave rise to a wide range of variations such as: the stack house, a one-room house with a second floor above; the dog-trot type, consisting of two spaces separated by an open area in the middle all under one roof; and the saddlebag, consisting of two spaces (one perhaps having originated as a side addition to a one-room cabin) separated by a chimney at the center.[2] The first known use of the term "log-cabin," distinct from "loged hows," can be traced to 1750.[3] Log cabins are historically made by stacking logs with saddle notches, whereas the log house uses square-hewn timber with hewn notching.

1
Side Entry

2
Gable Entry

3
Central Fireplace & Chimney

4
Side-Loaded Fireplace & Chimney

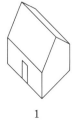  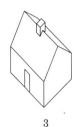 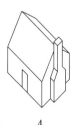

1   2   3   4

Cabin Character

Massing, materiality, and composition of elements such as windows, doors, and walls are characteristics of the cabin type. Character is something else. The origins of figural character—as opposed to literal character, which is the result of making markings to resemble objects or symbols of language—can be found in the lexicon of natural science, which used the term to describe the sorting of species by their differences. Before the mid-18th century, character in architecture was likewise a metric by which to measure deviations of a building from an "ideal" type. However, in the mid-1700s, changes in emphasis resulted in new means of classifying architecture based on a building's conveyance(s) and affects. This encouraged a consideration of an individual building's affective impressions and its "fit" within a larger collection of buildings.[4]

In 1745, an early scholar of architectural character by the name of Germaine Boffrand described character as the conveyance of a public building's interior function and use through its outward expressions. Boffrand suggested that buildings ought to convey specific moods, such as joy or sadness, as a relationship to the function of the building.[5]

Writing in the *Analyse de l'Arte* section of the *Cours d'Architecture* in 1771, Jacques-François Blondel described architectural character as a relation between the composition of a whole and the articulation of its parts. According to Blondel, this relationship affiliates with qualities such as male, light, pastoral, naïve, feminine, mysterious, grandiose, courageous, terrible, dwarf-like, frivolous, dissembling, ambiguous, vague, firm, virile, elegant, rustic, delicate, and many others.[6] Blondel claimed that these architectural associations could move human beings to contemplative inspiration.

Both Boffrand and Blondel used notions of physiognomy, the study of facial features, to develop their theories of character in architecture as expressions of passion emanating from the soul, and for Blondel this extended to include social status and rank as a relation to expression and function, eventually indexing cultural taxonomies: "[F]or example, a bulbous column base, replete with tori, might suggest the intemperate swellings of a decadent culture like Turkey, while a base with a gentle balance of fillets and cavetti alluded to the agreeable moderation of ancient Greece."[7]

Attempting to add clarity and precision to the topic of character in architecture, Quatremère de Quincy articulated three types of character in architecture—essential, relative, and distinctive—in his contribution to the *Encyclopédie Méthodique* of 1788, in which he noted that each of these types of character has a moral and a physical condition.[8] Relative character was principally concerned with conveyance of function or use through architectural form and expression, while distinctive character was concerned with the unique distinguishing features of individual buildings among the same type. De Quincy described essential character as the character type most conditioned by the influences of nature and most associated with strength and immensity in picturesque landscapes. He went on to state that buildings of presumably less developed societies more strongly convey an essential character than do those of more developed societies. De Quincy believed that artifacts of varying scales and uses—from buildings to pots—crafted by populations less connected to changes in civilization more easily received uninhibited influences from nature and tended more to register the qualities of their natural surroundings in their cultural objects, as compared to more advanced societies. De Quincy notably suggested that essential character could not be applied to a building through intellection, but was rather an intrinsic quality transferred to architecture through the culture that produced it.[9] In other words, essential character in architecture is encountered through an immediate and striking emotional sensation best perceived in elevational and contextual relationships, as opposed to the rational study of the plan or internal ordering. Furthermore, essential character was believed to be heightened by symmetrical compositions, fewer and smaller openings, expansive wall faces, heroic massing, and material uniformity.[10]

Despite differences among their work, it is logical to illustrate "character" through Étienne-Louis Boullée's and Claude-Nicolas Ledoux's work, given that the topic of character was introduced to the French academy through the teachings of Charles le Brun, Boffrand, and Blondel, whose students included Ledoux and Boullée. However, as a practicing architect, Ledoux had begun receiving commissions for new institutional types of public order in which he found Boffrand's and Blondel's systems of character misguided because they entrenched traditional conventions of known genres and expressions as "a proper framing for decorative program, [rather] than as a totalizing force that controlled the internal form and external expression of a building."[11] Furthermore, Ledoux favored the clarity of language over conveyance, stating that "[t]he character of the building should in no way be equivocal; the least knowledgeable spectator should be able to judge it."[12] In other words, for Ledoux, character ought to be singularly legible. Boullée favored an emotive response, which may naturally vary, stating that "the first sentiment we feel evidently stems from the way in which the object affects us. And I call 'character' the effects that results from this object and causes in us any impression whatever."[13] He believed in the power of nature to compel the senses and went on to claim that "[t]o embody character in a work is to use with efficacy all the means appropriate so as to make us feel any other sensations than those than should result from the subject."[14]

Historian and theorist Vittoria di Palma has remarked upon the aforementioned aspects of essential character in the context of Boullée's work, including his Cenotaph for Newton, which di Palma examines through the lens of Edmund Burke's writing about the artificial sublime. Burke described the artificial sublime as the transposition of sublime qualities found in nature (silence, immensity, vastness, contrasts in hue, etc.) to constructed images or objects, a process which produces an emotional state in a viewer, most often related to the effects of terror.[15] De Quincy himself never mentioned Boullée on the topic of essential character.[16] It is di Palma's contribution to examine the common affiliation of essential character with the artificial sublime and with the qualities found in Boullée's work, such as monumentality, contrasting tonalities, sobriety or somberness in mood, symmetry, strongly delineated profiles, geometric clarity, and material uniformity.

While de Quincy's theorization of essential character is often associated with a Boullée-like monumentality or a Ledoux-like institutionality, an alternative theory posits the isolated, diminutive one-room cabin as more closely affiliated with de Quincy's described qualities of essential character and perhaps also with Burke's artificial sublime. The cabin reflects influences derived from nature and impressed upon a cabin-dwelling culture; as such, it emanates notions of fortitude and individual power as terms associated with living in vast expanses of

hardly domesticated landscapes. In plan, the cabin does not manifest scholastic intellection but appears instead as a single room of geometric and functional uniformity. The cabin's most evocative effects are received *in situ*, seen elevationally or perspectively, typically exhibiting a symmetrical or near symmetrical principal façade with small openings contained within a legible whole of material consistency. The cabin is characterized by isolation and austerity that for many evokes a sober mood, and while its scale may not be heroic, its non-monumentality imbues the cabin with the power of an isolated event in a vast landscape. Perhaps we see Boullée—whose work coincided with the French Revolution and stood symbolically for intellectual reason, science, and rationality—as a protagonist for de Quincy's essential character because as a discipline architecture is predisposed to monumentality as a symbol of disciplinary power, especially when seen in the realm of public architecture aligned with societal or political revolution. The one-room cabin, however, provokes curiosity and peculiarity that is unique to isolated rooms within vast landscapes. It evokes impressions that are typically more primal than political, more provocative emotionally than rationally, and more sensorial in elevation or perspective (*in situ*) than in plan.

Cabin character is understood here primarily through the lens of de Quincy, whose scholarship remains an intriguing, though anachronistic, model for understanding character in contemporary culture. Essence, in particular, within contemporary architecture—and global culture—is undoubtedly slippery territory. In contemporary architecture, character has assumed alternative meanings and expressions often having less to do with conveyance of use, impression of a specific universal mood, physiognomy, or qualities distinguishing one thing from a collection of similar things. Today, character could be said to affiliate more closely with *dramatizing*—not in the sense of a theatrical performance, but in the sense of an aesthetic technique embedded in mediated culture that intertwines architectural form, experiences, representation, and imagery with social, contextual, political, and environmental content and that lures open, pluralistic associations rather than unequivocal impressions.[17]

Dramatizing is both a technique and an effect. As a technique, it fosters manipulations, abstractions, perversions or exaggerations to conventions, forms, and representations already animate in the world. As an effect, it elicits associations with pluralistic identities, contingencies, and constituencies through which new vocabularies are both applied and constructed. Dramatizing implies that there is no longer a prerequisite for stable monumentality, fixed canonization, or historic iconicity to affect or compel mass culture. Instead, the practice of dramatization assumes that collective, fleeting mediation, experience, and open associations hold the power of influence and garner the attention of myriad audiences. In one sense this moves toward the pluralization of architectural expressions in contemporary culture. However, it also spurs alternative methods of working and attitudes towards representation which tend to *professionalize, elementalize, personify, infantilize, animalize,* or *environmentalize* architecture by increasing ambiguity between meaning, expression, purpose, and audience.[18]

Architecture is *professionalized* when critical attention is drawn to mundane aspects of buildings, to their mediated state in an advertising economy, or to the instruments of service (documents) of architecture as a legal practice. This focus in attention affirms the existing architectural lexicon and its inherited conventions or procedures as it tends to resemble a conceptual art practice that works on its own mediums, techniques, and representation of otherwise common aspects of practice. This, however, does not necessarily mean disciplinary autonomy, but rather often develops previously unknown audiences outside of the field through its non-alienating appearances.

Architecture is *elementalized* when familiar elements—roofs, walls, windows, chimneys, etc.—are intentionally manipulated into similar forms or expressions without sacrificing legibility as the originating element. Elementalizing architecture often entails working in the context of the cultural heritage of a particular place populated by a collection of similar architectural forms or codes; it also entails a disciplinary desire to pervert familiar things into novel arrangements.

Architecture is *personified* by an underlying humanist impulse that relates the body to the built environment. Whether through technological interaction or socially active formalism, humanity is made legible following the desire for forms of collectivity and

social enterprise. Sometimes personification is literal, with buildings or work that appears in likeness to a human figure, whereas other times it is a collective experience of situations or appropriations to the built environment.

Infantilizing architecture is a disarming type of personifying architecture that imbues form, space, and material with a playful innocence and humorous undertones. Similarly, to *animalize* architecture is to affiliate form, space, and material with non-human peculiarities or primal figures. Alternately, animalizing architecture may also refer to a material science that imagines architecture as computationally derived from the animal and vegetal worlds.

Finally, architecture is *environmentalized* through the universalization and commodification of aestheticized systems associated with ecology, science, and material expression. This practice reflects both humanity's perils and its simultaneous faith that crisis can be overcome through the rational address of its cultural constructions, typically as a virtue of technology or science. A more compelling approach prioritizes aesthetics as a cultural practice of critique through environmentalism as a means of working between the physical materiality of architecture and environmental matter and representation.

The cabin can be seen as a conceptual support that highlights and modifies character and its dramatization in architecture. While form, composition, scale, ornament, and material are typically considered the hallmarks through which to evaluate, manipulate, or provoke character associations, the relationship to the ground further defines character. Whether an object submerges into or pushes away from the ground, whether the ground exerts pressure back onto the object deforming it, or whether the ground itself deforms around the object are meaningful in character analysis. Professionalized architecture tends to consider the ground as horizontally abstract, as an infinite plane upon which the profession's conventions and assumptions can be stationed. The ground and the table may be the same, but neither should be mistaken for an implied attitude of ontological flatness or stability within the profession itself; in fact, professionalizing character often highlights the instability and disparities

of practice and conventions. Elementalized architecture treats the ground as having a uniform orientation, thus providing a consistent datum against which to evaluate intentional deviations to familiar elements within a collection of legible buildings; elements assume a particular orientation—upright, tipped over, upside down, misplaced, or correctly located with respect to the ground. Personifying architecture tends to consider the ground as inherited and previously constructed, yet open to—even requiring—reconstruction; the ground contains particular histories of human habits and occupation that can be leveraged for social action, transformation, or projective collective experiences. Infantilizing architecture reveals the ground as a supple substrate in which the object receives the inverse pressure of the ground, becoming deformed against it; it is only with sufficient maturation of the object that the ground will begin to record its presence. Animalizing architecture tends to consider the ground as sufficiently stable to support the building's pushing away from

it. This pressure is often expressed through the use of legs or top-heavy masses, but objects may also exert downward pressure that deforms the ground. Environmentalizing architecture demands of the ground the qualities of solidity marked by human-made history, but only so as to illustrate its fragility; it is forever caught in a binary of peril and possibility. It is worth noting that these classifications relate most appropriately to work with strong figuration. For compositions or organizations such as piles, loose-fit aggregations, or scatter-plans, character associations often hinge on the qualities of spatial gaps and part-to-part relationships.

Almost Isomorphism in Logged Cabins and Their Mediated Spectacle

The cabin exhibits an in-the-round relationship with its physical context in which frontality manifests through intuition as a result of the basic impulse to give a front to a building through the

1.2

Plan of absolute isomorphism (interior and exterior surfaces are offsets of each other).

1.3

Plan: Crossed corners yield relative isomorphism (note: corners are draw as square hewn timber of equal width for purposes of clarity).

1.4

Plan: Absolute isomorphism occurs if the inside corners are constructed as offsets of the exterior plan profile.

1.5

Plan: Inverted isomorphism occurs if the implied negative square of the crossed corners inverts to the interior as a positive figure.

1.6

Plan: Mirrored isomorphism occurs if the implied complete square of the exterior crossed corners are mirrored to the interior.

1.7

Plan: Mirrored isomorphism also occurs if the crossed corners of the exterior are mirrored to the interior.

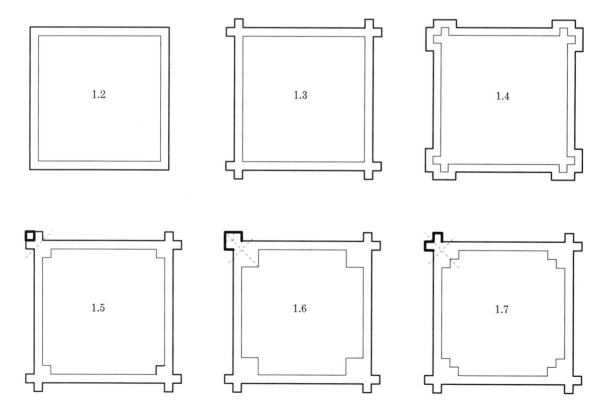

22

1.8
A stacked log cabin in cross section exhibits qualitatively similar, yet different interior and exterior contours due to the irregularity of individual logs in the stack.

1.9
Cross Section: Individually symmetrical logs per each wall create identical interior and exterior contours.

1.10
Cross Section: Using individually symmetrical logs in both walls creates identical interior and exterior contours with a symmetrical interior.

1.11
Cross Section: Offsetting the exterior profile of a stacked log wall outward creates a less crenelated surface.

1.12
Cross Section: Offsetting the interior profile of a stacked log wall outward creates a nearly uniform thickness with different interior and exterior contours.

1.13
Cross Section: Copying the exterior profile of a stacked log wall either inward or outward creates a condition of isomorphism.

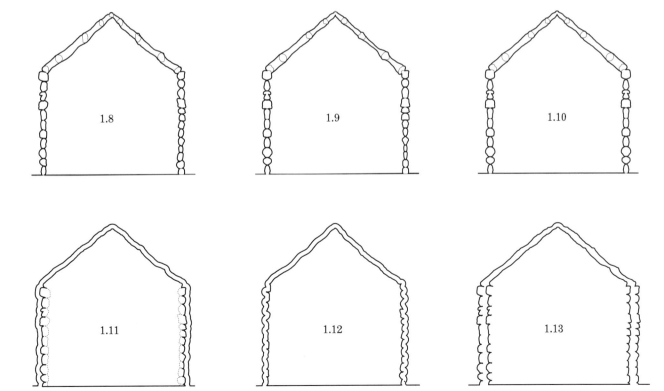

1.8

1.9

1.10

1.11

1.12

1.13

1.14—One-room building in a vast landscape.
Photograph courtesy of Dylan Krueger.

composition of a primary façade containing the door. In early cabins only the front façade was intentionally composed, as evidenced by the door and occasionally by window symmetry or the inclusion of a porch. In some instances, and especially as the cabin type spread westward in the 18th and 19th centuries, the orientation of the front became increasingly calibrated to climatic and geographic conditions. However, because the early cabin was a one- or at most two-room space, there was no subsequent internal sequencing or spatial divisions to create more rooms. The lack of internal divisions makes frontality less strange in the cabin than in other residential types because any location of the door in any one of the walls permits entry to the same interior space. Thus, frontality is not a condition that establishes subsequent internal order, but rather a single room can accept any side equally as the front. It follows that the cabin exhibits the

greatest degree of isomorphism between the inside and the outside when compared to other residential types. Isomorphism, rare in contemporary architecture, is an equivalence and uniformity of interior volume and exterior form. Because the cabin is most often one room bound by corresponding walls without internal spatial divisions, it exhibits nearly absolute isomorphism, making the (usually) four walls of the cabin one of the most striking architectural events of separation between an interior room and an ambient environment. However, upon further examination, contradictions arise concerning the degree of isomorphism in the cabin, especially in the log cabin, where the variability of log walls produces three contradictions:

Contradiction 1: Crossed-Corners (plan)
While the cabin might at first appear isomorphic, an unsung instantiation of the corner problem disrupts this. The crossed-log corners make the outside corners a half cross in plan and the inside corners a half square, or approximately a 90-degree angle. While crossed corners disrupt absolute isomorphism between the interior and exterior, they are also one of the cabin's structural and formal defining features.

Contradiction 2: Stacked Walls (section)
The log cabin represents an unassuming problem of stacking in architecture. Placing uneven and dimensionally unequal parts one atop another results in cabin walls of variable thickness with a non-uniform wall section. Despite its material uniformity, the log cabin wall lacks uniform dimensions, making log cabin walls unique among other residential wall types as the contours of the cabin set against its exterior surroundings differ from the contours of the interior room.

Contradiction 3: Symmetry (elevation)
The cabin is often associated with symmetry. Before the incorporation of chimneys this association was mostly accurate. The side-wall fireplace and chimney, however, produce an asymmetrical room, creating both visual and spatial hierarchies. The asymmetry introduced by a side-wall fireplace and chimney is the driving factor behind the addition of a second room, making the fireplace and chimney at the center of a two-room cabin and returning to a symmetrical composition once again. The side-wall fireplace and chimney anticipate addition.

The architectural discrepancies between the inside and the outside revealed by logged cabins demonstrate why the single room generally, and the log cabin specifically, is valuable for evaluating isomorphism in architecture. As exterior form and interior volume condense to the smallest threshold of difference, they amplify, rather than diminish, unresolved legibility between the inside and the outside. Furthermore, condensing the threshold between exterior form and interior volume within a vast terrain raises a fundamental question related to character: do the walls contain the space and qualities of the room in a vast landscape, or does the space of the room determine the location and qualities of the walls? This chicken-egg dilemma is heightened as a building approaches isomorphism.

While the cabin is the primary exemplar because of its residential capacity, so too could the shed, the barn, the ice fishing or hunting hut, or the outhouse relate.

Transgressive Mediation

The cabin has a surprising B-side—a hugely transformed modern (re)incarnation. No other residential type exhibits such a degree of formal and spatial transformation from its typological origins to its current status in contemporary culture. While it is true that modestly built cabins still exist and are still constructed today, a quick Google search or five minutes spent watching a televised home renovation show will quickly dilute the legacy of the ruggedly independent "American spirit" of yesteryear's cabin with portrayals of the cabin as a site for unbridled, often corporatized architecture.

During the post-recession period of 2012–2019, a plethora of T.V. shows returned attention to the cabin (and the tiny home) as a source for entertainment and DIY inspiration. At the time of this writing (10/20/2018, 8:58am) HGTV programming concentrating on the cabin (not including tiny homes) includes *Cabin Reno, Log Cabin Living, Log Cabin Kings, Living Country, Lake Home & Cabin Show, Montana Home, Mountain Life, Building Wild, Building Alaska, Buying Alaska, Cabin Truckers, Blog Cabin, Maine Cabin Masters, Rocky Mountain Reno, Rustic Renovation, Rustic Rehab, Timber Kings,* and a variety of particular episodes on shows like *Extreme Home Makeover, Build Small Live Anywhere,* and *Old Home Love.*

1.15—One-room building with vertical logs in a vast landscape. Photograph courtesy of Dylan Krueger.

Twentieth-century French philosopher Guy Debord has described models of taste production and consumption as spectacle, writing that "in societies where modern conditions of production prevail, life is presented as an immense accumulation of spectacles. Everything that was once directly lived is now merely represented in the distance."[19] On the one hand, these shows might suggest a reinvestment in modest architectural and social values originally associated with the cabin's lifestyle of independence and nature's impressions on dwelling transferred by those who build it. On the other hand, the abundance of television programming targeting predominantly urban and suburban populations with depictions of the cabin as an architecturally exuberant, technologically modernized economic commodity spurred by psychological nostalgia contradicts de Quincy's qualifications of essential character, while seeming to support Debord's

Semiotic Square for the cabin and its inter-
relations between character, context, politics, and
monumentality.

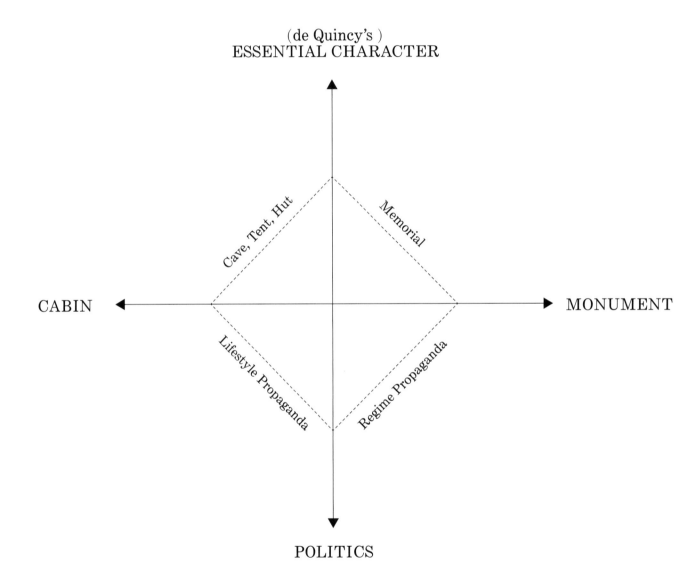

(de Quincy's)
ESSENTIAL CHARACTER

Cave, Tent, Hut

Memorial

CABIN

MONUMENT

Lifestyle Propaganda

Regime Propaganda

POLITICS

spectacle-to-commodity culture. Cast in a historic light, the cabin is a residential type that exhibits cultural, contextual, economic, architectural, and political transgressions and transformations. The cabin shifts from an isolated event of domesticity to a mediated source of entertainment. This is the cabin's fourth contradiction: societally commodified isolation.

Character and Contradiction

The cabin is a small, isolated event in a vast landscape. It is historically picturesque in its vivid, at times unusual evocation of a cultural imagination captured by scenography that heightens the cabin's quotidian qualities and molds lasting impressions of isolation, independence, and fortitude. If these associations are accurate for the cabin at its historical origins, then they are also accurate of the cabin's current-day susceptibility to transgressive appropriations of a mediated culture that stand in contrast to its historical imaginaries. The cabin was historically understood to be both physically and morally removed from the cultural and political life of the city. This quality enables us to read the cabin through the lens of de Quincy's essential character.

In 1840, however, the cabin's connotations began to shift. The cultural perceptions of the cabin and its affiliated moral and physical character were enfolded into a presidential campaign orchestrated by the Whigs for their favored

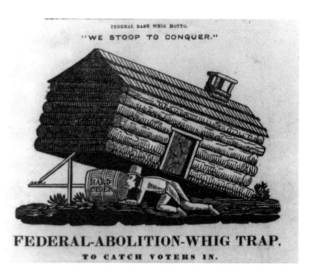

1.17—Anti-Whig campaign ad from 1840 titled *Federal-Abolition-Whig trap, to catch voters in.* (Library of Congress)

candidate, William Henry Harrison. The cabin became explicitly political. Incumbent president Martin Van Buren started the conversation about the cabin by leveraging his alliance with Democratic newspapers, asking them to print campaign ads mocking Harrison's modest way of life.

Central to the mockery was the assumption that the cabin represented a means of living unworthy of presidential candidacy. As one paper wrote, "[G]ive him a barrel of hard cider and settle a pension of two thousand a year on him, and my word for it, he will sit by the side of a sea coal fire and study moral philosophy."[20] Whereas the

1.18—Pro-Whig illustration from the 1840 Presidential election titled *Harrsion & Tyler* showing Harrison welcoming a soldier to his log cabin and another enjoying hard cider as a response to incumbent candidate, Martin Van Buren's ads depicting Harrison unfit for Presidency due to his lifestyle characterized by cabin dwelling. (Library of Congress)

Democratic newspapers portrayed the cabin and its associated lifestyle as a political demerit, suggesting that it was insufficiently sophisticated for a future President, Harrison and the Whigs turned it into a virtue, celebrating Harrison as "a simple frontier Indian fighter, living in a log cabin and drinking cider, in sharp contrast to an aristocratic champagne-sipping Van Buren."[21] The contrast is clear: we see similar rhetoric in today's mud-slinging political attacks between "coastal elites" and "fly-over states."

Harrison gained widespread support from influential political leaders and from broader populations who began to disregard the incumbent's derision of the cabin and instead began to associate the cabin with a new image of the American spirit characterized by fortitude, independence, moral ethics, and integrity. Harrison won the election in a landslide, ingraining a new imaginary of the log cabin as part of America's political sphere. Harrison, however, caught a cold that turned to pneumonia, and after just 32 days as President of the United States, he died. The mystique of the American cabin, however, lived on. Five elections later, Abraham Lincoln was elected President with a well-known background as a cabin-dweller. Fifty-six years later John Lloyd Wright, while working on the Imperial Hotel with his father Frank in Japan, invented what would later be called Lincoln Logs.

The toy cabin furthered the cabin's mystique and was used as propaganda bolstering the cabin's virtuous identity as a symbol of patriotism during WWI. Marketed as a symbol of societal values of American independence, the original packaging of Lincoln Logs revived the idea of character in architecture—or at least in the cabin—as a position of morality, touting that "interesting playthings typifying the spirit of America."[22] The toy cabin came with instructions for building models of not only Lincoln's Kentucky cabin, but also an American cabin borrowed from literature, Uncle Tom's Cabin.

Perhaps more than any other residential type, the cabin, even with its political history, has retained pluralistic associations with underpinnings in the popular image of an American dwelling affiliated with the moralistic virtue of physical isolation and the cultural construction of solitude. Still considered to represent independence, the cabin remains a residential type characterized by contextual—and perhaps cultural—repose from the frenetic multiplicities of urban life. Yet, because of these inherent qualities and popular appeal, the cabin is susceptible to typological and cultural appropriations, from politics to entertainment. That so much has become of a single room in a vast terrain is an enduring architectural celebration that illuminates distinctions between previous understandings of character and those we explore today that privilege open associations that expand the architectural lexicon through formal and spatial dramatizations.

1
Judith Flanders, "Log Cabin History: The Secrets of Making a Home," *The History Reader: Dispatches in History from St. Martin's Press,* September 9, 2015, http://www.thehistoryreader.com/modern-history/the-making-of-home-secrets-of-log-cabin-history/ (accessed October 12, 2018).

2
Edna Scofield, "The Evolution and Development of Tennessee Houses," *Journal of the Tennessee Academy of Science* 11 (1936), 229-240.

3
Ibid.

4
Michel Foucault, *The Order of Things: An Archaeology of the Human Sciences* [1971] (New York: Vintage Books, 1994), 159.

5
Anthony Vidler, "The Languages of Character" in *Claude-Nicolas Ledoux: Architecture and Social Reform at the End of the Ancien Régime* (Cambridge: MIT Press, 1990), 19-20.

6

For additional terms see Anthony Vidler's renowned treatise, *Claude-Nicolas Ledoux: Architecture and Social Reform in the Ancien Regime*. This book offers a wealth of scholastic content on Ledoux and his contemporaries with many parts dedicated to character. In this chapter, I use abbreviated versions of the terms to which Vidler dedicates countless pages.
Anthony Vidler, "The Languages of Character" in *Claude-Nicolas Ledoux: Architecture and Social Reform at the End of the Ancien Régime* (Cambridge: MIT Press, 1990), 19-20.

7

Michael Hill and Peter Kohane, "The Signature of Architecture': Compositional Ideas in the Theory of Profiles," *Architectural Histories* 3(1) (2015), Art. 18.
See also Vidler, *Claude-Nicolas Ledoux*, 19.

8

For a complete history on Quatremère de Quincy see Sylvia Lavin's book, *Quatremère de Quincy and the Invention of a Modern Language of Architecture* (Cambridge: MIT Press, 1992). Her book represents the most comprehensive understanding of de Quincy's work, which I address here with the utmost abbreviation.

9

Vittoria Di Palma, "Architecture, Environment and Emotion: Quatremère de Quincy and the Concept of Character," *AA Files* (2002) No. 47 (London: Architectural Association).

10

Ibid.

11

Vidler, "Institutions of Public Order: The Rhetoric of Character" in *Claude-Nicolas Ledoux*, 145.

12

Translation by Anthony Vidler in *Claude-Nicolas Ledoux: Architecture and Social Reform at the End of the Ancien Régime* (Cambridge: MIT Press, 1990), 145. Vidler quotes from Claude Nicolas Ledoux's *L'architecture considérée sous le rapport de l'art, des moeurs et de la legislation* (Paris: L'imprimerie de H.L. Perronnneau, 1804), 118-119.

13

Étienne-Louis Boullée, *Architecture: Essai sur l'art* (1789-99), ed. Jean-Marie Perouse de Montclos (Paris: Herman, 1968), 73. See also Vidler, *Claude-Nicolas Ledoux*, 145.

14

Boullée, *Architecture*, 73-74. See also, Vidler, *Claude-Nicolas Ledoux*, 145.

15

Edmund Burke, *A Philosophical Enquiry into the Origin of Our Ideas of the Sublime and Beautiful* [1757], ed. James T. Boulton (London: Routledge and Paul, 1958).

16

Though de Quincy did not mention Boullée specifically, he did speak directly to monumentality, stating that "[t]he word monument, the idea that it express and the luxury or magnificence attached to it, is suited above all to those great establishments that enter first in line for the needs of peoples and which a strong instinct for decorum has called for art to impress with an external character to mark their importance and advertise their purpose to the spectator."

Antoine-Chrysostome Quatremère de Quincy, "Caractére" in *Encyclopedia Méthodique: Architecture*, Vol. 2, 1801.

Translation by Anthony Vidler in *Claude-Nicolas Ledoux: Architecture and Social Reform at the End of the Ancien Régime* (Cambridge: MIT Press, 1990), 145.

17

The use of the term dramatizing is related to, though should not be confused with, terms that appear in past scholarship on the topic of character such as "rhetoric" (see Vidler, *Claude-Nicolas Ledoux*, 146-147). Whereas Vidler outlines a correlation between rhetoric as a device for amplification, joined by the sublime (noting that Ledoux was more influenced by the writing of Edmund Burke), I use dramatizing as both a technique and an effect, one of either of which could be amplification, but which also includes multiple others and does not require the joiner of the sublime.

Vidler, *Claude-Nicolas Ledoux*, 145.
When discussing Ledoux, Vidler notes that he was committed to the unequivocal aspects of architectural language such that anyone could assess it.

18

This is not an exhaustive list, but rather is limited here to six broadly related terms that attempt to loosely bracket methods, representation, and physical output within a conceptualization of character in contemporary practice. This list of terms, couched under the rubric of dramatizing as described in this essay, is itself a slippery provocation and does not cover the entirety of the contemporary field. Individual projects produced within individual practices vary between these conceptual terms. This list is conceived in the spirit of an expansion of Blondel's myriad (I believe 64) genres of character in architecture, but it moves emphasis away from singularly deducible qualities (such as male, light, pastoral, naïve, feminine, mysterious, etc.) to internal working methods, representation, and the kind of pluralism that a culture of visual sharing entails.

19

Guy Debord, "The Culmination of Separation" in *The Society of the Spectacle* [1967], trans. Ken Knabb (Canberra: Hobgoblin Press, 2002), 4.

20

The White House, "William Henry Harrison," WhiteHouse. gov, https://www.whitehouse.gov/about-the-white-house/presidents/william-henry-harrison/ (accessed August 20, 2018).

21

Ibid.

22

Christopher Klein, "The Birth of Lincoln Logs," *History*, August 29, 2018, https://www.history.com/news/the-birth-of-lincoln-logs (accessed September 22, 2018).

Context Amending & Context Offending in the Mountain House

The typical mountain house exhibits steeply sloping roofs with deep eaves, large and numerous windows, a heavy-to-the ground appearance, and an ordered plan with internal room divisions. The mountain house is more geometrically complex than the cabin. While the term *mountain house* suggests remoteness in sparsely populated states like Idaho or Utah, mountain houses are also found in more densely populated areas such as Santa Monica, Malibu, and Oakland, California; Albuquerque, New Mexico; and Colorado Springs, Colorado to name a few. The evolution of the mountain house from the cabin is difficult, if not impossible, to pinpoint in terms of a specific timeline, event, or building. However, today it is clear that scale and internal spatial sub-divisions of a rationalized plan are distinguishing features from the one-room cabin. Additionally, it is the contextual prefix 'mountain' that has come to define the type, complicating any notion of clear-cut formal, spatial, or organizational conceptualizations. Because of this contextual qualifier, this chapter is anomalous in relation to the others in this book as it uses specific buildings by specific architects to convey specific ideas as a method of demonstrating broader architectural debates.

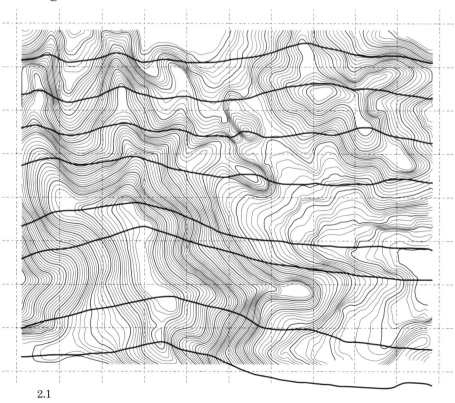

2.1

2.1
Mountain topography with contours, overlaid grid, and section profiles for reference to subsequent drawings in this chapter.

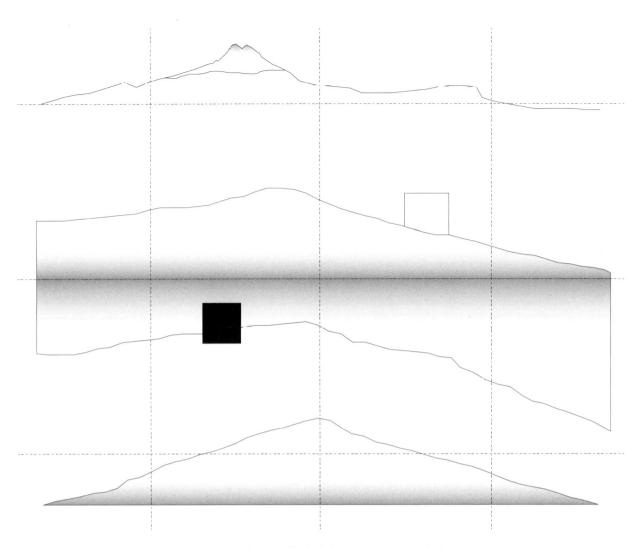

2.2—Context-Offending / Context-Amending conceptual diagram.

Context-Amending
& Context-Offending

The mountain house is not so much a proper type as it is a genre; that is, its identity relies on context in a way that distinguishes it from other residential types defined by form, space, and order alone. Consider, for example, the verb-noun relations in the terms *farmhouse* and *mountain house*. In the former, *farm* acts as a verb (*to farm*), which joins with *house* as a qualification of human labor involved in farming, substantiating the relationship between the house and its context. In the mountain house, however, mountain is a noun that contextualizes the geography of the house rather than qualifying its functional or human endeavors. This house is defined not by its support for an action, but by the geophysical qualities of the land on which it sits.

The same is true of any genre-based house qualified by its context, such as the desert house, beach house, or tree house. The semantics here underscore the ambiguity of the relationship between the mountain and the house. Simply put, mountains are inherently challenging environments for domestication. The qualities of a mountain—wild, slow, geologic—are contrasted against the comforts of the house—domestic, efficient, cultural. In fact, the mountain and the house have almost no conceptual overlap. Thus, the architecture resulting from their superimposition navigates a spectrum of contextual negotiation: on the one end, the architect might blend the house in with the mountain's qualities; on the other end, the architect might choose intentionally to distinguish the house from the mountain. These two poles are what I refer to as *context-amending* and *context-offending*.

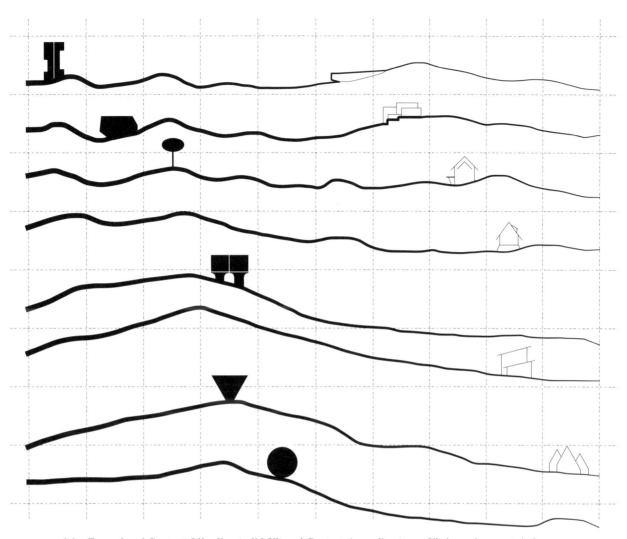

2.3—Examples of Context-Offending (solid fill) and Context-Amending (open fill) forms in mountain houses.

In the first instance, the house amends the mountain with the likeness of its own qualities, emulating the mountain scene through architectural blending and blurring. This amendment occurs through two versions of mimicry. The first is *tectonic mimicry*, evidenced by rooflines that approximate the shape-silhouette of a mountain, overhangs and outriggers that extend into the surrounds, heavy massing with natural materials, and irregular plan compositions that accommodate or settle into topographic complexities to complete the act of contextual blending. The second version of mimicry, *embeddedness*, treats topography as a thickened surface into which the house is inserted through techniques of cutting and through plan compositions that burrow into natural topography to achieve the effect of blurring. This often results in natural vegetation seamlessly covering the distinction between roof and ground, visually challenging the distinction between building and landscape. Both of these forms of mimicry are techniques of *context-amending*.

Alternatively, the house may be intentionally distinguished from the mountain by *offending* context. Context-offending manifests in geometrically distinct massing or profiles that contrast with the natural topography. Context-offending houses typically minimize tectonic expression and employ materials and colors that contrast against the natural surroundings. Plan compositions in context-offending houses depart from geographic and topographic mimicry and often exhibit clear geometric footprints. These are all techniques of *context-offending*. Whereas context-amending architecture arrests the physical qualities of its context and transposes them into constructed likenesses

2.4—Hearst's Wyntoon Estate (1906), Bernard Maybeck.

2.5—Sculptured House (1963), Charles Deaton.

through techniques of aesthetic *blending* or *blurring* of one thing into another, context-offending architecture manifests a will for differentiation, juxtaposing contextual circumstances with an attitude of aesthetic *bending* of one thing away from another.

The contrasting techniques of context-amending and context-offending are illustrated by differences in two neighboring bridges: the Golden Gate Bridge and the Bay Bridge, both located amidst the San Francisco Bay fog. The Bay Bridge amends its context: it is painted gray in an explicit attempt to blend the bridge into the fog, with the result that the bridge seems alternately to disappear within and emerge from the fog. The bridge coloration, taking its cues from the natural environment, favors aesthetic experiences that compound ambient qualities into a uniform environmental image and reinforce existing contextual imaginaries. Conversely, the Golden Gate Bridge offends its context: it is painted orange (International Orange, to be exact, as specified by architect Irving F. Morrow) in order to contrast starkly against the fog. In fact, International Orange is a color developed by NASA for that specific purpose—to distinguish designed objects from their surroundings. The intentional differentiation of the bridge color from the ambient environment sharpens experience through contrast that unhinges the existing contextual identity. While context-amending is often considered a hallmark of environmentally responsible or contextually sensitive architecture, it is often offending contrast that fosters new

spatial, cultural, social, and environmental habits. Context-amending architecture tends to reinforce existing circumstances, while context-offending architecture tends to re-author them, or offer new ones altogether.

Bernard Maybeck's Wyntoon Estate, built in 1906 for Phoebe Hearst and her son William Randolph Hearst in Siskiyou County, California, is an earlier manifestation of context-amending with tectonic mimicry. At Wyntoon, bulky massing beginning with round stone walls at the ground dissolves as the house attenuates into a series of sharp-gabled, hipped, and dormered peaks—a composition of parts that blends with the surrounding crop of trees and appears in silhouette as the shape-diagram of a mountain. Once described as "a disheveled harmony" as a corollary to its natural surroundings by the *Architectural Review*, Wyntoon achieves contextual blending through a technique of agitation, especially among its various roofs.[1] After Maybeck's building burned down, Julia Morgan was commissioned to design the new Wyntoon, completed in 1933. Morgan's house deploys techniques of both amending and offending context. While the roof's color matches the adjacent trees, the house is oriented to the river, and the shed dormers maintain tight shadow lines, its overall symmetry and bulky unattenuated massing are unmistakably context-offending qualities.

Examples of context-offending are found in Charles Deaton's 1963 cantilevering saucer, the Sculptured House, better known as the Sleeper House, in Genesee, Colorado, so called for its role in

2.6—Bradford Residence (1988), Bart Prince.

2.7—Whiting Residence (1991), Bart Prince.

Woody Allen's 1973 film, *Sleeper*. In the Sculptured House, a futuristic ellipse (described by Deaton as a "friendly, cooperative mushroom"[2]) soars over the edge of the mountainside, evoking a foreign object, perhaps a foreign mushroom, that has descended on the landscape from another world. Stark white chroma distinguishes the house from the surroundings, and its surface continuity eliminates tectonic distinctions between roof, wall, and floor, emphasizing massing over material-contextual blending or tectonic assimilation. Context-offending houses stand out: they appear abruptly and announce differences between context and residence.

2.8—Prairie House (1961), Herb Greene.
Photograph by Robert Alan Bowlby.

More challenging distinctions between the qualities of a house and its context occur across a breed of "organic" architectural constructs conceived by a collection of predominantly Southwestern architects. Bart Prince's Whitmore Residence (2004) in Glorieta, New Mexico; the Price Residence (1989) in Corona del Mar, California; Bruce Goff's Youngstrom House (1968) in Lake Quivira, Kansas; and Herb Greene's Joyce Residence (1959) in Snyder, Oklahoma, all can be said to confuse distinctions between amending and offending context.[3] These same architects have also worked in prairie contexts to similar effect. For example, Greene's Prairie House (1961), often fondly called the Prairie Chicken House, illustrates the exaggerated, even playful qualities often found in "organic" architecture and perhaps represents the abstracted country-counterpart to Venturi's Duck that was popularized later in the 1960s. Formally, materially, and phenomenally, these houses amend context through techniques of tectonic mimicry, material expression, and contextual geomorphic likeness. Yet, they do so with such exuberant manifestations that they also bear marks of context-offending architecture.

Often dubbed "organic architecture" for their amorphic, naturalistic massing, poetic written descriptions, and phenomenological materiality, these mountain (or hill) houses often exhibit qualities of geomorphic impressionism. Consider Bart Prince's Whiting Residence (1991) in Sun Valley, Idaho, in which heaving and swelling of form and space falls in rhythm with the background hills. Or another example: Prince's Scherger / Kolberg Residence (2005) located at the base of the Sandia Mountains in Albuquerque, New Mexico, where Prince drew inspiration from circular ceremonial

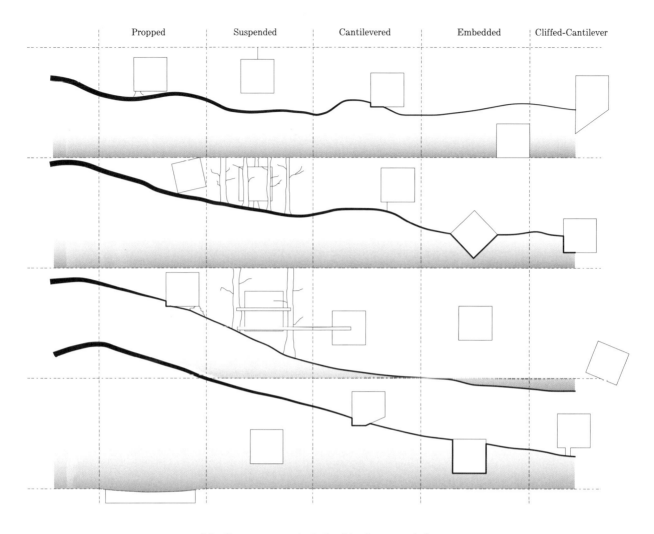

| Propped | Suspended | Cantilevered | Embedded | Cliffed-Cantilever |

2.9—Common ground relationships in mountain houses.

ruins cut into the Chaco Canyon landscape by the Anasazi. Prince describes the house as "leaving the site undisturbed so it read and flowed through the house, along with snakes, coyotes, and deer."[4] Steel roof beams extend beyond the house, ascending to "tie the structure and sky together" while approximating the mountain peak beyond, and the plan reveals a strong radial organization anchored by a 270-degree circular entry court, which sits in stark geometric contrast to natural topographic features even as walls radiate outward and into the landscape.[5] Prince's nearby Bradford Residence (1988) also makes architectural moves to blend with its context through tectonic mimicry and geomorphic impressions, yet it is known locally as The Spaceship, suggesting alien, context-offending qualities that stand out from its context.[6] These instances of "organic" architecture with their dichotomous and profoundly exaggerated qualities necessitate a third category of relationships between the mountain house and its context. I refer to this approach as *context-hyperextending*.

While other residential types sometimes manifest qualities of amending or offending their context, the mountain house most acutely reveals these distinctions through scalar, material, massing, and tectonic relationships with the distinctive features of the mountain. Apart from the mountain house, other houses with distinctive natural surroundings such as desert houses, tree houses, and beach houses are most likely to be describable through the qualities of context-amending or context-offending—or, in a few extraordinary instances, context-hyperextending.

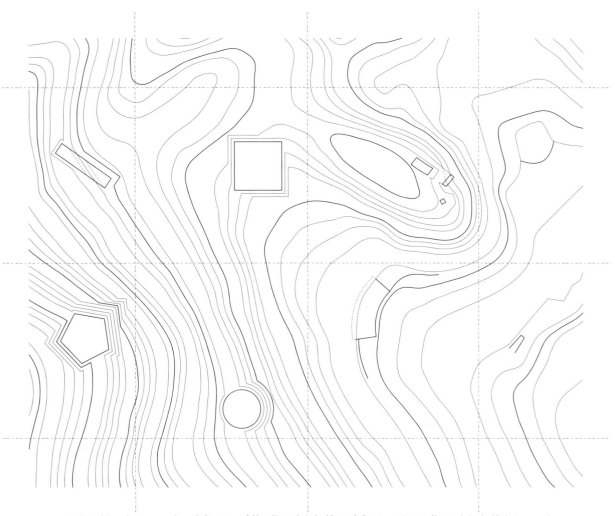

2.10—Site plan examples of Context-Offending (left half) and Context-Amending (right half) interventions.

Variations on Frontality:
Sidedness and Orientation

The mountain house often manifests a variation on frontality: sidedness. Sidedness reveals competing hierarchies among two or more sides of a four- (or more-) sided object. In the mountain house, sidedness results from its relationship to a sloped topography. Because two principal façades of the mountain house, the upslope and downslope façades, are more or less parallel to the contours (perpendicular to the slope), the other two, the "sides," are perpendicular to the contours (parallel to the slope). This relationship emphasizes the elevations that are parallel to the contours while reducing the visual and formal impact of elevations that are perpendicular to the contours. Thus, the upslope elevation most often appears as the front with regard to approach and entry, which typically

occurs from the upslope side. The downslope elevation, however, appears as the front with regard to contextual hierarchy, which typically prioritizes the downslope face for views and natural light. The parallelism of the upslope and downslope façades creates two fronts responding to distinct spatial and experiential criteria with competing hierarchies. This is sidedness. Sidedness is distinct from frontality because it has less to do with the legibility of frontalizing elements like a porch or a door, and instead concerns the perceptual, formal, and spatial juxtapositions bracketed by two parallel elevations, no matter the distance between them. In mountain houses, slope is the principal site condition responsible for creating sidedness between the upslope and downslope elevations.

Sidedness is most pronounced in context-amending houses where the downslope elevation is typically obligated to maximize views and the

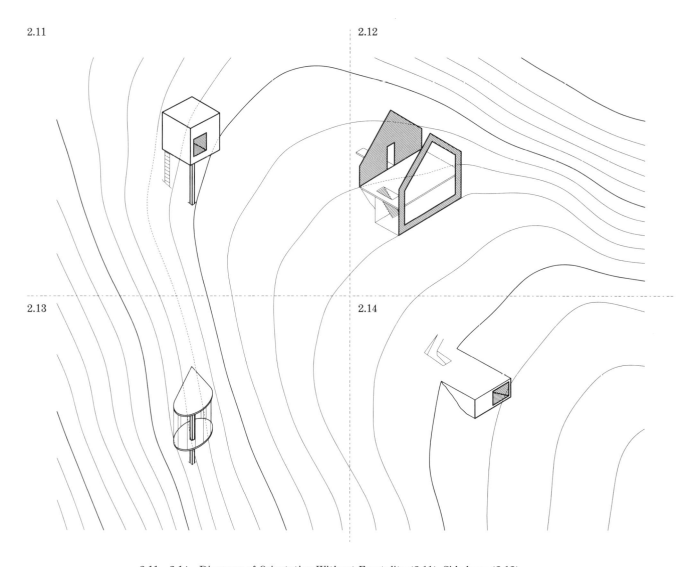

2.11 – 2.14—Diagrams of Orientation Without Frontality (2.11), Sidedness (2.12),
Orientation Without Frontality or Sidedness (2.13), and Embedded Orientation Without Frontality (2.14).

upslope elevation is conditioned by the approach and entry sequence. In context-amending houses with tectonic mimicry, the downslope elevation tends to mimic the mountain shape-silhouette through variations on the gable roof, and it is not uncommon to find protruding decks that further mimic the mountain's silhouette. In context-amending houses with topographic embeddedness, the upslope elevation may be only partially visible (or may appear as a landscaped roof), while the downslope elevation appears to be emerging out of the natural topography. The differences in these two conditions of sidedness are equally legible in plan and elevation, but most pronounced in section. It follows that context-amending houses tend to amplify sidedness, whereas context-offending

houses tend to diminish it. By diminishing sidedness through planimetric, formal, spatial, and material composition, context-offending houses might be expected to return to a condition of frontality. However, rather than exhibiting frontality, context-offending houses tend to disclose a preferred orientation through their internal arrangements as opposed to the specific legibility of a front. In other words, context-offending houses can most often be characterized by a specific orientation without frontality or sidedness.

In eschewing frontality or sidedness, context-offending houses may instead orient interior experience toward contextual externalities without immediately disclosing these intentions in massing or formal expressions. Such houses reveal their

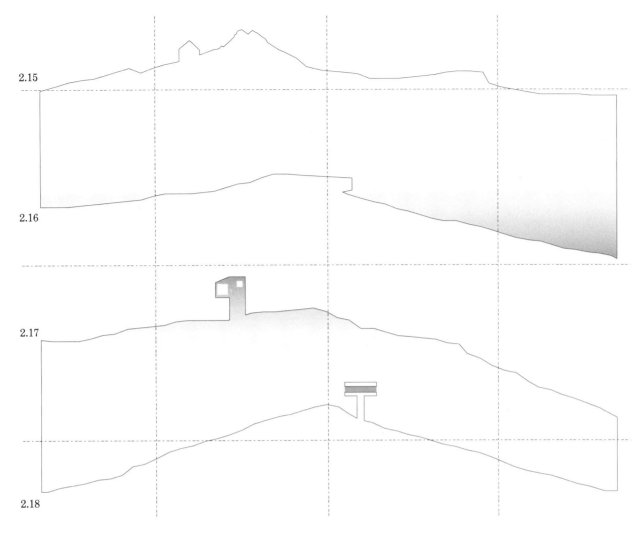

2.15

2.16

2.17

2.18

2.15 – 2.18—Diagrams of *Context-Amending*; Sidedness and tectonic mimicry (2.15),
Context-Amending; Embedded Sidedness (2.16), *Context-Offending*; Orientation Without Frontality (2.17),
and *Context-Offending*; Without Sidedness or Orientation (2.18).

preferred orientation through plan, window placement, and calculated deviations in the uniformity of massing that exposes, frames, acknowledges, or orients toward a preferred focus. Johnston Marklee's Hill House (2008) is an example of specific orientation without frontality or sidedness, whereas the Sculptured House or John Lautner's Chemosphere is not. While all three houses are context-offending houses, the Hill House reveals particular moments of discrete attention to external foci and topographic sensitivities in which internal order corresponds to the precise location of elements and massing. Conversely, the Sculptured House and the Chemosphere foster omni-oriented panoramas with no particular external foci; these houses express care for the ambient totality of contextual surroundings

rather than orienting toward discrete moments of attention.[7] Whereas context-amending houses typically demonstrate sidedness as a condition of the upslope and downslope elevations, context-offending houses tend to exhibit either orientation without frontality or sidedness, or omni-orientations.

Taking Sides

The distinction between context-amending and context-offending conjures long-standing debates concerning architecture's manifestation in physical contexts characterized by natural features and geophysical qualities. While this distinction hinges on a potentially reductive binary, its polemic is useful for illuminating ideological differences between different methods of integrating the physical qualities of a site into an architectural expression. On one end of the spectrum, a phenomenological, vernacular, or Critical Regionalism-inspired approach prioritizes a building's inscription into its site, giving it the "capacity to embody, in built form, the pre-history of the place, its archaeological past and its subsequent cultivation and transformation across time."[8] These houses develop precise, site-specific techniques and sensitivities for intersecting architectural interventions with topographic, geologic, and vegetal continuities of natural landscapes. Context-amending houses are polychromatic and most often appear in likeness to "singular peaks," "stepped hills," "mountain ranges," "cuts and canyons," and vegetated sloped landscapes that blend with local circumstances.[9]

On the other end of the spectrum, a belief in the creative-intellectual powers of architecture both to re-author physical contexts and to inspire new perceptions of culture as a virtue of differences between human artifacts and natural conditions advances notions that contradiction supports meaning.[10] Context-offending houses are most often monochromatic and contrast against natural formations with Platonic or primitive geometries, such as spheres, cones, cylinders, cubes, pyramids, and ellipsoids or geometric abstractions to these primitives so as to be *almost* spherical, cubic, and so on.

These two poles were represented during a heated debate between Peter Eisenman and Christopher Alexander at Harvard GSD in 1982. Throughout the discussion, the primary divide hinged on Alexander's claims for "feeling" in architecture and Eisenman's call for "intellection." At one point, while discussing gable roofs and feelings, Alexander remarked:

Why does this taboo [of the gable roof] exist? What is this funny business about having to prove you are a modem architect and having to do something other than a pitched roof? The simplest explanation is that you have to do these others [roofs] to prove your membership in the fraternity of modern architecture. You have to do something more far out, otherwise people will think you are a simpleton. But I do not think that is the whole story. I think the more crucial explanation is that the pitched roof contains a very, very primitive power of feeling. Not a low pitched, tract house roof, but a beautifully shaped, fully pitched roof. That kind of roof has a very primitive essence as a shape, which reaches into a very vulnerable part of you. But the version that is okay among the architectural fraternity is the one which does not have the feeling: the weird angle, the butterfly, the asymmetrically steep shed, etc.—all the shapes which look interesting but which lack feeling altogether. The roof issue is a simple example. But I do believe the history of architecture in the last few decades has been one of specifically and repeatedly trying to avoid any primitive feeling whatsoever. Why this has taken place, I don't know.[11]

Eisenman responds by saying:

This is a wonderful coincidence, because I too am concerned with the subject of roofs. Let me answer it in a very deep way. I would argue that the pitched roof is—as Gaston Bachelard points out—one of the essential characteristics of "houseness". It was the extension of the vertebrate structure which sheltered and enclosed man. Michel Foucault has said that when man began to study man in the 19th century, there was a displacement of man from the center. The representation of the fact that man was no longer the center of the world, no longer the arbiter, and, therefore, no longer controlling artifacts, was reflected in a change from the vertebrate-center type of structure to the center-as-void. That distance, which you call alienation or lack of feeling, may have been merely a natural product of this new cosmology ... Le Corbusier once defined architecture as having to do with a window which is either too large or too small, but never the right size. Once it was the right size it was no longer functioning. When it is the right size, that building is merely a building. The only way in the presence of architecture that is that feeling, that need for something other, when the window was either too large or too small.[12]

Alexander stands on the context-amending side with concern for comfort and feeling, whereas Eisenman, borrowing from Le Corbusier, is on the context-offending side with the belief that architecture's impact requires difference.

Mountain houses sharpen the contrast between context-amending and context-offending because of the perversity of the contradiction between their context and residence. The amending-offending spectrum naturally scales to larger constructs, from civic, commercial, or other types of buildings to infrastructure. While it may at first appear that context-amending houses, buildings, or infrastructures satisfy the imperatives levied by commodified sustainability, ethical responsibility, and contextual sensitivity, it follows that they also run the risk of reinforcing cultural, social, political, or environmental habits by simply blending in. The artifice of blending and amending does not inherently promote the reshaping of habits, policies, and relationships; it could be said that it both affirms and mutes them by assimilating contextual contingencies into domesticity. By the same token, context-offending houses, buildings, or infrastructures may seem to disregard environmental imperatives, contextual specificity, or ethical temperament, yet it follows that they retain the capacity for altering or raising awareness of cultural habits by standing out. Context-offending enables alternative modes of seeing, interpreting, understanding, imagining, and intervening in the world. By standing out and "offending," this architecture refuses to affirm a cultural, environmental, or political status quo; it applies pressure on inherited circumstances while enabling the possibility for new ones. Context-hyperextending works similarly through the use of form, space, and material to intensify local contextual and cultural conditions through highly expressive reflections on context. Wrapped in aesthetic, ethical, and environmental ideologies, whether explicit or implicit, the decision to blend or to bend, to amend, to offend or to hyperextend endures debate across cultural and generational distinctions as an unending source of unresolved legibility in architecture.

1
"House of Mrs. Phoebe A. Hearst in Siskiyou Co., Cal.," *Architectural Review* 11 (1904) (Boston: Bates & Guild Co.), 64-66.

2
Jack Atkinson, "The Deaton Sculpture House," *Arts & Food*, September 1, 2018, https://artsandfood.com/2018/09/the-deaton-sculptured-house-aka-the-sleeper-house.html/ (accessed March 15, 2019).

3
In particular, Bruce Goff and Herb Greene developed an approach to architectural practice and pedagogy at the University of Oklahoma in the 1950s—'60s known as The American School that sought an authentic American model of education and practice during s a time when most schools in the U.S. were influenced by either the French Beaux Arts or German Bauhaus–or industry and abstraction. For more information, see the Christopher C. Gibbs College of Architecture at the University of Oklahoma, "The American School," Architecture.OU.Edu, https://architecture.ou.edu/the-american-school/ (accessed March 22, 2019).

4
Joseph Giovannini. "Bart Prince Creates a Light-Filled Residence in New Mexico." *Architectural Digest*. Accessed February 16, 2019. https://www.architecturaldigest.com/story/prince-article-102008

5
Ibid.

6
Ibid.

7
It should be noted that the Sculptured House, though known for its cantilevering saucer, also has a large, less visible portion sited in a context-amending manner.

8
Kenneth Frampton, "Towards a Critical Regionalism: Six Points for an Architecture of Resistance" in *Postmodern Culture*, ed. Hal Foster (London: Pluto Press, 1983), 26.

9
In the book, *Landform Buildings* (Lars Muller Publishing, 2011) Stan Allen notes correlative terms between architectural form and natural, geologic formations, which share some relation to what I call context-amending in houses. Not all terms in Allen's book apply to context-amending houses, and some of the terms are more appropriate to context-offending.

10
The idea that contradiction supports meaning is a summation of Robert Venturi's book *Complexity and Contradiction in Architecture* (Museum of Modern Art, 2nd edition, 1977). The direct relationship between meaning and the terms of contradiction, such as ambiguity, imprecision, double-meanings, conjunction, and so forth occurs 38 times in the book, revealing an underlying notion that meaning is sharpened through contradiction.

11
Christopher Alexander, "Contrasting Concepts of Harmony in Architecture: The 1982 Debate Between Christopher Alexander and Peter Eisenman," *Katarxis 3* (London, 2004), http://www.katarxis3.com/Alexander_Eisenman_Debate.htm (accessed December 4, 2018). First published in *Lotus International* 40 (1983), 60-68.

12
Ibid.

Dramas of the Purlieu & Strange Frontality in the Farmhouse

FRONTALITY

1

In sculpture: a composition in which the front view is complete without additional information from lateral views. In painting: the depiction of an object, figure, or scene on a plane parallel to the plane of the picture surface.

2

The orientation of a building such that it exhibits an identifiable front, typically resulting from the visibility of the front door within a principal façade composition.

The Farmhouse typically exists in a liminal, cultivated space between wilderness and urbanity. It can be difficult to identify a farmhouse as distinct from other types by its massing and elements alone, and it has a wide variety of sub-types. However, the farmhouse has a specific contextual imperative—it must be a residential base for cultivating crops—that distinguishes the farmhouse from other types. Historically, farmhouse subtypes often overlap with those of the cabin, including the New England Saltbox, side-gabled pre-railroad farmhouses (also known as Folk houses), New Netherland farmhouses, Delaware River Valley farmhouses, Pennsylvanian farmhouses, Virginia and Maryland farmhouses, and farmhouses of Appalachia—succeeded by Southwestern farmhouses, French-influenced farmhouses, plains farmhouses, and the eventual dawn of the contemporary farmhouse.[1]

Most often, farmhouses were designed by farm women, who were historically responsible for the domestic operations of the farm and therefore also took on the role of architect. While each geographic region's style varies in its organizational and formal tendencies, the logics of construction and materiality are consistent distinguishing features. A handful of other unifying traits are broadly shared across the various iterations of the farmhouse. For example, farmhouses traditionally have a gabled roof, are painted white, and are arranged with a porch at the front, a kitchen at the back, and a fireplace and brick chimney at both ends or somewhere in the middle of the house. The characteristic white exterior was historically the product of lime paint, used to prevent mildew from growing on the wood siding. Lime quickly became the most widely used paint because of its disinfectant and insect repellent properties and because it was cheap to make, easy to apply, and effective both in function and in unifying the external appearance. Similarly, the signature red color of the American barn arose from a readily available material: rust. When combined with oil, rust produces an orange-red hue and prevents decay by preventing the growth of mold or moss which can concentrate moisture in the barn wood.

Dramas of the Purlieu

Perhaps no other American residential type is encountered across such a broad spectrum of representational and psychological dramas as the farmhouse. The farmhouse simultaneously evokes an idealistic nostalgia for a "simpler time" and conjures memories of the hardships endured in pursuit of an agrarian lifestyle. Consider the cultural and representational gaps between the 1970s television portrayal of an earnest and endearing fictional family's Depression-era rural lifestyle in *The Waltons* and the reality of utter environmental and social decay during the 1930s Dust Bowl. Though *The Waltons* has long been off-air and appears markedly quaint in retrospect, the double connotations of a simpler lifestyle and an enduring hardship are habituated in the public imaginary of rural America, of which the farmhouse is the most dramatic architectural manifestation.

The duality of the farmhouse in the public imagination goes further, evoking the enchantment of the sublime and the anxiety of the horrific. This dichotomy between sublime allure and horrific fear has been visualized in classic movies including *The Wizard of Oz* (1939) and *Psycho* (1960). In the former, the cultural comforts of the farmhouse and its tight-knit familial space is dreamily upended by an uncanny, ruptured familial space of horror thick with anxiety and urgency.

The farmhouse symbolizes both dwelling and cultivation in the marginal landscapes between urbanity and wilderness where "we feel not instructed or edified but awakened in an emotional way; we either want to be part of it or avoid its independence and get back to a more comfortable urban environment."[2] This relationship between the farmhouse and its rural yet cultivated setting is best characterized by the term *purlieu*. In 15th-century Britain, the term *purlieu* was used to describe land at the far perimeter of an estate that remains partly wild and is never fully domesticated despite being part of the estate.[3] Purlieu is a liminal space between the worlds of domestication and wilderness, between comfort and mystery. This implies both perceptual and subjective psychologies, as well as the proximity between the farmhouse's rural setting and the urbanized space of the city and suburb. Because the purlieu can never be fully domesticated, it often conjures mystery, fear, and anxiety in those furthest from it, yet for those accustomed to its nearness it tends to be a space of comfort, enlightenment, and enchantment. The farmhouse's occupation of the contextual margin between domestication and wilderness suggests that its representational plurality is provoked by its dual existence as a space for dwelling

3.1—Ranch and farmland near Cheyenne, Wyoming.

act of nature, whisking Dorothy away on a fantastical journey, after which she returns home in an enlightened state after three clicks of her heels. Conversely, Alfred Hitchcock repeatedly used the farmhouse as a site of intrinsic fear, perhaps most notably in *Psycho*'s Italianate farmhouse. In Hitchcock's work the farmhouse is often the and for cultivating the countryside. This contextual drama is enhanced by the farmhouse's status as a quintessential object in a field. No other residential type enjoys, or is burdened by, such objecthood while also supporting cultivation of the surrounding field.

The farmhouse is perceived paradoxically as both turning toward and turning away. It is held in the public imaginary as both comforting and alienating; confrontational and quiet; remote and exposed. It is a residential type that stages perceptual contrasts between its own qualities and its remote setting; between wilderness and urbanity. To dwell in a farmhouse is to oscillate between the opposite positions of being forever surrounded and being continuously isolated.

Strange Obligations to Frontality

As objects in a field, farmhouses rarely bear the urban or suburban pressures of public address or neighborliness. Nevertheless, despite myriad in-the-round possibilities, farmhouses commonly exhibit frontality in the manner of residential types found in more populated areas. Whereas the cabin, as previously discussed, exhibits frontality through the symmetry of a principal façade, the farmhouse does so by virtue of its orientation. The front porch, in particular, is a frontalizing element that discloses orientation and in the case of the farmhouse is typically oriented toward the access road or driveway. The exact origins of the American porch are not known. In Britain, a "porch" is a fully sheltered entrance, similar to what Americans call the foyer. It is generally accepted that the enclosed porch arose in response to two major functional needs: the shedding of dirty outdoor wear and protection from seasonal variations in temperature, from hot summers to rainy springs and snowy winters. Yet, the open porch is something of a confusing element when searching for a point of origin. Nevertheless, today the front porch is a transitional element between the interior spaces of dwelling and the exterior world of labor and environmental circumstances.

Despite the ambiguity of its origins, the porch has historically figured heroically in the representations and connotations of the farmhouse. American landscape designer Andrew Jackson Downing described the porch as a principal element of the farmhouse in his pattern book of 1850, *The Architecture of Country Houses.* According to Downing, "the porch or veranda of the farmhouse should not only be larger, but also simpler, and ruder, and stronger than that of the cottage because there is more manly strength in the agriculturalists life than in that of any other class."[4] The irony, of course, in this statement is that it was far more common that women designed the family farmhouse. Nevertheless, Downing continues: "In raising the character of the farmhouse, the first step above the really useful is to add the porch, and the bay window, since they are not only significant of real but of refined beauty."[5] For Downing the porch was one of three principal elements (alongside the bay window and the chimney) specific to a farmhouse in its conveyance of the "truth" and "strength" of agrarian livelihood. Downing's rather grandiose proclamations provide insight into the farmhouse's strange yet lingering obligation to frontality as a morally symbolic and culturally virtuous representation of a previous era's ideological relationships between architecture and culture. But this does not account for either 1) the contextual circumstances of the farmhouse or 2) the spatial consequences of the porch. Contextually, the porch cleaves the farmhouse from the open surrounding as a frontispiece within an ambient field. Spatially, the porch defers the internal order of the house to the infrastructural contingencies of access.

The Porch Cleaves

The porch cleaves the farmhouse from its surrounding context by making legible a front within an otherwise a-frontal circumstance. The porch is effective as an objectifying element because of its clear legibility as a directional frontispiece, allowing it to fix the farmhouse's orientation within an in-the-round context. A veranda—a wrap-around porch, which may or may not give access to the front door—also cleaves the farmhouse from its context, but it does so through sidedness, rather than frontality. A *full* veranda entirely surrounding a square-plan (or circle, or any symmetrical plan) house, is an exception: in such a situation, rare as it may be, the square or otherwise symmetrical plan's internal order is not conditioned by the veranda itself, nor does the veranda disclose frontality or sidedness to the house. Any inflections or deviations to the square plan or the full veranda, however, will create frontalizing hierarchies, and thus the probability for contextual cleaving returns. It does not absolutely follow that the absence of a porch or veranda merges the farmhouse with its context.

3.2
Diagram of an object in a
field with omni-orientations.

3.3
Diagram of an object in a
field exhibiting frontality
by virtue of a frontalizing
element, like a porch.

The porch has the effect of deferring internal spatial arrangements of the farmhouse to infrastructural access through its frontalizing orientation toward the access road or driveway, creating a spatial tension between the casual, utilitarian space of the porch and the formal, ceremonial space of the room immediately inside the front door: the parlor. The most formal room in the traditional farmhouse, the parlor is directly inside the entrance with secondary spaces like the living room near the middle and service spaces like kitchens and bathrooms nearer the back of the house. Intended for welcoming and conversing with guests on a casual basis as well as on rare occasions such as weddings, funerals, and small public events, the parlor was typically outfitted with a small quantity of family belongings of importance such as pictures, instruments, glassware, and the nicest furniture. The parlor's position at the front of the house anticipates visitation, yet it is also the most contrary room to set adjacent to the porch. Though by now it may feel customary in contemporary architecture to move so abruptly between such contrasting spaces, in the context of a house under no obligations to frontality and with such rare occasions for parlor-room festivity, this contrasting adjacency creates a spatial drama between inside and outside—between the most informal utilitarian space of the exterior and the most formal space of the interior. The parlor was so special that it eventually became unfavorable, as Mrs. E. H. Leland noted in *Farm Homes: In-Doors and Out-Doors* in 1881:

> Just here I want to enter my humblest protest against any parlor that pinches and stints other rooms in order to exist ...It is bad taste and bad morals to make most anything answer for family use day after day, while the best room is sacredly reserved for outside people, people who are not greatly benefited, after all, for when do we not observe that it is the simple, easily served meal that we enjoy, and not the stiff atmosphere of a seldom-used room.[6]

The farmhouse's status as an object in a field is underscored by the tendency, throughout the history of the farmhouse, to create additions through *telescoping* as needs change, families grow, or ownership changes. Telescoping additions are legible by two or three descending scales of the same or similar forms, resulting in the impression that they might all retract sequentially back into the original form. The most common telescoping addition is an addition to one of the original side-gabled ends of the main house, in the form of that same side-gabled end but scaled down by one-third. If a second addition is made, it is typically added to the opposite gabled end of the original house, therefore maintaining the original house as the center of the new whole. Telescoping additions tend to reinforce existing frontality despite altering the composition of the whole.

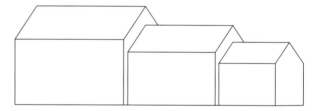

3.4—Diagram of telescoping additions.
In farmhouses, the middle mass is often the original house.

Today, additions are made more commonly through constelled accumulation. This is characterized by the accumulation over time of detached buildings such as guest houses, detached garages, barns, sheds, feed bins, or landscape elements such as swimming pools, fences, or retaining walls. Whereas telescoping additions tend to reinforce the object-in-a-field status, constelled accumulations diffuse the status of individual objects through multiple structures that implicitly define the spaces in-between as shared areas for socializing, playing, and labor distinct from the larger operation of farming. The spaces between buildings are multivalent, activated as both leisure space and work yard, spaces for equipment maintenance and social engagement, animal husbandry and sport. Constelled aggregations often may appear organizationally ad hoc, as loose arrangements composed by multiple structures of variable uses and scales in relative proximity and which easily accommodate new additions and appropriated uses without the

3.5 (top) and 3.6 (bottom)
Constellated farm properties located near Burns,
Wyoming, in which houses, barns, coops, silos, vehicles,
farming equipment, tires, lumber, and other materials
are collected, sorted, and stored.

3.7 (left)
and 3.8 (right)
AS BUILT_Constellated
farm properties located near
Palmyra, Iowa.

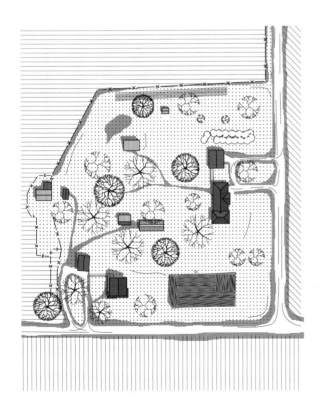 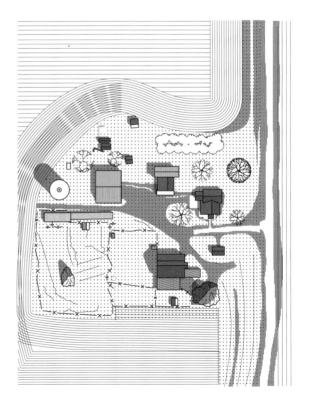

3.9 (left)
and 3.10 (right)
AS BUILT_Constellated
farm properties located
near Washington, Iowa,
and Fredricksburg, Iowa.

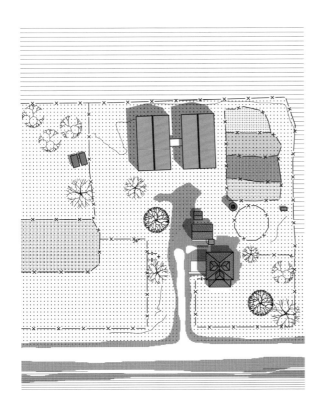

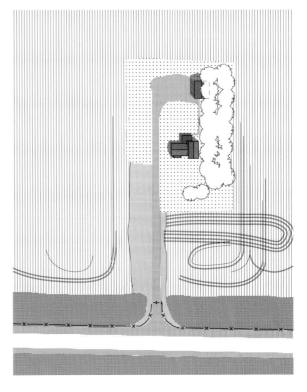

Constellated farm fields range from having clear hierarchies of order to an expansive field of ad hoc accumulations.

3.11
Double Lots: two multi-building properties with individual access but without visible divisions between the two properties, thus appearing as one constellation on a single property.

3.12
Overlapping Clusters: loosely defined zones in which a key building in one zone simultaneously serves functions in another zone.

3.13
Mosaic Allocations: one property sectioned by fences or retaining walls in which different cells are allocated specific functions and buildings.

3.14
Flag Lots: a flag-shaped area accessed by a long driveway from the main road that is surrounded by arable land.

3.15
Gridded Flags: a flag lot internally organized by a grid.

3.16
Broken Flags: a flag lot with a broken boundary, out of which materials, buildings, equipment, and machinery migrate.

Aggregation Tendencies in Constellated Farm Fields.

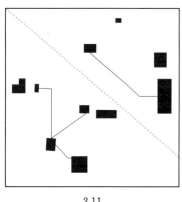

3.11

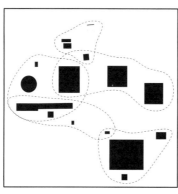

3.12

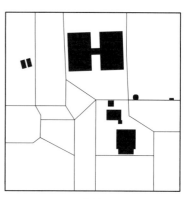

3.13

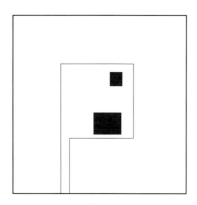

3.14

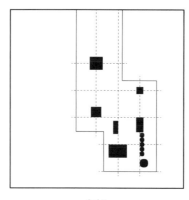

3.15

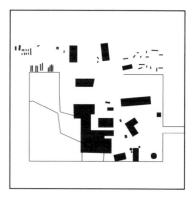

3.16

3.17
Odd Lots: adjacent properties with multiple buildings that cluster at intersections or corners but which do not exhibit visible divisions.

3.18
Soft-Body Clusters: adjacent zones that each have internal functional affinities but that do not overlap or share functions with nearby zones.

3.19
Banners: striations in which each band maintains distinct, linear logics of distribution among elements, natural features, and buildings.

3.20
Unsorted Mosaics: dense collections that appear to share sufficient formal and spatial similarities so as to be considered a contiguous whole.

3.21
Confetti 1: an a-hierarchical, provisional arrangement of diverse and dissimilar parts whose proximities reveal novel affiliations in which the addition or subtraction of parts is easily accommodated and does not damage existing relationships.

3.22
Confetti 2: multi-scalar superimpositions that become layered through the loose scattering of parts and in which the addition or subtraction of other parts does not damage existing relationships.

Aggregation Alternatives in Constellated ~~Farm~~ Fields.

3.17

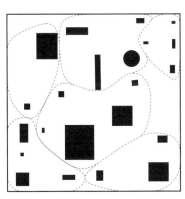

3.18

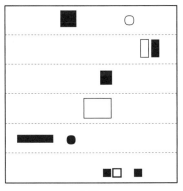

3.19

3.20

3.21

3.22

3.23—AS BUILT_Farmhouse in central Iowa. This is a typical condition of many farmhouses in which the porch orients towards the access road or driveway, deferring internal order and external address to infrastructural access.

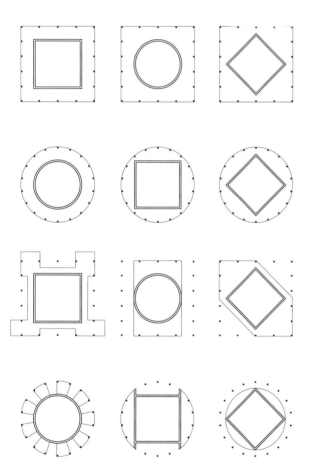

3.24—Diagrams for contextually non-cleaving & non-deferring porches or verandas as omni-oriented elements.

requisite for shared formal, material, or functional relationships. The loose arrangements of constellated fields are bound as an archipelago of sorts, or a field within a field—a sectioned-off territory of *stuff* within the larger site of the farm. Strangely, even constellated conditions rarely forgive the main house's apparent obligation of frontality.

Despite what might initially appear as disorder, accumulation patterns among constellated arrangements can be loosely qualified through analyzing the relationships of individual buildings, barns, fences, open areas specific to animals, driveways, storage, and trees or shelter-belts as well as septic areas and wells. Six of these conditions common to constellated farm fields are double-lots, clustered overlaps, packed mosaics, flag lots, gridded flags, and scattered flags.

Constellated farm fields adhere to Stan Allen's definition that a field condition "could be any formal or spatial matrix capable of unifying diverse elements while respecting the identity of each" as "loosely bound aggregates characterized by porosity and local interconnectivity."[7] However, these fields do not share the same qualities or influences as flocks, schools, swarms, crowds, or herds also referenced by Allen, which properly belong to the study of behavior and mathematics and which Allen applied to the logics of the city as a lever for architectural organization.[8] Instead, constellated farm fields are distinct from Allen's *Field Conditions* in three primary ways:

1   It is not uncommon for objects to outnumber human or even animal subjects. The density and inter-relations of objects and subjects is inverted when shifting focus from the city to the farm. Built objects typically outnumber subjects, though they do tend to respond to the vectorial effects of local environment and time through the directional pressures of prevailing winds and gravity. While this does represent physical form under the influence of vectorial forces, the ramifications of their influence are predominantly structural rather than organizational, and therefore space between objects responds to different criteria. There are exceptions to this, such as windbreaks or snow fences.

2   Figure-ground relationships are proportionally temporal to the scale of the figure. A house or barn figure against the ground is classically stable, whereas the diminishing scale of objects—say,

descending from a barn to a house to a shed to machinery to a coop to a bin to a fence post to debris—makes the exercise of figure-ground a temporal act of descending proportionality. However, confusion exists here. Is stored grain included as a figure or part of the ground; is the silo an open or filled circle? What about a compost pile, or a manure heap, split and stacked firewood, stacked hay, or a windbreak of trees? The material of the ground in constelled farm fields often becomes figures, meaning for example, the manure heap or compost pile certainly biodegrades into ground, yet its location is typically fixed as though it were a figure. Yet, the shape or profile of the figure is temporally variable.

3   There is no requisite for self-similarity among adjacent parts as interval, repetition, and seriality are not fundamentally critical to the constelled farm field. Constelled farm fields are an amalgam of proximities without the requirement for self-similarities in form, materials, organizations, or scales. Thus seriality and repetition are not critical, and intervals between objects are not uniform or fixed; a small barn may be adjacent to a large arena, a chicken coop proximate to a line of trees, a house near a pool, a garage by a porch, or a storage silo beside a compost pile. Without the burden of seriality, repetition, or fixed intervals, it is possible to biopsy or objectify each part within the whole as a reducible condition. Each part has semi-autonomous agency and the capacity to accept myriad internal orders, external expressions, physical orientations, or appropriated uses without reducing the salient accumulations or transactions of the whole, even as material energies—from flesh and blood, to oil and rust, to produce and manure—filter through the constellation of buildings, pastures, open ground, and equipment.

It follows that constelled farm fields reveal alternatives to fields defined by relational densities and vectorial pressures such as flocking, herds, contingent forces, or environmental intensities and instead suggest other relationships through the accumulation of objects as a field: soft-bodies that press against one another with internal constituents, hard-bodies that pile up, bricolage that layers and superimposes or collages, striations that allocate and differentiate, and confetti that scatters as ordering strategies. Distinct from behavioral

analogies, these alternative field conditions found among farms accommodate layering, overlapping, superimposing, scalar contrasts, loose scattering, piling, and unfixed relationships—strategies that sponsor diversity and ambiguity in use, expression, alteration, and material economy. These field conditions layer labor, leisure, material economies, architecture, landscape, furniture, machinery, resource accumulation, animal husbandry, and storage as conditions for exchanges between human, animal, environmental, and vegetal processes.

Camouflaged Drama
In The American Purlieu

The "mundane" qualities of remoteness and quotidian architecture are often associated with the farmhouse. Indeed, historically the farmhouse was built modestly with locally sourced materials and composed with functional rather than formal, aesthetic, or ideological imperatives. Often the forms and aesthetics of early farmhouses reflect the primary obligation to shelter, but they do so in a manner that underscores the economic constraints endured by a farming operation. Yet, this reading is not the whole story. In fact, the farmhouse's evolution within the "American Garden," as the American countryside was once called, was complex not in formal appearances but rather in what the lack thereof conceals. When the American heartland was referred to as the Great American Garden it was considered as a sort of purlieu: frontier land that was neither fully domesticated nor fully wild, but with the promise of agricultural abundance. Over time this garden became a contradictory territory of science and religion, cultural sophistication and bucolic repose, deeply politicized and home to few politicians. It was the territory of agricultural experimentation like max-till and air-blasting—attempts to increase rainfall by releasing moisture into the air through tilling the soil and using dynamite to push rainclouds around the prairie—as well as the space of fervid religious affirmation. This dichotomy remains at the core of the American heartland. The ever-accelerating mediation of the land by high technology is manifested in advanced pesticides research and development, GPS-monitoring of crops, and complicated cases of access and rights to water. Meanwhile, emphatically bucolic nostalgia is cast over the

American countryside as visualized in photographic farm-scapes at sunset and as celebrated by country music's tales of coming of age in the American heartland.

The ancestor of these contemporary contradictory attitudes toward the countryside can be found in Nathaniel Hawthorne's written records of time spent at Sleepy Hollow in the woods near Concord, Massachusetts, in 1844. While recording the sounds he heard in nature—snapping twigs, rustling leaves, bird calls—Hawthorne included the whistle of a train in the distance.

> But hark! There is the whistle of the locomotive—the long shriek, harsh, above all other harshness, for the space of a mile cannot mollify it into harmony. It tells a story of busy men, citizens, from the hot street who have come to spend a day in the country village, men of business; in short of all unquietness; an no wonder that it gives such a startling shriek, since it brings the noisy world into the midst of our slumberous peace. As our thoughts repose again, after this interruption, we find ourselves gazing up at leaves, and comparing their different aspect, the beautiful diversity of green.[9]

While this may at first seem like an ancillary note within Hawthorne's eight-page record of the day, it reveals the interjection of technologically advanced machines into the pastoral scene. The machine's entrance disrupts romanticized conceptualizations of the American garden and brings the latter into closer proximity with urban, and eventually global, political spheres.[10]

Some 150 years after Hawthorne's recording near Sleepy Hollow, the intrusion of technology in the garden had advanced from the locomotive to possibly the most disruptive technological object— the Intercontinental Ballistic Missile—that was routinely concealed within subterranean silos by the U.S. Military. The cultural and political weight of the machine had grown much more sinister as the once ubiquitously bucolic American garden was strategically punctuated with war-gardens where advanced technology, global politics, and nuclearization were quietly—and quickly—tucked into the American purlieu. Between 1961 and 1967 alone, over 1,000 Minutemen missiles were planted in the American heartland—each with a 1.2-megaton warhead— not including the Titan missiles or the Peacekeeper

missiles.[11] Over 2,000 missile silos were eventually tucked into the American purlieu. The head of the Army Corps of Engineers, Senator Sidney Martin, noted that it was "the greatest construction effort in history."[12] This occurred almost exclusively in remote landscapes across Wyoming, Nebraska, Colorado, the Dakotas, and Missouri—all middle American landscapes familiar to the farmhouse. One class of missile—the Peacekeeper missile—was distributed in what are called Flights. One Flight consisted of ten missile silos, each with one missile containing ten warheads. Each of the ten missile silo sites in the flight was at least three miles from the others, and each flight had a Launch Control Center positioned approximately at its center. During the Cold War, large territories of American farmland were colonized into a nuclear heartland, some areas concealing more than 200 ICBM sites. Earlier missile sites, such as the Titan I, II, and III series, housed the Launch Control Center directly adjacent to three missile silos as a single operational complex. For obvious reasons of security, distancing the missile silo sites from each other and especially from the Launch Control Center became the predominant organizational strategy. While the missile silos themselves were built underground, reaching depths of over 300 feet, the Launch Control Center required a covert, camouflaged, and unassuming identity in order to conceal military personnel and operations that otherwise would appear dramatically out of place in the farmlands of America.

Perhaps counterintuitively, the qualities often associated with the farmhouse—modestly built, remote, unassuming, sparsely populated—were

3.25—A cow blends into the surroundings near an ICBM site near Cheyenne, Wyoming.

3.26—ICBM site in Flight Q near Cheyenne, Wyoming.

3.27—ICBM site in Flight Q near Cheyenne, Wyoming.

3.28—ICBM site in Flight Q near Cheyenne, Wyoming.

3.29—ICBM site in Flight P near Cheyenne, Wyoming.

3.30—Launch Control Center for Flight Q near Cheyenne, Wyoming.

3.31—Launch Control Center heli-pad for Flight Q near Cheyenne, Wyoming.

3.32—Launch Control Center for Flight P near Cheyenne, Wyoming.

3.33—Launch Control Center heli-pad for Flight P near Cheyenne, Wyoming.

desirable to the United States Military during the nuclear armament of the Cold War, and the farmhouse type took on a critical role in national defense operations precisely because of these qualities. As a technique of painting or patterning uniforms and equipment for the purposes of blending them into their surroundings, camouflage soon became associated with the farmhouse. The U.S. military applied the principles of camouflage to the farmhouse for the purposes of veiling the Launch Control Centers. Built to look like typical, nondescript farmhouses, the Launch Control Centers were an architectural over-painting, a veil over what was really being sheltered there.

The farmhouse was an ideal construct for the camouflaging and concealment of the Launch Control Centers for Intercontinental Ballistic Missiles. Its unassuming, deferred orientation to the access road effectively pointing at nothing, along with its deceptive contrasts between interior and exterior and its multivalent cultural representations of American life, rendered the farmhouse as deceptively non-threatening in the arena of global politics and nuclear armament. Yet, 80 feet below the floor of these houses two Missileers worked in 12-hour shifts over an operational period of 22 years with command over the ten ICBM missiles in 20 Flights near Cheyenne, Wyoming. Though the size of the transformers, the air shafts in the side yards, the heli-pad, and the tall fencing might indicate that these were not ordinary farmhouses, they did little to disclose the geopolitical imperatives that swirl around their creation in the American heartland. Leveraging the prosaic qualities of the farmhouse and the ambiguity of a context never fully cultivated yet never fully wild, these pieces of militarized architectural camouflage quietly hid some of the most sinister and advanced technology in human history.

The legacy of the Cold War has shifted the associations of the farmhouse—and the farm—in the American imaginary. It cannot simply return to an ambiguous state of apoliticism that initially facilitated its wartime transmogrification. In the wake of the 20th century, the farmhouse is unendingly associated with geopolitical maneuverings and subterfuge while still maintaining its previous pluralistic associations.

It seems possible that the next "machine in the garden" will be the deployment of automated, drone-led agricultural practices. In some areas, this is already underway. With the hypothesis of an automated, remotely controlled labor force tending to agricultural production and distribution, it is possible that the farmhouse will become increasingly divorced from its contextual responsibilities. However, it remains to be seen if the psychological and representational dramas that surround the farmhouse will give way to new public imaginaries, or if the farmhouse will retain its complicated multiplicities of cultural, political, and social representations in the American purlieu.

1
David Larkin, *The Farmhouse Book: Tradition, Style, Experience* (New York: Universe Publishing, 2005), 18-57.

2
Larkin, *The Farmhouse Book*, 9.

3
The term purlieu came into use in Britain in the 15th century to describe land under ownership but uncultivated and therefore subject to forest law. Today, the term is used more generally to describe areas surrounding a specific place. I refer to it here in its historical use.

4
A. J. Downing, "What a Farmhouse Should Be" in *The Architecture of Country Houses* (New York: D. Appleton & Co., 1850), 138.

5
Downing, *The Architecture of Country Houses*, 141.

6
Larkin, *The Farmhouse Book*, 96.

7
Stan Allen, "Field Conditions" in *Points + Lines: Diagrams and Projects for the City* (New York City: Princeton Architectural Press, 1999), 92.

8
Allen, *Points + Lines*, 99.

9
Leo Marx. "Sleepy Hollow 1844" in *The Machine in the Garden: Technology and the Pastoral Ideal in America*. (New York City: Oxford University Press, 1964.), 13-14. Quoting Nathaniel Hawthorne's July 27, 1844 recording near Sleepy Hollow.

10
Ibid.

11
Gretchen Heefner, "Introduction" in *The Missile Next Door* (Cambridge: Harvard University Press, 2012), 2, 50.

12
Heefner, *The Missile Next Door*, 87, 92.

Fig. 3.34 (Below)
Site plan for a farmhouse near Sedalia, Colorado.
Endemic Architecture, 2018.

Fig. 3.35 (Right)
First Floor Plan (1 of 3) for a farmhouse near Sedalia, Colorado.
Endemic Architecture, 2018.

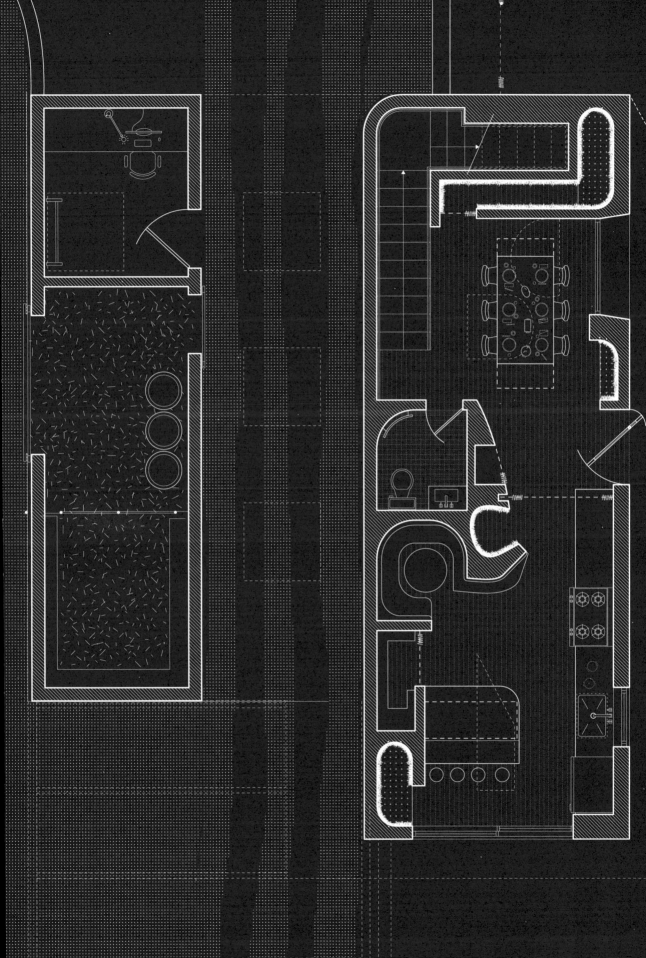

Fig. 3.36 (Below)
Elevations for a farmhouse near Sedalia,
Colorado. Endemic Architecture, 2018.

Fig. 3.37 (Right)
Second Floor Plan (2 of 3) for a farmhouse
near Sedalia, Colorado. Endemic Architecture,
2018.

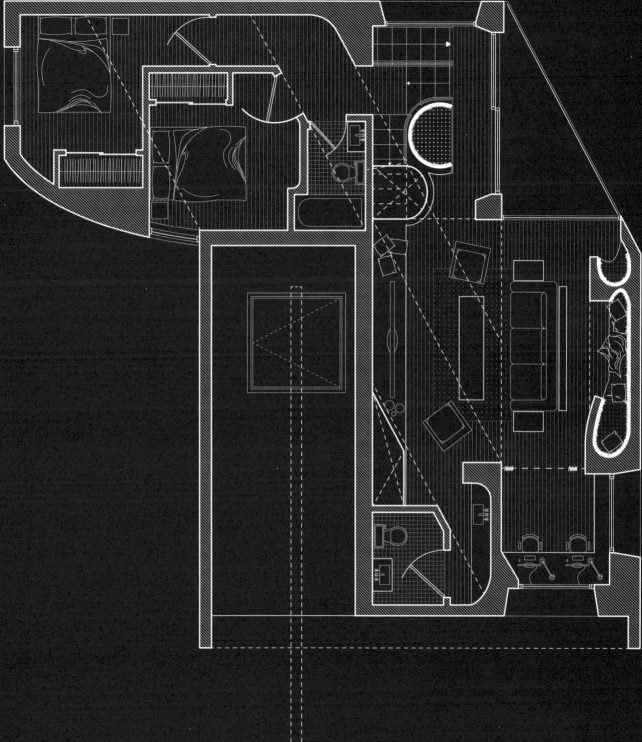

Odd Façades & Social Transformation in the Queen Anne House

CORNER

1

The place where converging lines or surfaces meet, forming an angle.

2

An architectural condition requiring the formal, spatial, and material resolution of an interior and/or exterior change in direction.

Prominent from around 1880 to 1910, Queen Anne houses are a subtype of Victorian characterized by steeply pitched roofs, a corner turret or tower, and a dominant front facing gable.[1] The façades of Queen Anne houses are typically asymmetric with a collection of elements including dormers, bay windows, towers, turrets, chimneys, and flared eaves, typically finished with wood shingles and clapboard. All of these houses include a half or full porch equal in height to the first floor. Queen Anne houses can be identified by their eclectic massing, including bulky roofs with a front gable, cross gables, or hipped roofs with cross gables below and multiple protrusions from the exterior surfaces. Whereas the ridge of a hip roof typically runs parallel to the front façade in other domestic types, in a Queen Anne house the ridge often runs front to back with a front and side gable located asymmetrically below. The orientation of the hip and location of the cross gables below add to the appearance and perception of bulky massing. Cross-gabled houses typically produce an L-shaped plan, though dominant front-gabled Queen Anne houses are more common, especially in urban contexts. Most Queen Anne houses exhibit a loaded enfilade in plan with an entry room, hallway, stairs, and kitchen along one side of the house, filling approximately one-third of the house's width. The other two-thirds of the ground floor plan comprise a four-room enfilade sequence with an entry room leading to a front parlor room, then a second parlor room, and finally a formal dining room with a breakfast nook at the back. Bedrooms are located on the upper floors.

1
Front-Gabled with Turret and Entry Porch.

2
Front-Gabled with Turret, Dormer and Wrap-Around Porch.

3
Tower with Recessed Porch.

4
Turret with Cross Gables and Wrap-Around Porch.

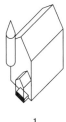

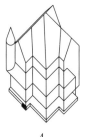

1   2   3   4

Westward Migration and
Material Economies

Perhaps no other residential type is more inappropriately named than the Queen Anne, as these houses have nothing to do with Queen Anne herself or the dominant Renaissance style that was favored during her reign in Britain (1702-1714). Promoted in the last quarter of the 19th century by a group of European architects, most notably Richard Norman Shaw, the Queen Anne type draws its principal influences from the late Medieval architecture popular during the reign of Queen Anne's predecessor, Queen Elizabeth (1558-1603). Today, Queen Anne houses have contradictory associations. On the one hand, they are associated with the lifestyle of the upper-class bourgeoisie; on the other hand, Queen Anne houses remind of a counter-cultural past, and sometimes even evoke haunted, or creepy sensations.

The Watts Sherman House, designed by H.H. Richardson and built in 1874 in Newport, Rhode Island, is generally considered the first Queen Anne house in the United States. The Watts Sherman House has a heavy appearance with rusticated stone, patterned brickwork, and thick massing. This material treatment was typical of East Coast Queen Anne houses, which were made of heavy, naturally colored materials such as stone and brick. As the type moved westward and southward, the materiality of the Queen Anne changed in response to local availability of materials and different climatic needs. The heavy materials of the East Coast Queen Anne were substituted with lighter materials—namely wood framing and ship-lap, shingle, or clapboard siding. In the Pacific Northwest, redwood timber was abundant and rot-resistant, and so materials shifted from stone and brick to redwood along the West Coast. This was especially true in San Francisco, where much of the current-day Embarcadero—including the San Francisco Giants baseball stadium, AT&T Park—was populated with industrial-era planing and sawing mills. Logged trees from Northern California and Oregon arrived at San Francisco mills where they would be planed, sawn, and milled into wood studs, ornamental details, shingles, lathe-turned balusters, columns, and so on. San Francisco became a place of innovation, where new sawing and planing technologies spurred dramatic increases in the production of Victorian wood parts.

By East Coast popular opinion these wooden Victorian houses were simplistic, cheap, thin, and lower-class versions of the East Coast Queen Anne. In particular, the application of exterior paint—something that might be done by any unsophisticated laborer—made them inferior in the minds of many East Coasters in comparison to the sophisticated natural surfaces of stone or brick. On the West Coast, however, such objections were rare, and the wood construction, especially the balloon frame, meant these Queen Anne houses could be built quickly and modified easily—crucial considerations for a burgeoning middle-class city. Seemingly infinite formal and ornamental variations and customization of intricate details could be achieved thanks to the mass production of wooden parts. The use of wood framing and wood-cut parts meant that houses could be constructed as more or less identical boxes with an ample variety of applied ornamentation, surface relief, and mass-produced yet customized detail. By the 1880s, wood-cut and milled parts and ornamental variations had become so widely distributed across the nation through an abundance of pattern books that the Queen Anne house, still largely unpopular among vanguard architects, was a preferred choice of the middle-class populace on both coasts and in cities across the country.

The relative speed with which a developer, contractor, or homeowner could order any number of pre-cut wooden parts from a pattern book and have them shipped by rail made Queen Anne detailing both affordable and compositionally customizable. By the early 1900s, nearly 48,000 Victorian houses had been built in San Francisco, most of them by developers building along the cable car lines emanating outward from downtown to the "suburbs." Shortly after the 1906 earthquake and fire, families and individuals began sub-dividing many of the remaining larger houses into two, three, or four separately rentable units—a spatial practice of residential sub-division which would later amplify the social impacts of the Gay Rights Movement, the Summer of Love, and cultural transformation through communal living in single-family houses.

4.1—The Cockettes inside their Oak Street house in San Francisco.
Photographs courtesy of Bud Lee Picture Maker (1971).

Odd Façades

Queen Anne houses, like the other houses in this book, have façades, not skins. The most obvious distinction between a façade and a skin is that a façade is a building's face, and faces reveal emotions and internal animations in ways that skin alone cannot. The term "building skin," pervasive in contemporary architecture, implies systematized, unified, or parametricized surface continuities and global wrappings that tend to absorb meaningful differences into a modulated or gradated system. By contrast, façades accommodate difference, idiosyncrasies, and discrete elements into only partially cohesive ensembles. While construction materials shifted from stone to wood in the Queen Anne's westward migration, the textural qualities of the exterior surfaces, particularly at the front, remained a defining feature. Whether by contrasting brick patterns and colors, rock textures and sizes, or shingle and siding patterns, Queen Anne houses exhibit delicate, low-relief material textures over bulky massing. In fact, Queen Anne houses used intentional irregularities in plan and elevation to avoid smooth, flat, or blank surfaces. Balloon framing was perhaps most significant in fostering these idiosyncratic effects because it enabled discontinuities in the wall structure through the easy incorporation of varied field-framed elements such as bay windows, niches, dormers, and turrets which may or may not correspond with interior functions.

Overhanging roofs, soffits, flared eaves, Dutch gables, dormers, witches' caps, finials, ornamented barge boards, hooded chamfered corners, chimneys, and front porches produce multiple receding shadows and variable surface depths in elevation. Perhaps the most notable description of these effects comes from turn-of-the-century San Francisco Bay humorist and author Gelett Burgess, who wrote in 1890:

> It should have a conical corner tower, it should be built of at least three incongruous materials, or better, imitations thereof; it should have its window openings absolutely haphazard; It should represent parts of every known and unknown order of architecture; It should be so heavily plastered with ornament so as to conceal its theory of construction; It should be a restless, uncertain, frightful collection of details giving the effect of a nightmare about to explode.[2]

Burgess's description of the Queen Anne house's outward address might also apply to the typical Victorian interior, decorated by collecting, accumulating, and displaying an abundance of materials, art, trinkets, and other stuff. The home of the Cockettes, a psychedelic drag theater group

69

formed in the 1960s, may be the most extravagant example of the Victorian homology between interior decoration and exterior qualities. The Cockettes styled the interior spaces of their Oak Street Victorian after their own costuming, as flamboyant expressions of gay and drag culture. Faux and real furs, exotic prints, long draperies, lush colors and wall coverings, eclectic furnishings, sprawling collections, plants, garlands, glitter, and so forth encrusted the interior space as if it were a stage set for burlesque, mimicking the exterior aversion to flat, smooth, and blank surfaces.

Celebrated urban historian and philosopher Lewis Mumford recalled his own upbringing in Victorian interiors in a somewhat different light. He echoed the sentiments of many a clutter-averse modernist when he wrote that:

> No one can truly appreciate the appeal of modernism who has not lived in a closed and cluttered Victorian brownstone, with its living room packed with the weekend collecting's of a lifetime—china vases, Japanese figurines, cheap statues of crocodiles, elephants and dancing nymphs, and often, as in Elvina Mumford's sitting room, lamps and lampshades as frilly and pink-blossomy as Lilian Russell.[3]

However, both the Cockettes and Mumford believed in the revolutionary reorientation of social and cultural values, and while they may have been diametrically opposed concerning the merits of Victorian décor, they both understood architecture, performance, and aesthetics as central to this revolution.

Another Corner Problem

One of the more perplexing features of the Queen Anne house is the corner turret, or corner tower. Here, the typical 90-degree corner of the house is conjoined with a cylindrical protrusion—one of the more surprising architectural encounters in the history of the single-family house. No other residential type has a corner condition like the Queen Anne house. The turret protrudes from the corner at a distance above and detached from the ground, while the tower is vertically continuous with the house from the ground to the roof. Both have their origins as defensive elements in fortification.

Medieval castles often had turrets and towers, manned by archers and affording panoramic views to monitor oncoming threats. The corner turret or tower makes sense under these Feudalist terms. The Queen Anne house's turret or tower today retains no connotation of fortification and is instead seen as charming and quaint, even welcoming. While it is tempting to explain the functional adaptation of the turret from the castle to the house by imagining a less-than-noble class's desire to protect their own homes, or at least to symbolize the purveying eye of protection, or even more simply to enjoy panoramic views otherwise occluded by the corner, these possibilities do little to explain the strange variations the corner turret has endured since.

Relieved of militaristic duty, the corner turret or tower becomes a cylindrical interior frontispiece to the parlor room on the first floor and to a bed or sitting room on the second or third floors. Unlike the farmhouse, the Queen Anne house has a parlor which is entered from an entrance hall, rather than the porch, in a loaded-enfilade plan. The porch, entry, hall, bathroom, and stairs sit on one side of the plan, while the hall leads to a four- or five-room enfilade on the other side. As the tower or turret protrudes from the corner, typically opposite the entry, it creates visual and spatial ambiguity regarding the limits of interiority by eliminating the corner altogether. The tower or turret's articulation of the corner altogether avoids Modernism's concern for detailing the meeting of perpendicular planes and Renaissance architects' column-to-arch corner problem. In a Queen Anne house, the corner turret or tower creates a problem not of planar perpendicularity nor of re-entrance, but rather of ambiguity, as the corner is replaced by volumetric rotundity.

In contrast to the canonical Modernist and Renaissance corners, which were both dimensionally systematized and locationally discrete, the Queen Anne turreted corner is both dimensionally variable and locationally ambiguous. Dimensional variation occurs through changes in diameter and vertical elongations yet is not preconditioned by an overriding geometric or gridded dimensional system, such as structural bays or dimensionally standard units. Locational ambiguity arises depending on the turret's location in relation to the two adjoining walls. The turret or tower can occupy a range of locations with varying degrees of intersection with other house elements; it can sit in front of the roof, co-planar with the roof, co-planar with either adjacent façade, inset from both adjacent walls, or recessed from the roof. If, for example, a turret's center point is aligned in plan with the side wall but in front of the front wall, the house appears deeper and taller. If the turret's center point is aligned with the front wall but outside the side wall, the house will appear wider and shorter. The variations in dimension and location affect both interior volume and exterior massing. As such, the Queen Anne house's corner problem is formal, spatial, and organizational but never systematized by a structural grid.

Prior to the Queen Anne's bloated corner, one of the hallmarks of residential iconicity was the visible termination of the roof on each side of the front façade; the roof completed the figure by enclosing the whole. In fact, the junction between the roof and two perpendicular walls was the very definition of the corner. In the case of a house with a tower or turret, only one terminal side of the roof is visible, whereas the other is interrupted by an attached form with its own discrete roof. This raises another question about the turreted or towered corner: is the turret or tower a compound figure with the house, or is it an autonomous form distinct from it? In the case of the turret, perhaps this can be answered by looking at the bottom, where the 90-degree corner of the house and the turret bottom meet. If the turret's bottom attenuates to the corner of the house, the whole can be said to be a compound figure: the merging of the turret bottom to the house confirms the corner as a necessary condition for continuity between house and turret. If, however, the bottom is a bowl or a flat plane, or if it attenuates away from the corner, then it can be said to be an autonomous figure: the decoupling of the bottom from the house corner below denies the corner as a necessary condition for continuity, allowing each volume to be independently legible.

Whereas the origins of the tower and turret reside in the functional imperative of looking outward, most often the towered or turreted corner in a Queen Anne house is occupied by a sofa or chairs oriented for looking inward. The inversion of one's gaze while occupying the absent corner reflects a vast range of formal, spatial, and material perversions to the Queen Anne corner including:

1   Distributed Legibility:

The corner turret or tower is a relational part within the whole. For example, a dormer window is a constituent of a roof, as a turret or tower is a condition of the corner. However, as parts within a whole, the tower and turret introduce locational ambiguity with variations on organizational, aesthetic, and compositional effects. For example, in neighboring houses the location of the tower introduces difference. On the left, the tower is protruded forward, thus altering the roof lines, relationship of tower to gabled front, and the appearance of bulk so as to appear wider and taller, whereas on the right the tower is recessed behind the gable, creating the opposite effects. Turrets and towers are modifiers of formal, spatial, and façade differences.

4.2—Neighboring houses with towers in Alameda, California.

2   Almost Familiar Forms:

Turrets' and towers' plurality of individual forms are one of their most salient qualities. Turrets and towers are so dear to the Bay Area that even the most modest of houses often tries to incorporate one, revealing a vacancy in our lexicon for what to

4.3—House with a tower in Oakland, California. (Is it a tower?)

71

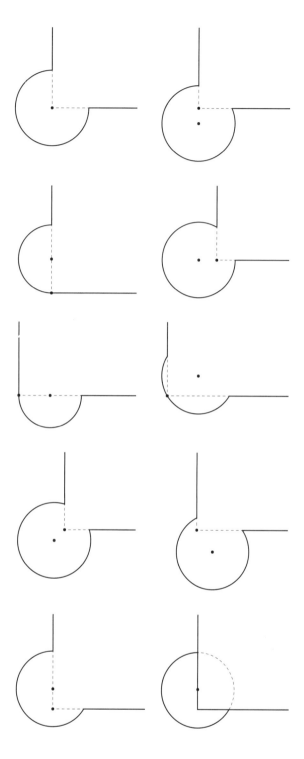

4.4—Locational ambiguity of the Queen Anne corner turret occurs in plan as a relationship between the diameter and the location of the center of the turret in relation to the adjacent walls.

call the results. In some cases, the proportion and scale of the turret (or tower; sometimes it's unclear) supersedes its host, diminishing the house in favor of an over-scaled, ghastly bloated turret-tower-like form of scalar misquotation.

3 Functional Maybes:
Turrets and towers are historically affiliated with specific function(s), yet their current-day status can be described as *functional maybes*: maybe they function, maybe they don't. The corner turret is no longer obligated to its militaristic history. It engenders functional (and representational) confusion and sometimes what we might call critical banality—architectural elements that appear so prosaic or common to the local context they can be seen anew as a form of criticism of that very same context's cultural or political underpinnings. In fact, there is perhaps no less accountable entity in American residential architecture than a windowless, uninhabitable corner turret.

4.5—Neighboring houses with nonfunctional turrets in San Francisco, California.

4 Contextual Infidelity:
Turrets and towers tend to convey contextual indeterminacy—even contextual ambivalence—rather than regionalism or contextual identification. Despite their local endearments and inscriptions in local codes, they are contextual infidels. For

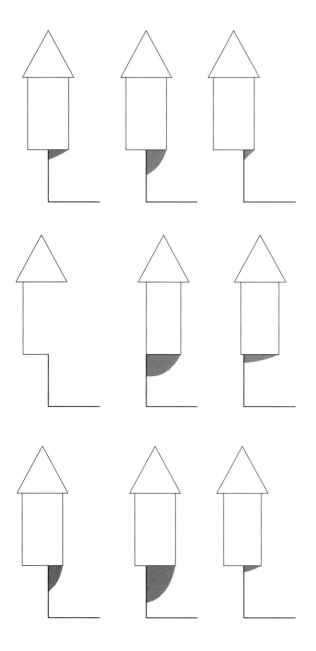

4.6—Locational ambiguity of the turret in plan (see 4.4) impacts the expressions of the façade making the house appear wider, thinner, taller, shorter, protruding, or receding, depending on its location in relation to the adjacent walls.

example, a photograph of a house with a turret is unlikely to reveal a particular context as turrets so easily migrated across cultural context—despite the fact that they are often pointed out as defining characteristics of cities and neighborhoods by local populations. In other words, to distinguish a Chicago from a San Francisco turret or tower requires additional terms of contextual evaluation.

From Counter Culture to Conservative Preservation

During WWII, San Francisco became a hub for members of the U.S. Military who were dishonorably discharged for their sexual orientation. Gay historian John Lougher states that apartment buildings in various parts of the city underwent "queerizing" in the 1940s, and more gays gravitated to the Queen City of the West in the 1950s to avoid the homophobia of much of the rest of the nation. It was in the 1960s, however, that "gay men's artistic and restoration sensibilities began to burst forth in San Francisco."[4] At the same time, during the late 1950s through the early 1980s Victorian houses in the San Francisco Bay Area were, unlike today, cheap to rent and often occupied by younger, progressive, counter-culture populations. While the Cockettes communed on Scott Street, Janis Joplin resided in an apartment on Ashbury Street just blocks away from the brightly painted purple house where the Grateful Dead spent the Summer of Love (and where the famous drug bust of 1967 took place).

In fact, many of the endearing architectural Victorian qualities that appeal to tourists, planners, preservationists, and residents of San Francisco today are the appropriations of counter-cultural expressions of gay and drug culture and the social transformations of the 1950s through 1980s. For example, one of the Bay Area Queen Anne's most noteworthy qualities is the exuberance of color, as noted by Elizabeth Pomada and Michael Larsen in *Painted Ladies: San Francisco's Resplendent Victorians*, "Drugs, media, and the counterculture have made this an age of color. A revulsion against the sterile, inhuman, intimidating monoliths spreading like architectural ooze over the downtown landscape helped foster the need for the enduring stability and character of the Victorians."[5] Because Victorians on the East

4.7
AS BUILT_A turret located behind the gable and in front of the front façade wall in San Francisco, California.

4.8
AS BUILT_Turret on a hipped roof
corner in San Francisco, California.

4.9
AS BUILT_A turret with a flat top
located adjacent to a chimney in
Alameda, California.

If turrets were hybridized with other
nearby elements they would produce
compound figures at the corner of the
house, confusing internal functions
through external expression.

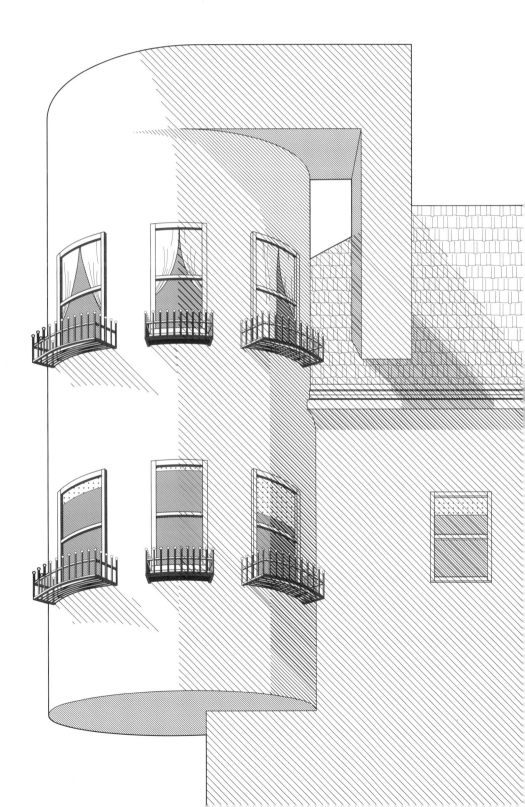

4.11
AS BUILT_When the bottom of a turret attenuates to the corner of the house, like this one in San Francisco, California, the turret and the house read as a compound figure.

78

4.12
When the bottom of a turret attenuates
away from the corner of the house it reads
as an autonomous form that is distinct
from the house, having its own internal
and external expressions.

4.13
If the fascia were swept across the
façade, it would extrude the turret with
it, creating roof that cannot be properly
named; it is part mansard, part gable,
part witche's cap, and part clerestory—
but none of these alone.

4.14
AS BUILT_The turret (cylinder), protruding gable top (triangular prism), and witches' cap (cone) merge at one point, unifying each part while simultaneously differentiating between them in San Francisco, California. These intersections recall Luis Monduit's geometric drawing series of intersecting primitive forms, titled *Some Penetrations of Solids* in which it is only possible to name specific primitive parts —cylinder, cone, etc.—but the whole that results from intersecting primitive forms is unnameable.

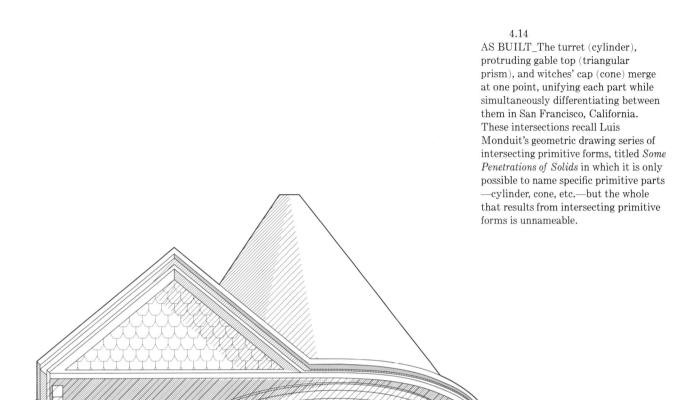

4.15
The flare detail is common in Queen
Anne houses, revealing a technique for
avoiding flat and smooth surfaces by
belling the exterior wall outward where
it crosses the interior floor. Flare details
are also commonly found on turrets.

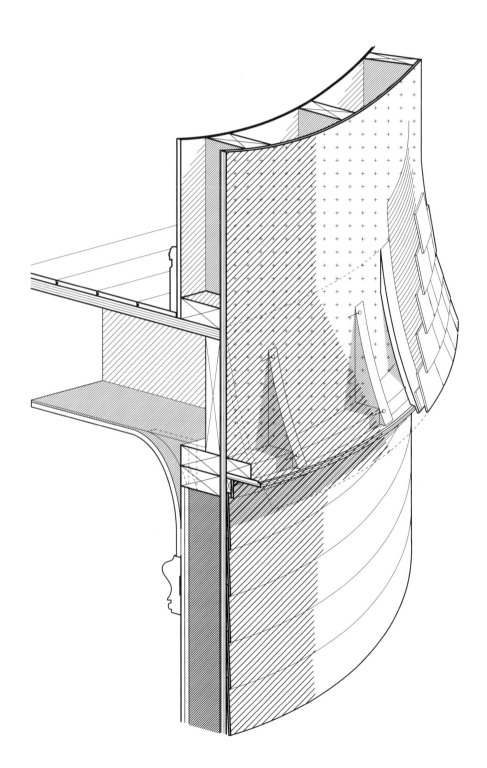

4.16
Though rare, turrets are sometimes found on the back corner of houses, like this one in Alameda, California.

4.17
The side elevation of this Slanted-Bay
Victorian house (revealed only when the
neighboring house was torn down due to
fire) in the Alamo Square neighborhood
of San Francisco, California, shows
a comparatively ad hoc composition
of windows, egress, and mechanical,
electrical and plumbing equipment
with a tacked-on rear addition that is in
violation of building and preservation
codes.

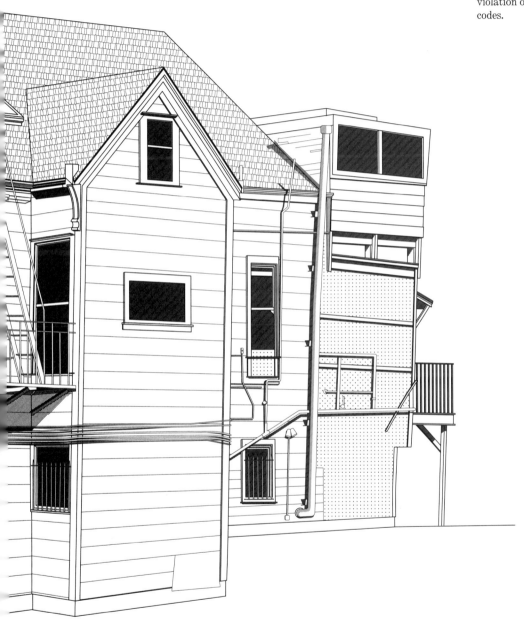

86

4.18
AS BUILT_The side elevation of this house
in the Alamo Square neighborhood of San
Francisco, California, reveals the disparity
between the regulations levied on the front
façade and the compositional freedom of
the side elevations.

Coast had historically been constructed using natural materials, they exhibited natural colors from varieties of stone and brick. However, the Bay Area Queen Anne housing stock, as well as the Bay's other Victorian varieties, opened the façade to a wide array of alternative architectural and cultural expressions from the composition of architectural form to individual preferences in the color of paint. Because roughly 17% of the population was openly gay during the post-war decade of the 1950s, San Francisco represented one of the nation's highest concentrations of gay culture, a fact which directly impacted the expressive qualities of the Victorian houses of San Francisco. "Gay men have been at the forefront of San Francisco's colorist movement from its beginnings in the early 1960s. They saved many of the city's degraded Victorians in distressed neighborhoods, buying them 'VOV'—vacant, open, and vandalized—and camping out inside while getting going on rehabilitation. ... The exteriors were the first things to be revived."[6] As groups of friends and gay couples banded together to rent out entire houses, the houses themselves figured prominently in the Gay Rights Movement as residents painted over the more subdued palettes that originally mimicked natural colors with bright, multi-colored palettes associated with gay culture and individual expression, serving also as visual calls for equality and social transformation. The Victorian houses of San Francisco, and the Queen Anne type in particular, are rare manifestations of a highly articulated, high-relief, and high-contrast Pacific Northwest architecture representing populations committed to cultural change and social equality.

Ironically, today San Francisco's Victorian houses, specifically the Queen Anne and Italianate varieties, are cornerstones of the city's notorious preservation polices—to the point that the Planning and Preservation Code even stipulates acceptable paint colors worthy of "preservation" in many neighborhoods, while requiring an application for a Certificate of Appropriateness in others. How ironic is a hearing on a Certificate of Appropriateness, given the social and cultural histories of the Victorians' counter-cultural tendencies! Most often, the colors permissible today are not the vibrant, saturated colors of the 1960s, but a more subdued, homogenized palette. What were once domestic symbols of social transformation and cultural influence on the national consciousness of human rights have been aesthetically molded into static representations of

architecturally conservative planning and preservation policies so tightly regulated that they no longer allow for the individualist self-expression that endeared these Victorian houses to a broader culture during times of social and political transformation. As a result of their aesthetic, cultural, historic, and economic value, many neighborhoods are heavily protected and maintained by the San Francisco Planning and Preservation Code—and the formation of these historical districts and their inscriptions into code have created socio-economic divisions and self-referential expressions that sharpen the contrast between the city's preferred image of itself and its need for evolving residential policies.

Perhaps surprisingly, the origins of this code trace back to the 1960s, during which time urban renewal prioritized tearing down Victorian houses, Queen Annes in particular, and replacing them with International-Style Modernism. Eventually the Victorian housing stock would fall from 48,000 to only 10,000. While the Preservation Code's intention was merely to stave off the effects of demolition on neighborhoods, the eventual slide into aesthetic regulation stands in contrast to the history of exuberant expressions found in the Victorians. Today, multiple code restrictions limit everything from color and shape to bureaucratic oversight by a special aesthetic task force composed of four city planners who make subjective judgments on any proposed alterations with regard to its likeness to existing Victorians in a particular neighborhood. This all begs the question: what is being preserved by this code? It seems clear that the preservation code is not designed to preserve San Francisco's greatest heritage—that of social transformation and the cultural expression of generational, political, artistic, environmental, and economic circumstances as manifested through architecture. The restrictiveness of the preservation code, intended to maintain particular aesthetic qualities for the purposes of "public health, safety, and welfare and for the enrichment of human life ... by fostering knowledge of the living heritage of the past" stands in stark contrast to the history of the Victorian house in general and the Queen Anne in particular as sources for social transformation and architectural imagination.[7] This is made all the more perverse by the preservation policy's obsession with the front-façade. It is not uncommon to encounter a house whose neighboring house has been torn or burned down, revealing strange compositions of the side façades and illegally built rear additions to all varieties of Victorian houses. The contrast between the demand for compliance of the front façade with regulatory preservation codes and explicit irreverence to the very same codes on the sides and backs of houses underscores the idea that preservation, to the City of San Francisco, exists independently of shifting cultural influences, social transformations, interiority, or alternative means of expression and is more simply understood as counterfeiting a compositional image divorced from its own urban heritage and cultural, social, and architectural origins.

Planning and preservation commissions routinely regulate architectural styles, forms, and materials under the banner of preservation. In nearly every instance, questions arise about what exactly is being preserved and for whom. By what metrics should we assess the value of cultural heritage in residential architecture? San Francisco's Queen Anne houses have been reduced to an aesthetic image which dilutes their legacy, and capacity, for social transformation and elevating cultural awareness. They have become commodified and codified by practices of bureaucratic exclusion and limitation, stemming the exuberant impulses that spurred the typological modifications in the first place and later evolved it half a century later. If one of the intentions of the preservation code is to preserve knowledge of the past through architecture, then one could reasonably expect the code to illuminate, even to promote, social transformation through gay culture, drugs, and media. The area's historic roots in social upheaval and the Gay Rights Movement create friction against today's appropriated historic preservation, which tends to affiliate with the high-end rental market of San Francisco.[8] Such bureaucracy limits the preservation of what was fundamentally a project in heterogeneity.

The Queen Anne residential type has never been favored among avant-garde architects, though it has long been beloved by constituencies unconcerned with the discipline of architecture.[9] In San Francisco, as in many cities, the current-day policies levied on these houses are often perceived as limiting the contemporary architect to the forms or expressions of the past. In fact, the general lack of a theory of preservation among architects leaves a critical aspect of the built environment under the domain of bureaucracies intent on the idea that preservation is an act of stable retrospection.[10] While the avant-garde in art, music, and architecture is typically ambivalent to the affinities of broader culture, such a legacy of formal, spatial, and material expression, corner problems, mass customization, and manufacturing innovations along with a history of social and cultural transformation, makes the Queen Anne house an ideal source for both critiquing preservation and provoking alternative models of it that are both retrospective *and* projective.

1
The principal type, Victorian, covers the time-frame approximately equivalent to the reign of Queen Victoria (1837-1901).

2
Gelett Burgess is quoted on a poster at the Haas Lilienthal House, SF Heritage, 2007 Franklin St., San Francisco, CA 94107 (attended tour September 20, 2018).

3
Donald Miller, "Architecture as a Home for Man" in *Lewis Mumford: A Life* (New York: Grove Press, 1989), 181-183.

4
Will Fellows, *A Passion to Preserve: Gay Men as Keepers of Culture* (Madison: University of Wisconsin Press, 2004), 132.

5
Elizabeth Pomada & Michael Larsen, *Painted Ladies: San Francisco's Resplendent Victorians (*New York City: E.P. Dutton, 1978), 7.

6
Fellows, *A Passion to Preserve*, 132.

7
Section 1001 ("Purposes"), the San Francisco Planning Code Article 10: "Preservation of Historical Architectural and Aesthetic Landmarks," last updated 2019. Available through the American Legal Publishing Corporation at http://library.amlegal.com/nxt/gateway.dll/California/planning/article10preservationofhistoricalarchite (accessed September 17, 2018).

8
A central aspect of this is NIMBYism characterized by a population that co-opts the preservation code to avoid the addition of new forms or and expressions seen as undesirable.

9
Clement Greenberg articulated differences between the avant-garde and kitsch in art, noting that the avant-garde tends to work on its own mediums, while kitsch is familiar to the point of being quaint or easily consumed. This reference calls into question the Victorian house's typically kitsch associations, suggesting instead that perhaps it can be understood as avant-garde. Clement Greenberg, "Avant-Garde and Kitsch" [1939] in *Art and Culture* (Boston: Beacon Press, 1961).

10
In OMA's preface text, "Cronocaos," for the 12th Venice Architecture Biennale Rem Koolhaas advocates for an architectural theory of preservation and its social and architectural implications in post-war culture. He calls for new models of mediating between preservation and development, which I also echo here.

4.19
Left: Composite plan made by cutting and pasting diagrams
for turrets, bay windows, corner bays, and side yard recesses
found at varying scales in the San Francisco Planning and
Preservation Code. Endemic Architecture, 2018

4.20
Right: Plans for a Queen Anne house in San Francisco,
California. Endemic Architecture, 2018

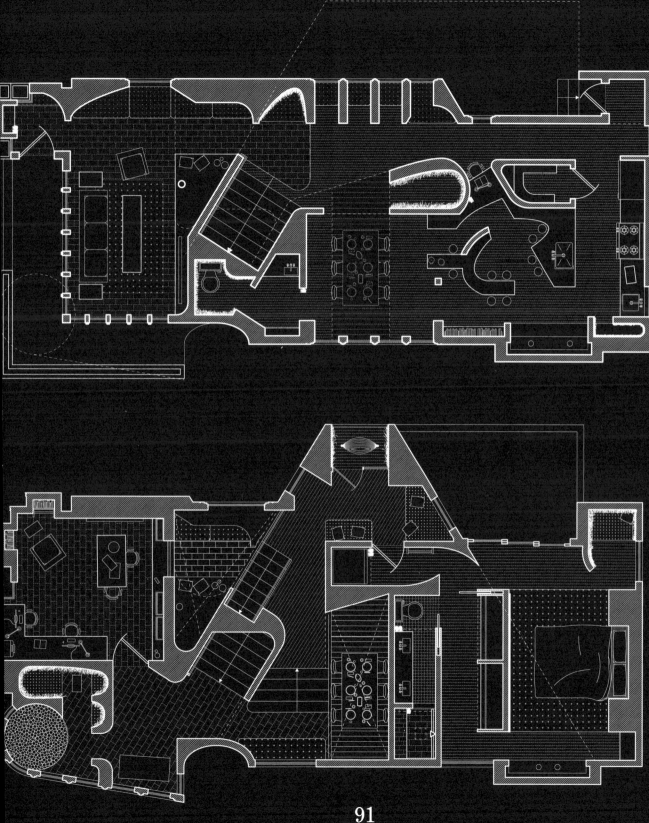

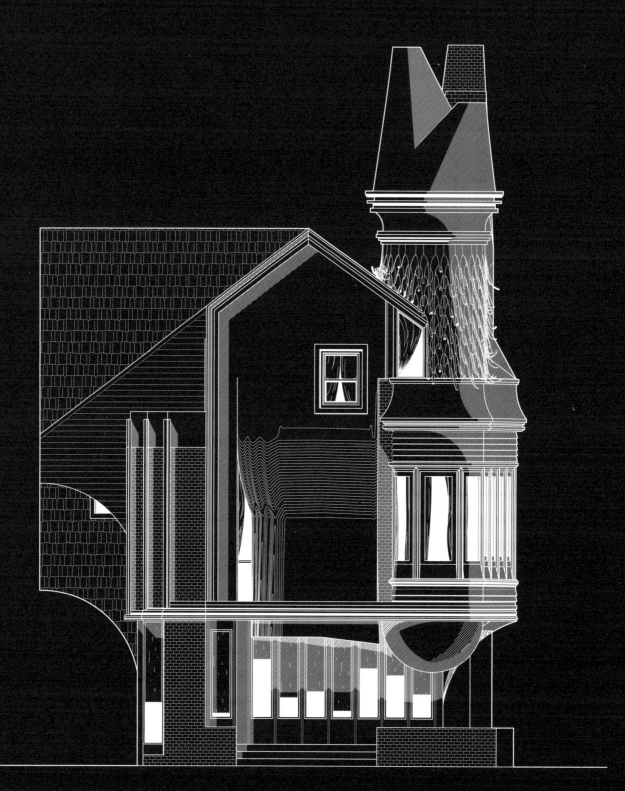

Kit Homes & The Mathematics of the American Foursquare

KIT

1

A set of articles or equipment needed for a specific purpose.

2

A [typically] mass-produced assortment of materials used to construct a particular thing. Parts are easily modified, augmented, or interchanged, and parts from one kit may be swapped with parts from another kit, thus introducing variations into a systematized logic of distribution and assembly.

The American Foursquare is typically a two-and-a-half-story house with a hip roof and central dormer, often featuring dormers on each side as well. It has a square or nearly square plan with a large front porch and a two-by-two room composition that gives the house its name. The American Foursquare is typically 24' × 24', 24' × 26', 26' × 26', or 26' × 28'. If the plan varies from a square, it is always deeper than it is wide. The American Foursquare was an evolution of the Prairie and Craftsman styles, as the Queen Anne and Colonial Revival styles were waning in the late 1890s. Originating in the Midwest, the American Foursquare most often had a balloon frame, with a later shift to a platform frame. It was a common type for farmhouses, suburbs, and cities alike. Its Midwestern origins were registered in early names for the style as it emerged locally—for instance, the Prairie Box, Cornbelt Cube, or the Denver Box—before it was called the American Foursquare.[1]

The American Foursquare began appearing in catalogs and plan books before 1900 as a kit home. Builders continually sought to simplify the house's plan and structure to make it affordable for a growing middle class, and many Foursquares adopted more open floor plans between 1905 and 1915. The Foursquare was one of the most widely built residential types of the early 20th century due to its simple form and standardized plan. It could easily adopt material and ornamental variations and could even be adapted to a one-and-a-half-story variant.

1
American Foursquares are typically differentiated on the exterior by the location of front steps, front door, and the number of windows on the 1st and 2nd floors.

Compounding Rowe's Complex

In his canonical essay "The Mathematics of the Ideal Villa" (1947), Colin Rowe theorized the proportioning and organizational systems that underlie many Palladian villas. In his essay, Rowe performed a comparative analysis of Le Corbusier's Villa Stein at Garches and Palladio's Villa Malcontenta. Rudolf Wittkower used the same primary terms of analysis as Rowe in his own analysis: he used the villas' plans to construct a generalizable system of regulating lines that condition organization and form through a structural-spatial grid. Whereas Rowe purposefully distanced the villas' ordering logics from cultural and historical circumstances by advocating for a transcendent language of form and proportion as a virtue of mathematical (universal) 'truths', Wittkower was concerned with historical formal analyses associated with humanist ideals in architecture. Rowe observed that Malcontenta and Villa Stein are each 8 units in length, 5.5 units in width, and 5 units in height with projecting elements occupying 1.5 units in depth. He went on to note that Palladio's structural system requires the second floor to have the same plan as the floor below, whereas Le Corbusier's framing system allows a free arrangement of stacked floors, introducing asymmetries in plan and elevation. This system, according to Rowe, allowed Le Corbusier to subvert the Palladian tripartite façade with elevations divisible by four. Rowe continued:

> Palladio sought complete clarity of plan and the most lucid organization of conventional elements based on symmetry as the most memorable form of order, and mathematics as the supreme sanction of forms.... Le Corbusier admires Byzantine and the anonymous architecture of the Mediterranean world; and there is also present with him a purely French delight in the more overt aspects of mechanics. The little pavilion on the roof at Garches is, at the same time, a temple of love and the bridge of a ship.[2]

Twenty-five years later Rowe turned away from an ideal mathematics of form and organization and towards collage. In both his introductory essay to *Five Architects* (1972) and his book *Collage City* (1978), coauthored with Fred Koetter, he argued for heterogeneity and shifting hierarchies

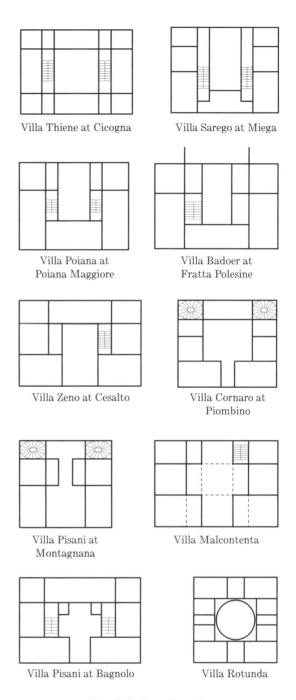

Villa Thiene at Cicogna

Villa Sarego at Miega

Villa Poiana at Poiana Maggiore

Villa Badoer at Fratta Polesine

Villa Zeno at Cesalto

Villa Cornaro at Piombino

Villa Pisani at Montagnana

Villa Malcontenta

Villa Pisani at Bagnolo

Villa Rotunda

5.1—Palladian villa grids, redrawn from Rudolf Wittkower.

as formal and organizational strategies in favor of mathematical reducibility. In his analysis of the ideal villa, Rowe's claims required a belief in certain mathematical truths, whereas his later texts again endorsed a formal analytic project through ahistorical composition, but this time around he endorsed heterogeneous collage rather than ideal ordering.[3]

In 1994 Greg Lynn gave his own now canonical take on "The Mathematics of the Ideal Villa" in his text "New Variations on the Rowe Complex," in which he rethought mathematical systems of organization that do not align with ideal types. Lynn's assessment was that irreducible, anexact forms "would resist transcendent and universal ideological proclamations precisely because they cannot be idealized and reproduced identically" and that "methods of differential organization do not necessarily need to calcify into fixed typologies."[4] Borrowing from non-human behaviors such as swarms and animal transportation systems, Lynn suggested that deviations arising through variation build "consistency, continuity, and identity through differentiation."[5] In particular, he cited ant communities as an exemplary counterpoint to idealized mathematical reduction. By recalling Kevin Kelly's work on pheromone trails of ants in the book *Out of Control: The Rise of Neo-Biological Civilization* Lynn noted that rather than traveling an optimal line between food source and ant hill, ants collectively employ a random walk mode in which some ants deviate from the path, thus introducing differentiations and deviations in which new food sources can be found. This led Lynn to identify Rowe's "blind spot" as an inability to acknowledge differentiation among ordering logics.

Rowe and Wittkower would likely both have been familiar with variations on American Foursquares, but neither mentioned them in their analyses, despite the plausibility of incorporating them into the disciplinary fold of proportional tendencies and ordering grids among square- or rectangular-cell plans with cubic massing. Perhaps they ignored the Foursquare because its variations never amounted to an ideal type or because the internal divisions of the American Foursquare are asymmetrical and therefore deviate from explicit proportional systemization. The American Foursquare may also have been too commonplace, too sub-Architecture, too easy to order from a Sears Roebuck catalog, or too provincial to wield influence or to be considered appropriate company

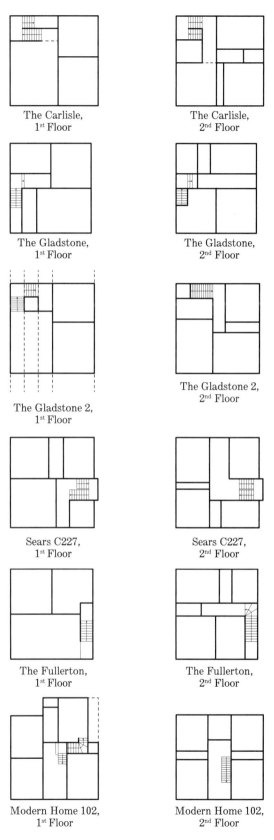

The Carlisle,
1st Floor

The Carlisle,
2nd Floor

The Gladstone,
1st Floor

The Gladstone,
2nd Floor

The Gladstone 2,
1st Floor

The Gladstone 2,
2nd Floor

Sears C227,
1st Floor

Sears C227,
2nd Floor

The Fullerton,
1st Floor

The Fullerton,
2nd Floor

Modern Home 102,
1st Floor

Modern Home 102,
2nd Floor

5.2—Sears Roebuck American Foursquare kit home plan diagrams.

for the likes of Palladio or Le Corbusier. Although Lynn also made no mention of the Foursquare, his parable about ants' introducing individual deviations in order to avoid reduction to linearity can be borrowed to describe variations in the Foursquare house.[6] Lynn foregrounded his claims by stating that he "would posit a parable that combines both mathematical reduction and diversification in a single continuous system" and concluded by noting that "this type of differentiation is not opposed to but continuous with the mathematical and the systemic, forming one system, the continuity of which is punctuated with moments of reduction and simplification, proliferation, and free differentiation."[7] Lynn did not clarify whether there are durational limits on the terms of continuity or on the reach of systemization, leaving us to assume that the ant trail is sufficient evidence for an architectural condition of systematized continuities exhibiting moments of idiosyncrasy, differentiation, and isolated reduction.[8]

Ultimately, Lynn advocated for topological form-making processes that are anexact yet rigorous, borrowing from Edmund Husserl's *The Origins of Geometry*. Techniques such as slicing rather than punching to create openings—or using undulating tessellations rather than A-B column grids to supply structural support—correspond to non-ideal geometries. Indeed, Lynn explicitly revealed his distaste for reductive processes divorced from the influences of external contingencies and his preference for continuous systems exhibiting both simplification and differentiation at the scale of individual buildings. The provincial, mass-produced, and circumstantial articulations of the American Foursquare are presented here as a fresh and contestable middle ground between Rowe and Lynn. By turning conceptualizations of systematized continuities exhibiting moments of idiosyncrasy, differentiation, and isolated reduction away from biological and topological formal affiliations and toward the production processes of residential construction in kit homes over a relatively short period of time, we can biopsy some of the key terms, like *continuity* and *systemization*, that define Wittkower's, Rowe's, Eisenman's, and Lynn's theoretical lineage.[9]

Continuity & Isolated Reduction

Whereas Lynn concentrated on the effects that field-based contingencies exert on the formal manifestations of a discrete object, it is also possible to reverse this gaze and consider the effects that a collection of objects exert on an expansive field. This ushers in a durational alternative to fixed typology: genealogy.[10] Genealogy is the study of trait modification occurring over time and in shared proximities, indexing evolutionary shifts rather than momentarily fixed conditions, singularities, or idealization. Following cultural, social, environmental, and technological variations, genealogy reveals both continuous reductions and amplifications that vary in degree rather than in kind, typically manifested through the expression of individual parts within a larger whole.

The American Foursquare evolved out of modifications to the Queen Anne and revivalist styles of the Victorian period by simplifying their planimetric and elevational agitations into a four-square plan with cubic massing. Also borrowing from the Craftsman style and the Prairie School, the American Foursquare is a recombinant residential architecture whose continuities and idiosyncrasies are best seen in a genealogical relationship to the forms, elements, and expressions of other, time-proximate houses, as well as to the evolving expressions within a particular type.

Continuity is a matter of the degree of difference and duration of modifications made over time by individual deviations within in a collective field. Assessing continuity requires an understanding of preceding and following modifications and variations that reflect shifting cultural attitudes, technological advancements in construction, changing needs, and—most importantly—individual preferences in expression through color, elements, composition, materials, additions, and renovations. This last category of change by individuals is analogous to the ants' random walk mode referenced by Lynn. Disparities in the private economics and proclivities of homeowners, architects, and contractors further proliferate deviations in an opportunistic process, preventing linear reduction to an ideal type.

5.3
American Foursquare kit
homes listed in the Lewis
Manufacturing Catalog,
Homes of Character, in 1920.

The ORLANDO

The PIPING ROCK

The CORONADO

The REGAL

The LANCASTER

The MARENGO

The SHELDON

The PORTLAND

The MALVERN

The CARLISLE

The PRINCETON

The CANTON

The REVERE

The KENDLETON

The NEW SHERIDAN

The ROSEMONT

The RALEIGH

The ROCHELLE

The GOULD

Systemization & Differentiation

As in the case of the Queen Anne houses of the late 1800s, the emergence of pattern books, catalogs, and kit homes ironically fulfilled a Modernist ambition for mass customization and prefabrication. The American Foursquare's relationship to machine industrialization, technological advancement, labor, mass production, and customization corresponds even more closely to Gropius's or Le Corbusier's tenets of Modernism. Le Corbusier, for example, championed the machine, industrial efficiency, interchangeable parts, and customization through standardization, while Gropius championed prefabrication. Le Corbusier's 1920 Citrohan House was imagined to be efficient like a car, easily built in series and made available to the masses. However, the Citrohan House not only seemed to prohibit individualized expressions, but also suppressed the possibility for meaningful idiosyncrasies in form, façade, and material through dogmatic stylization and Modernist idealization. American Foursquares, often built in multiples by averagely skilled field labor piecing together mass-produced, machine-made, industrially delivered, standardized yet customizable and orderable parts—from shingles, to balusters, to windows, to cornices, to rugs, to moldings, to lamps, to tables, to wallpaper, to paint color—did the opposite: they opened up the possibility of mass-produced houses with individualized expressions.

Kit Boxes / Box Kits

In 1906, Frank Kushel was managing Sears's China merchandising department when he was tasked with the dubious job of dismantling the company's catalog-ordered building materials department due to declining revenue. However, as Kushel began this process he became convinced that the department could become profitable if Sears changed the way building materials were sold. Kushel proposed to Richard Sears that instead of dismantling the building materials department they should shift from selling assorted parts to selling entire homes as consolidated packages that included everything from nails to windows, staircases, and paint. Kushel branded his proposal "The Modern Homes Program," and in 1908 Sears Roebuck published its first *Book of Modern Homes and Building Plans*.

In 1911 Sears recognized that the growing middle and working class, who comprised the primary demographic looking to buy kit homes, were increasingly ignored by the conservative banking industry, so the company began a program to finance the homes they sold. The terms were 25% down and as little as 6% interest for five years or higher rates for fifteen years. By undercutting the banks, Sears Roebuck made kit homes accessible to wider populations. Prior to 1914, the kits specified lumber that had to be cut in the field, but in 1914 the company began releasing kits with ready-cut, factory-fit framing, saving an estimated 40% on labor. "The lumber was stamped with the Sears name and numbered on the ends of the boards to correspond to numbers on the floor plans, so mistakes in assembly were less likely – though far from impossible, as many extant Sears houses testify by otherwise inexplicable deviations."[11] The Sears Roebuck kit homes were also popular in industrial towns, such as Carlinville, Illinois, "where Standard Oil of Indiana built a million dollar development for employees of Schoper Coal Mine."[12] The last *Modern Homes* catalog was released in 1940, though the program had already begun to fail due to defaulted mortgages and the Great Depression.

Pattern books and kit-of-part houses enabled mathematical and material systemization of delivery and construction while avoiding identical reproductions due to individual preferences and differentiations made in the field. This process was enabled by newer manufacturing technology, such as wood planing and sawing, as well as the standardization of building material sizes and specifications, such as standard lengths for studs and plywood. Particularly important was the balloon frame, and later the platform frame. The ease and expedience with which houses could be framed—whether by field-cutting lumber or by factory-fit pieces—enabled on-the-spot variations introduced by local laborers responding to homeowners' changing preferences or in-the-field problem solving. In fact, the balloon frame and platform frame allowed systematized continuities to exhibit moments of idiosyncrasy, differentiation, and isolated reduction.[13] Contrary to the types of systemization Lynn wrote about, here systemized continuity is achieved through the use of prefabricated parts, the wood frame, and dimensional standardization. Moments of differentiation occur freely through the comparatively easy incorporation of variations

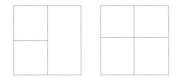

5.4 (above)
1:2 and 2:2 American Foursquare plan diagrams of a three-room and four-room arrangement.

5.5 A–E (right)
Because the American Foursquare is geometrically composed with a 1:2 or a 2:2 arrangement of squares treated as independent cells, it opens the possibility for aggregation abstractions that hypothesize alternative plan arrangements for a foursquare house.

PP. 102–103

5.6
AS BUILT_An updated Fullerton close to the original design in Denver, Colorado.
5.7
AS BUILT_Hillrose in Griffith, Indiana, with a removed front porch, added small entry vestibule and planters, and wood siding replaced with vinyl.
5.8
AS BUILT_Hillrose in Bridgeport, Connecticut, with an added upper floor room over the porch.
5.9
AS BUILT_Modified Fullerton in Aurora, Illinois, with an enclosed porch and added air-conditioning window units.
5.10
A rare pop-top Foursquare in Denver, Colorado.
5.11
AS BUILT_Hillrose in Oak Park, Illinois, with an enclosed front porch, making a new interior room.
5.12
AS BUILT_Hillrose near Convoy, Ohio, close to the original design with a modified foundation and porch handrails.
5.13
AS BUILT_modified Fullerton in Elgin, Illinois, with an added front room, relocated entry, and re-finished with stucco.

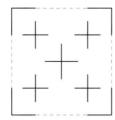 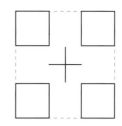 

5.5A—Plus Plans: Perpendicular walls at mid-points or corners of the four cells create hybrid enfilades.

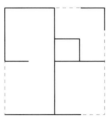 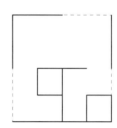 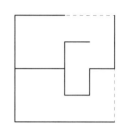

5.5B—Incomplete Squares: Perpendicular, incomplete walls of square cells produce ambiguous interior enclosures.

 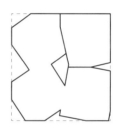 

5.5C—Clipped Figures: Rotating the cells within a binding perimeter can produce internal courtyards with a pocketed perimeter.

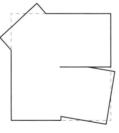 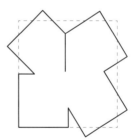 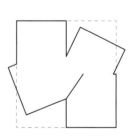

5.5D—Complete Figures: Rotating the cells in breach of a binding perimeter can produce complete figures with a protruding perimeter.

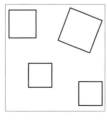 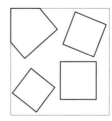 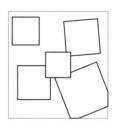

5.5E—Scattered: Loose-fit arrangements isolate rooms within a uniform volume.

5.6

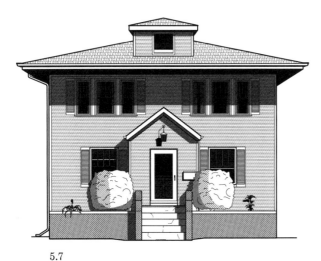

5.7

5.8

in form, elements, materials, rooms, walls, and façade composition by local field laborers. Sears Roebuck, for example, released fourteen balloon- or platform-framed American Foursquare kit homes between 1908 and 1940. With the average kit home including 25 tons of material and 30,000 parts shipped by railroad, the Sears Roebuck kit homes were as much a system of industry logistics, labor, and material dissemination as they were affordable single-family houses. The most obvious differentiations over time occur in changing materiality and the addition of new rooms. Wood siding was replaced as vinyl siding became popular in the 1980s, and PermaStone replaced a lot of real stone. Dormers, chimneys, windows, eaves, roofs, and the most commonly modified element of all—the porch—varied as additions were tacked on, porches were enclosed or removed, tops were popped, and rear additions expanded the house into the back yard. These elements help to resist idealization as individual homeowners modified, renovated, or otherwise altered houses over time in ways that would be impermissible on canonical or culturally protected works. These individual modifications proliferate collective differences through an opportunistic process reflecting changing needs, environmental circumstances, taste, economics, and regional affinities.

Many companies, including Gordon VanTine and Montgomery Ward, made Foursquare kit homes. Aladdin Kit Homes had a particularly wide variety of options, as did Lewis Manufacturing, who listed 23 American Foursquare variations in their 1920 *Homes of Character* catalog, which declared that "the ugly façades of costly stone and the distracting ornament and jigsaw decoration of the houses of the last generation are gone. We know now that simplicity with good lines is more to be prized than ornament without them."[14] The introduction continues, "Gone is the parlor with its hideous contorted furniture, the custom of leaving the best room in the house utterly unused except on rare occasions."[15]

The concluding paragraph of the introduction states that "the hundred Lewis designs with their varying sizes and opportunities for endless variations in material and color schemes give the builder every chance to express his own tastes."[16]

5.9

5.11

5.12

5.10

5.13

103

5.14 – 5.21

The logic of the American Foursquare kit home as a collection of
discrete parts—modified by individuals both upon construction and
over time—suggests a strategy of combining Foursquare kit homes
that otherwise do not belong together. These drawings are not rigorous
enough to be considered under the rubric of *kit-bashing* because there
has been no attention paid to individual parts within the original kits.
Instead, the modifications and deviations evident in the small collection
of AS BUILTS are taken as completed wholes that have previously
undergone alterations to the kit. They have then been combined here
as first- and second-floor halves, combinations which are absurd as
a projection of actual possibility yet which underscore the idea that
systemization can breed differentiation and that continuity depends
on the degree of difference.

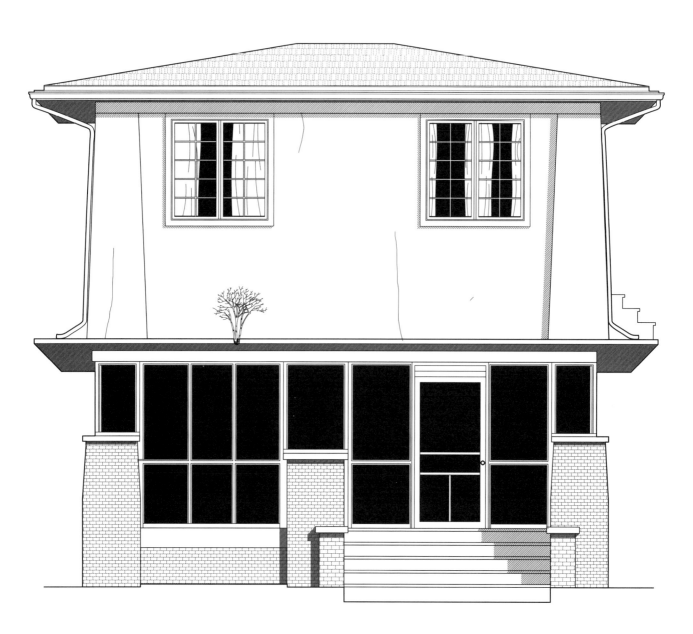

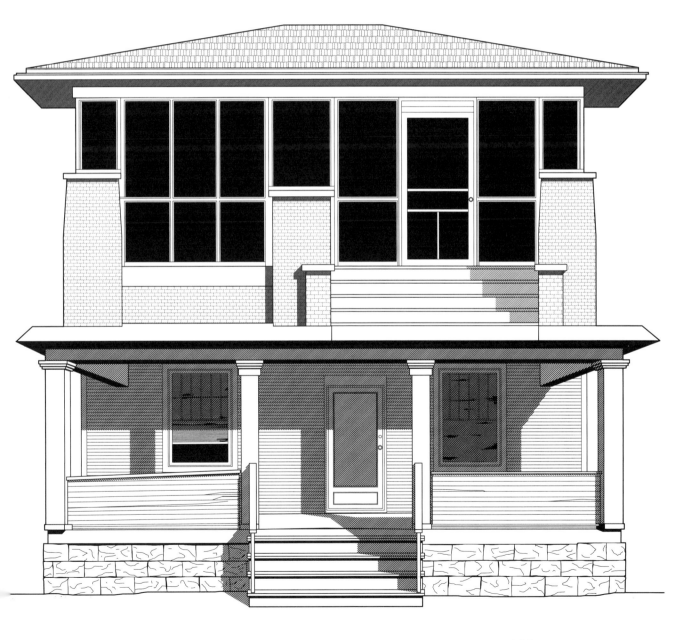

Centers, Peripheries, Centripetal and Centrifugal Rectangles and Squares

Even if we recognize the tiring perils of reductive grid analyses, a curiosity lingers that such analysis can help satisfy. Although the architects of the American Foursquare did not explicitly draw influences from Palladio, Palladian villas and the American Foursquare nevertheless share a blockform with a distinct condition between their centers and peripheries. The first distinction between an American Foursquare and a Palladian villa is obvious: the kit homes do not follow classical proportional harmonics of symmetry. Rather, the American Foursquare tends to use midpoints along the exterior walls as origin points for spatial division, yielding a 1:2 (1 rectangle, 2 squares) or a 2:2 (4 square) room plan on the ground floor and typically a 2:2 (4 square) room plan on the second floor. The resulting 1:2 or 2:2 plan quadrants on the first floor are treated locally, as independent cells determined by programmatic allocations. This leads to a lack of internal symmetry as each quadrant exhibits its localized rules that are often distinct from the other cells. This geometry stands in contrast to the global symmetry of Palladian villas, where the center becomes an accessible (approximate) square. In the American Foursquare the opposite is true, as the center is occluded by either intersecting walls or a wall dividing two or more rooms.[17]

The first ramification of de-spatializing the center of the American Foursquare, the point at which all four square cells meet, is that it requires the house to have a specific front. As the center is relieved from spatial, circulatory, or programmatic occupation, the perimeter must satisfy the necessary spatial sequencing beginning with entry in one of the cells, thus manifesting a clear frontality. By contrast, consider Villa Rotunda, in which each of the four elevations appear equally as the front, and upon entry from any side one arrives at the center. While not all of Palladio's villas are in-the-round like Villa Rotunda, and they exhibit frontality to greater and lesser degrees, the possibility for spatial occupation of the center suggests that entry could be achieved from any side, through which one will always arrive at the center, de-emphasizing the idea of a single front. On the other hand, the American Foursquare's spatial negation of the center forces a choice of frontality to which the other three cells must respond. Similarly, from civic buildings

to stadiums, and from government facilities to institutions, whether or not the center is publicly occupiable relates directly to the exterior expression of frontality and public address.

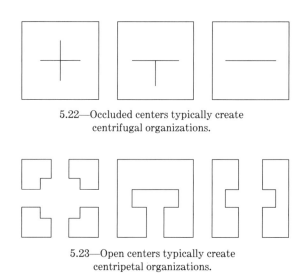

5.22—Occluded centers typically create centrifugal organizations.

5.23—Open centers typically create centripetal organizations.

A second, related ramification of neutralizing the center of the American Foursquare plan is centrifugal circulation, which moves from the inside out.[18] The American Foursquare tends to push circulation to the perimeter, evidenced by the consistent location of the stair against perimeter walls. In this context, centrifugal circulation promotes thermal comfort within first-floor rooms due to the proximity of non-circulatory space to a centrally located fireplace. Circulation through a Palladian villa, on the other hand, tends to be centripetal and moves toward the center, where the stairs are typically located—though there are a few exceptions to these general rules, such as the Sears Roebuck Modern Home No. 102 (1908), whose stairs are found near the center, and Palladio's Villa Pisani at Monatagnana (1552) in which spiral stairs occupy two corners.

Prairie Boxes and Primitives

The American Foursquare originated in the Midwest and, as previously noted, was colloquially called the Prairie Box or the Cornbelt Cube. Its status as a Midwestern cultural touchstone was not lost on Frank Lloyd Wright, or his contemporaries like Walter Burley Griffin and Marion Mahony Griffin, both of whom worked in Wright's office

5.24
While finding the center-periphery relationship of a square is an easy task, it becomes a spatial paradox when the spatial boundary is re-configured by the omission of the stair, creating an irregular figure. At least two centers can be geometrically defined in such instances:

1—an average center of all vertices, marked with a plus sign.

2—an average center of all edges, marked with a dot.

The center-periphery duality reveals shifting internal hierarchies among the four cells of the American Foursquare that depend on the location of the stair rather than fixed grid divisions.

Notably, the average center of the vertices typically aligns with the front door in Foursquare houses, thus revealing a surprising relationship between the location of the stairs and the location of the front door.

Superimposing the six house diagrams (bottom row) produces an irregular grid pattern with a stair in each quadrant, which would imply a separate entry into each cell from the exterior.

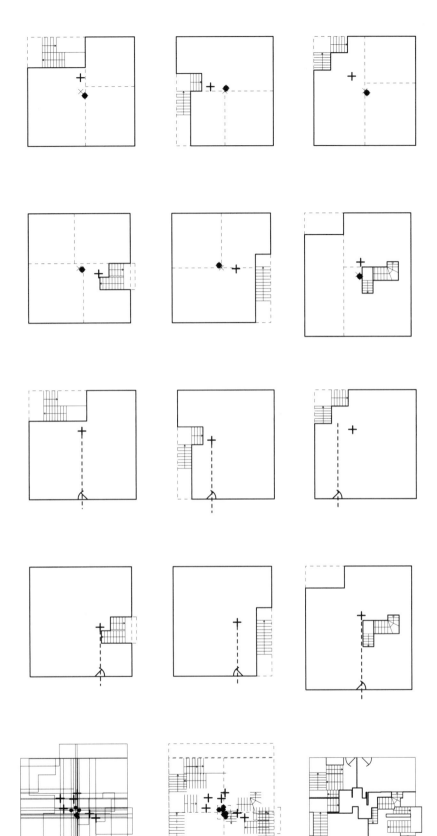

113

for a time.[19] Wright's Robert Lamp House and "A Fireproof House for $5,000" are both examples of Foursquares that exhibit aspects of the Prairie style.[20] Similarly, Wright's projects for American System-Built Homes (1912-1916), of which over 900 drawings were made (more than any other project in his archive), were prefabricated houses meant to deliver high-design affordable housing to the public. Some are still standing today in Milwaukee and Chicago. Wright's Foursquares exhibited the notable relocation of the entrance to the side of the house so that the entire front could serve as a living room. Much of Wright's residential work, including his Foursquares, included a central fireplace used to distribute heat equally to adjacent rooms.

It may seem to be a bit of a stretch to dovetail the American Foursquare, Kushel, and Wright into the Wittkower-Rowe-Eisenman-Lynn conversation about Palladio and Le Corbusier, but some of the shared affinities and discrepancies between the Foursquare and the more canonical precedents are worth observing under the rubric of unresolved legibility. Palladian villas and the American Foursquare share mathematical and rational underlays, including cellular ordering logics, manifested through cubic massing and gridded (or cellular) plans. The mathematical and rational extends beyond form and order in the Foursquare to include the logistics of mass production, standardization of parts, distribution, and construction technology.

Recalling Lynn's parable of the ants' randomized walk mode, the collection of American Foursquares, accrued over time, across the Midwest in particular, reflects individual freedoms, preferences, differentiations, and idiosyncrasies that manifest precisely because of systematized continuity in construction materials, factory production, design seriality, transportation, and labor. This may be true for houses in general, but it was the American Foursquare that most dramatically transitioned American residential architecture from a Victorian moment to a Modernist one. In fact, Foursquares were once also called Transitional Period homes; this 'transition' occurred not only in the Midwestern low-middle- and middle-class areas of Chicago, Milwaukee, Minneapolis, Cleveland, Cincinnati, and Denver, among other Midwestern cities, but also in the farmlands of Iowa, Illinois, Indiana, Ohio, Wisconsin, Minnesota, and Michigan. The Midwest was once coined the Great American Garden, or the countryside between the East and West coasts, prompting an analogy of the American Foursquare as "the countryside villa" for Midwestern middle-class America at the turn of the century. But this analogy is trite. In fact, the American Foursquare represents an abundance of non-idealized, mass-produced, middle-America houses characterized by distinctive features, transformations, and modifications made to a basic cube using standardized parts and labor.

1

Paul Duchscherer and Linda Svendsen, *Beyond the Bungalow: Grand Homes in the Arts and Crafts Tradition* (Layton, Utah: Gibbs Smith Publishing, 2005), 25.

2

Colin Rowe, *The Mathematics of the Ideal Villa and Other Essays* (Cambridge, MA.: MIT Press, 1976). Originally published in *Architectural Review*, 1947.

3

Rowe's shift in emphasis from formal hierarchies to collage as noted with regard to the three texts herein has been well documented, including by Greg Lynn in "New Variations on the Rowe Complex."

4

Greg Lynn, "New Variations on the Rowe Complex" in *Folds, Bodies, & Blobs: Collected Essays* (La Lettre volée, Bruxelles, 1998), 213-214. First published in *Any Magazine*, New York: ANY no. 7/8 (1994): 38-43.

5

Lynn, "New Variations," 214.

6

That Lynn does not mention the American Foursquare is much less surprising than any lack of attention from Wittkower or Rowe, given that the bulk of his argument rests on Rowe's scholarship, not on the analysis of buildings designed by Palladio or Le Corbusier. Moreover, any residential construct that leads to proper naming and fits within a model of formal typology would be unlikely to satisfy Lynn's concerns for differentiation.

7

Lynn, "New Variations," 218.

8

Greg Lynn uses the behavior of ants, borrowed from Keven Kelly's book, *Out of Control: The Rise of Neo-Biological Civilization* (Reading, Mass.: Addison-Weslery, 1994), as analogous to architecture that I paraphrase here by pulling from various parts of Lynn's text as systemized continuities with idiosyncrasy, differentiation, and isolated reductions.

9

Here again I refer to Lynn's invocation of Kelly's ant parable. However, I use it here through an appropriation of the parable to the construction industry that allows for reinterpreting the terms of *systemization, continuity, differentiation*, and *reduction*.

10

The term genealogy has recently been revisited by Kenneth Frampton in his book *A Genealogy of Modern Architecture* (2015) as a framework for comparative analysis of examples of modern architecture through their relationship of typology and context. I use the term here in a slightly different manner, to describe evolving modifications made to defining features such as porches, materials, massing, etc. within a broadly framed type, the American Foursquare. The distinction is that the parts, or elements, are the modifiers of continuity and isolated reduction, not programmatic type itself nor its specific context. Kenneth Frampton, *A Genealogy of Modern Architecture:*

Comparative Critical Analysis of Built Form (Zürich: Lars Müller, 2015).

11

James Massey and Shirley Maxwell, "The Story on Sears Houses" *Old House Online*, January 29, 2013, https://www.oldhouseonline.com/house-tours/story-sears-houses (Accessed November 10, 2018).

12

Ibid.

13

Here again I refer to Lynn's use of Kelly's ant parable, summarized as systemized continuities with idiosyncrasy, differentiation, and isolated reduction.

14

Lewis Manufacturing Company, *Houses of Character*, (Bay City, Michigan: Lewis Manufacturing Company, 1920), 5.

15

Lewis Manufacturing, *Houses of Character*, 6.

16

Lewis Manufacturing, *Houses of Character*, 7.

17

When discussing differences between John Hejduk's seven Texas Houses, Peter Eisenman refers to centers and peripheries with specific regard to Texas House 4. In this house, the addition of a second floor moves the reading away from one of horizontal extension and instead toward a three-dimensional frame that contains a volume within which vertical circulation occupies the center, creating pressure in the vertical plane that moves from the center to periphery. See Peter Eisenman's "In My Father's House Are Many Mansions" in *Inside Out* (New Haven: Yale University Press, 2004), 121-124.

18

In the same essay from *Inside Out*, Eisenman uses the terms "centripetal" and "centrifugal" to describe two opposing modes of circulation. I recall it here in relation to the location of stairs in American Foursquare houses.

19

Marion Mahony Griffin was the author of many drawings produced in Frank Lloyd Wright's office, many of which are often wrongly attributed to Wright as the illustrator.

20

"A Fireproof House for $5000" was first published in *Ladies Home Journal* in 1907.

HOUSE
FOR SALE
BY OWNER

Receding Façades & Traditional Cosmetics
in the Ranch House

PHYSIOGNOMY

A person's facial features or expression, especially when regarded as indicative of character or the supposed art of judging character from facial expressions.

FAÇADE

The expressive face of a building, especially the principal front that looks onto a street with an outward appearance that is maintained to convey or express use or value.

Prominent in the 1950s and '60s, the ranch house is identified by a low-pitched roof, broad low-to-the-ground massing, an informal open plan without a parlor room, fewer divisions between rooms, and an asymmetrical façade composition. The ranch house has four primary roof variations: hipped, cross-hipped, side-gabled, and cross-gabled. The ridge of a side-gabled or side-hipped roof runs parallel to the front façade, resulting in a rectangular plan, whereas cross-gables or cross-hips result in an 'L' plan. Although the ranch house is typically a single-story, in the Northeastern United States, split-level and tri-level variations on the ranch house appeared in the 1940s and '50s due to higher property costs. Perhaps no other domestic type is more associated with mid-century American domesticity than the ranch house. Also known as the Rambler, this post-war, family-oriented, Federal Housing Administration (FHA) subsidized residential type became so integral to the burgeoning commuter neighborhoods of the 1950s and '60s that it remains a dominant feature of many American cities and suburbs today, from Atlanta to St. Louis to Los Angeles. As the most aggressive manifestation of mid-century domesticity, the ranch house emerged alongside definitive shifts in post-World War II American culture, including the invention of T.V. dinners, rampant gender-biased appliance advertising from companies like General Electric, increased distribution of home and garden magazines promoting a casual family-oriented interior, the dawn of color T.V., and an exodus from cities to suburbs by a predominantly white population spurred by bank lending practices and FHA subsidies.[1]

Open floor plans encouraged visual and auditory continuity between the kitchen and living room, yet much of the ranch house's popular aesthetic appeal was rooted in its traditional exterior appearance. The ranch house's aesthetic origins can be traced to the Spanish Colonial houses of the Southwestern United States, but they were popularized by California builder and designer Cliff May. In 1946, May partnered with *Sunset Magazine* to publish a book titled *Western Ranch Houses*, which articulated the history of Spanish Colonial houses in the Southwest and included architectural drawings and ideas for a new version of the ranch house. By the 1950s the ranch house had become the dominant American housing type.[2]

Faces & Façades

Faces have a complicated history in terms of architectural legibility—one that is admittedly slippery to address today. Dating back to ancient Greece, physiognomy was the practice of reading a person's face (often considered the human corollary to a building's façade) as a means for interpreting their inner 'soul'. At its origins, this was primarily a religious occupation, though by the early 1900s it was more broadly associated with spirit and aesthetics, while maintaining an affiliation to expression and meaning.

In 1688, Charles Le Brun delivered a theory of the eyebrows based on René Descartes's assertion that the impressions of the soul are received in the pineal gland.[3] Le Brun noted that the eyebrows are the nearest facial feature to the pineal gland, and thus when the soul "was attracted towards something outside itself, the pineal is stimulated and the eyebrows raise; when the soul is repulsed, the eyebrows lose contact with the pineal gland and begin to descend."[4] While Le Brun was concerned with the individual and his or her unique facial expressions, over a hundred years later Quatremère de Quincy applied the concept of physiognomy to collective cultural temperament, or how the "emotional proclivities of a nation are manifested in its built works."[5] In the early 19th century, Georg Wilhelm Friedrich Hegel emphatically denied the value of physiognomy and phrenology, turning instead to phenomenology.[6] By distinguishing experience and phenomena from being and consciousness, Hegel effectively discredited the idea that facial expressions register an inner soul. In 1907, Georg Simmel authored an essay titled "The Aesthetics of the Human Face," in which he claimed that personality and meaning manifest through the aesthetics of the face, as opposed to the body, because the face is the mirror to the soul. Simmel notes that

> Bodies differ to the trained eye just as faces do; but unlike faces, bodies do not at the same time *interpret* these differences. A definite spiritual personality is indeed connected with a definite, unmistakable body, and can at any time be identified in it. Under no circumstances, however, can the body, in contrast to the face, signify the *kind* of personality.[7]

Simmel further noted that exaggerations, deviations, or transformations to any facial part within the face can lead to discomforting effects. Colin Rowe leveraged similar logic in the 1980s as a criticism aimed at what he considered Modern architecture's effacement as a result of the free plan and free façade. Rowe once stated that "when considering intercourse with a building, its face, however veiled, must always be a desirable and provocative item."[8] Salacious undertones aside, Rowe's claim was that a building can only compel a visitor to enter if its façade provokes a strong sensation or emotion, like desire. Furthermore, he believed that the façade ought to reflect the building's internal animations—what one might call its soul in a civic and experiential sense, rather than a religious one. Rowe went so far as to say that a building without a face was soulless. It was not that long after that early explorations of the digital turn in architecture entailed a turn away from the façade and toward the building skin, which tends to smooth out differences and idiosyncrasies unique to façades through systemization, gradation, or modulation. The resulting buildings have little to no lingering semblance of a face, but are instead all skin.

This account of faces—and façades—in architecture is quite abbreviated, but it is nevertheless useful for introducing unresolved legibility vis-a-vis the façade and its historical theorizations related to the face. However, a mere application of Le Brun's physiognomic theories of eyebrows to the post-war ranch house would likely not stand up under scrutiny—though it could be said that the ranch house's massing and façade appear not unlike a knitted brow, which would imply a general feeling of repulsion or withdrawal. Perhaps slightly more believably, one might consider the ranch house through Simmel's aesthetic indicators of personality and meaning, or return to Rowe's cause-and-effect relationship between the house's public address and internal animations. In many ways, these readings are all embedded in what follows, and yet none of them stands alone as a theoretical resolution in the ranch house residential type and of the qualities common to its façade. Instead, these various readings relating faces and façades, culled from across four centuries, afford a wide lens to reconceptualize the composition of massing and tectonics of this residential type as recombinant expressions evaluated through the detachment of elements from the whole. In other words, the ranch house succeeded in doing what previous residential types most often intentionally avoided with their compositional tendencies for symmetry, frontality, and contextualization: by contrast, the ranch house disturbed the legibility of a face through the seemingly independent consideration of parts within the whole of a façade. The face is not removed, but rather recomposed. It is not a face concerned with the disclosure of internal animations, but rather with obscuring interiority. The ranch house's face recedes and compresses; it spreads out and sinks in. Spatial contradictions and scalar juxtaposition of elements are hallmarks of the mid-century ranch house. Though these qualities may at times be deceptively subtle, they tend to propagate idiosyncrasies. These contradictions are achieved through four façade features: the location of the front door, the roof-to-wall relationship, window scales, and compaction of the vertical dimension.

Four Façade Features

1 Front Door Withdrawal

Whereas most residential types typically convey a welcoming front by virtue of a raised entry, a protruding porch, or the front door's overt visibility and centrality, the ranch house tends to exhibit a more ambivalent public address. Most notably, the front door tends to be inconspicuous, obscured by an asymmetrical composition, low roof, variegated material palette, and broad massing. The front door is often even invisible on the front elevation when it is set into the short side of an L plan. Thus, the ranch house seems uninterested in unsolicited visitation. It is one of the only single-family residential types without a visible front door in its front elevation. This would likely trouble Rowe, for even if he felt enticed to enter, the comparative difficulty of locating the door would contradict the experiential invitation or internal animations.

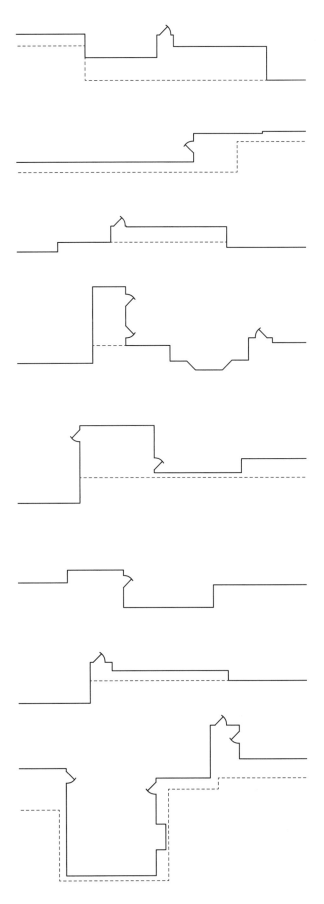

6.1
Ranch house plan profiles showing front façade crenelations. The receding and protruding planes produce the quality of front door withdrawal into the depth of the plan. In some cases, multiple front doors can be read, while in other cases there is a visual absence of the door in the front elevation.

119

When the door is visible on the front façade of a ranch house, it is typically recessed deep into the plan, set alongside a more dominant element like a chimney, or tucked into a recessed corner beside a protruding attached garage. The receding door conveys an inward withdrawal that distances the public address from the familial interior—cleaving the inner world of the house from the outer world of the city or suburb.

Even when the door does not recede inward, confusion is often encountered through the presence of multiples. Although it does not have multiple interior units, this ranch house in Denver, Colorado, appears to have two front doors.

6.2—Ranch house in Denver, Colorado, that appears to have two front doors.

2 Window Stress

Because the ranch house's front door is often deeply recessed or not visible at all on the front elevation, the composition of windows—especially the picture window—is often the most pronounced feature. The front door's invisibility or retreat shifts attention to the picture window, amplifying the gaze into the home by passersby as well as the gaze outward by homeowners, rendering the picture window as a suburban device for bi-directional surveillance. The receding front door and the picture window contradict one another, as the one diminishes the appearance of physical accessibility while the other visually amplifies it. In ranch houses without a picture window, the window composition is often characterized by a number of smaller windows that appear awkward in their proportional relationship to the broad massing. This arrangement suggests a more unidirectional view, as looking out is encouraged but looking in is limited or difficult. The subtle yet peculiar arrangement of doors and windows in the ranch house façade betrays the casual family-oriented interior with the anxieties of a post-war suburban culture newly removed from the social and political life of the city, as evidenced by the emphatic mediation of gaze and view.

3 Descending Roofs, Shallow Eaves and the Independence of Walls

The standardization of building materials in the 20th century, such as framing lumber and plywood, increased the efficiency of construction, but it also limited the ceiling height of most ranch houses to just over eight feet. This corresponded with shallow sloping roofs, fostering an effect of vertical compaction of the front façade. The shallow-pitched roof further exaggerates the vertical compaction of the house's walls by appearing to exert a downward pressure against the presumed solidity of the ground, giving the windows the appearance of horizontal scalability and vertical compaction—of simultaneous tension and compression. The low-pitched roof typically has boxed, clipped, or flush eaves that amplify the front door's inconspicuousness and the compaction of the front façade. Like a haircut that lacks volume and falls flat on one's face, shallow eaves produce a flattening effect that diminishes the hierarchical status of other features, like the door. Instead of a

6.3 (left)
Boxed (top), clipped (middle), and flush (bottom) eave details add to the appearance of a compacted front façade in the ranch house, especially when combined with slab-on-grade foundations and front door withdrawal.

6.4 (opposite)
Cropping and masking ranch house façades reveals underlying compositional tendencies while emphasizing the distribution of elements, such as windows, doors, chimneys, and roofs.

120

protruding porch or raised entry, the ranch house achieves depth by the recession of individual walls inward from the eave, giving the appearance that the already compressed walls move independently from the roof above. In other words, shallow eaves make walls appear as independent planes able to move freely in a manner seemingly detached from the eave, soffit, or roof. This lends a crenelated quality to the front façade plan profile.

4 Lying Low

The foundation further contributes to the impression of a compacted vertical dimension, as the previous era's masonry wall or pier foundations, which created a buffer zone between the mass of the house and the ground, were replaced with slab-on-grade foundations in the ranch house residential type. The slab-on-grade foundation technique was developed and readily deployed by the U.S. military during WWII for fast construction requiring very little excavation and adaptability to a variety of terrains. As a consequence of the slab-on-grade, the ranch house appears both literally and perceptually closer to the ground. The front stairs, ubiquitous amongst previous residential types, were eliminated as the floor of the house became effectively continuous with the ground. The result is an informal interior with a reduced transition between inside and outside as the floor becomes sectionally equivalent with the ground.

The ranch house's façade composition recedes and compresses. It does not add up to complete the whole of a face as read through Le Brun, Simmel, or Rowe—but neither can it be said to be illegible as a façade. The qualities of recession and compression reconfigure and distort the façade and the interior, but plasticity is also suggested through the free distribution of elements. Alleviated from rigid hierarchies, the façade and the interior sponsor myriad compositional expressions reflecting a broader cultural impulse to turn away, to spread out, to obscure. This calls to mind yet another study of facial features: Victorian sociologist Francis Galton's technique of photographic *averaging* for

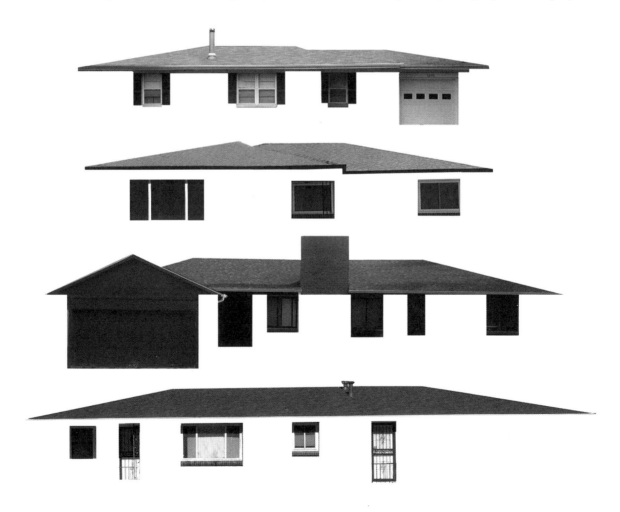

6.5 (top)
AS BUILT_A ranch house in Denver,
Colorado, in which the front door is deeply
recessed and the garage and chimney
become the most pronounced elements.

6.6 (bottom)
AS BUILT_A ranch house in Littleton,
Colorado, in which the front door is recessed
and smaller in scale than the adjacent
windows.

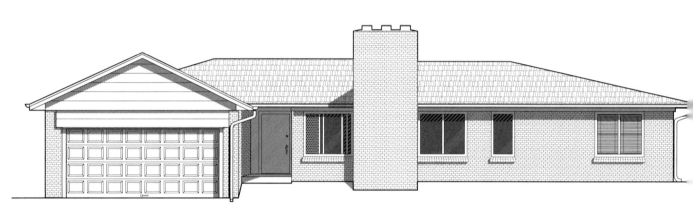

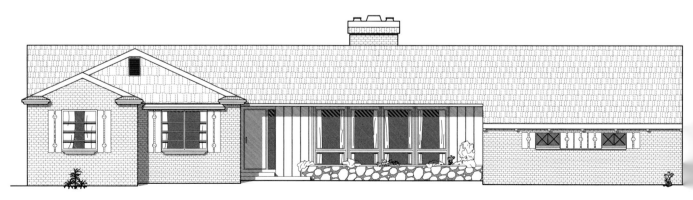

6.7 (top)
AS BUILT_A ranch house in Denver, Colorado, in which the front door is set into the short side of the cross-hip L plan, making it visually absent in the front elevation.

6.8 (bottom)
AS BUILT_A ranch house in College Station, Texas, in which the front door is set into the short side of the cross-hip L plan, making it visually absent in the front elevation.

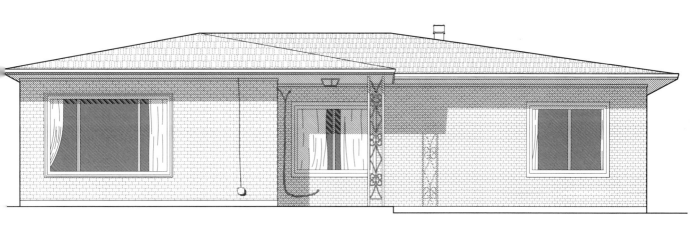

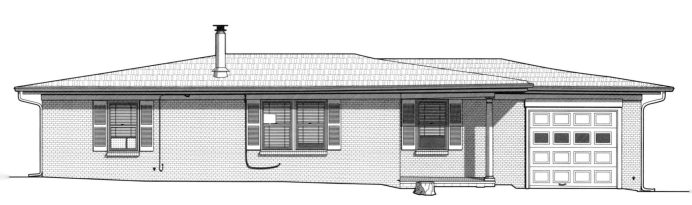

123

psychological analysis. Superimposing photographs of faces of prisoners, siblings, and various occupations, Galton's "Average Faces" attempted to discern common qualities among subjects of similar psychologies or occupations through facial comparison.[9] This technique muted unique, idiosyncratic features while amplifying shared ones. The resultant effects of superimposition revealed recombinant faces: blended compositions, blurred or smoothed features, and transfigured hierarchies.

Similarly applied here through drawing, these "Average Ranches" are composite elevations of the As Built drawings. Whereas Galton's photographic facial averaging tended to smooth differences into a unified whole, superimposing the compositional and tectonic qualities of the ranch house—and architecture more generally—tends to amplify the value and expressions of parts, construct idiosyncrasies, juxtapose materials, emphasize contrast, and highlight seams, offsets, and joints. As recombinant compositions made from quotations of otherwise familiar conditions, the newly "averaged" ranch house is susceptible to productive reconsiderations of its social, cultural, and architectural expressions without the onus of inherited ideas of suburban traditionalism.

A Cosmetic of Traditional Values

The ranch house can also be read in terms of its materiality. Banks, for example, were much more likely to approve loans for people purchasing houses with traditional exterior materials such as stone, wood siding, shutters, and brick. These materials were understood to represent fiscal responsibility and family values more than monochromatic or Modern materials like stucco did. Banks overwhelmingly supported traditional values as telegraphed through materiality. Not only were materials such as rock, clay, and wood affiliated with mid-century traditional suburban values, but so too were their visible effects of human assembly. Thus, exposed joints, grout lines, visible seams, and building material unitization—as opposed to the smooth seamlessness and gridded orders of Modernism—were also associated with tradition and comfort. Board and batten, another popular siding material of the ranch house, accentuates the seam between adjoining planar materials with protruding relief, like piping on a cushion. Seamlessness in exterior appearance, on the other hand, connoted synthetic fakery, risk, sterility, and corporate values over family values, and it was associated with an unwelcome cultural and political opacity in post-war America—at least according to lending institutions and popular suburban taste. However, the economic incentives for traditional materials required only the *cosmetic* of traditional values—an overpainting of familiar impressions of traditional building material onto an alternative space of Modernism. Perhaps inevitably, many of these materials were replaced over time with materials that merely represented traditional materials. PermaStone replaced actual stone, vinyl siding and vinyl shutters replaced their wooden precedents, and sheet brick replaced unit bricks.

This cosmetic of traditional values introduced variations on *flatness* as a characteristic of a new suburban residential aesthetic. This flatness should not be confused with blankness, nor should it be understood as compositionally reductive. It is provisional: there is no absolute cohesion between elements and materials in the ranch house's materiality or tectonics. The crenelated plan of the front creates multiple receding planes capable of accepting different materials—and material substitutions and alterations are easy because materiality is applied to isolated planes without an obligation to the coherence of the whole.

Redlined Ranch-Burbs

In addition to the increased publication of images and plans, a primary cause for the widespread popularity of the ranch house type was its FHA subsidy, which originated in the 1930s and was intended for small house types. After WWII the FHA lifted the regulatory mandate's limitation to smaller homes, and the ranch house began to grow in size and popularity until the ranch house and its variants became the most built and bought type of American houses in the 1950s-'60s. As builders successfully lobbied the FHA for guidelines permitting larger houses under the subsidy, the FHA in turn advocated for the construction of entire neighborhoods as consolidated efforts by single developers. As developers undertook the task of constructing such neighborhoods, elements like chimneys, porches, door locations, and picture window styles were used to modify the outward address of individual houses in order to avoid monotonous neighborhoods.

Banking practices, however, were discriminatory, and loans were approved for an overwhelmingly Caucasian demographic. At the same time that the GI Bill issued 67,000 mortgages in New York and New Jersey with fewer than a hundred mortgages taken out by non-whites, banks disproportionately denied minority populations mortgage loans through the practice of "redlining." Redlining was a practice used by the FHA to divide up otherwise contiguous neighborhoods based on data such as racial and ethnic composition for the purposes of limiting financial services without consideration of the resident's credit or qualifications.

The most important role of the Federal Housing Administration was it subsidized mass-production builders of entire subdivisions, entire suburbs. And it did so with a requirement that no homes be sold to African-Americans and that every home in these subdivisions had a clause in the deed that prohibited resale to African-Americans. So these two programs combined worked to segregate metropolitan areas in a way that they otherwise would not have been segregated. This was not an implicit program. It was not something that was hidden in any way. It was written out in the Federal Housing Administration's manuals that they gave to underwriters who were appraising properties for possible mortgage insurance. The involvement of the Federal Housing Administration in the development of these suburbs was very open, explicit and well-known. There was nothing secret about it. The Federal Housing Administration's justification was that if African-Americans bought homes in these suburbs, or even if they bought homes near these suburbs, the property values of the homes that they were insuring - the white homes that they were insuring - would decline and therefore their loans would be at risk. There was no basis for this claim on the part of the Federal Housing Administration.[10]

These discriminatory practices of government policy and the banking industry spanned the nation, from Levittown, Pennsylvania, to Daly City, California, and were most obviously manifest in the rapid construction of the suburban ranch house. In 1975 the Home Mortgage Disclosure Act was passed, requiring banks to disclose their lending practices, and other initiatives such as the 1968 Fair Housing Act intended to eliminate discriminatory lending practices—though by this time the costs of suburban houses were prohibitively high, and previously excluded demographics still could not afford them. Perhaps the ranch house's FHA-subsidized building campaigns and developer-driven mass production—inextricable as they were from its massing and composition of elements—invite a likeness to de Quincy's physiognomic understanding: as a post-war residential architecture, the ranch house reflected a cultural temperament of withdrawal from the social and geopolitical influences of the city, alongside increased attention to the internal worlds of entertainment and familial insularity.

Unsurprisingly, these subsidies and loan programs of the 1940s and '50s favored traditional appearances and normative aesthetics as they related to suburban culture, with the result that ranch houses overwhelmingly exhibit exterior materials of stone, brick, concrete block, clapboard siding, and board and batten siding. These materials were often recombined, making the ranch house one of the most mixed-and-matched residential types with regard to the material palette. The width of lot sizes also increased as use of the automobile increased, rendering the compact lots and houses of the "streetcar suburbs" of the early 20th century less viable as residents took to driving their own cars. The confluence of subsidized

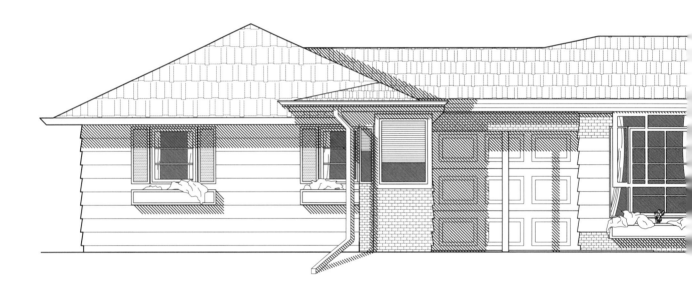

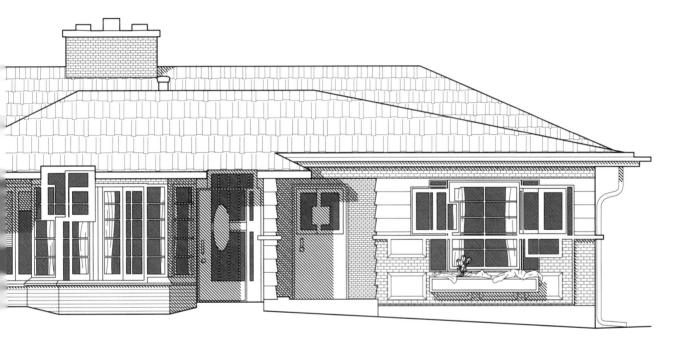

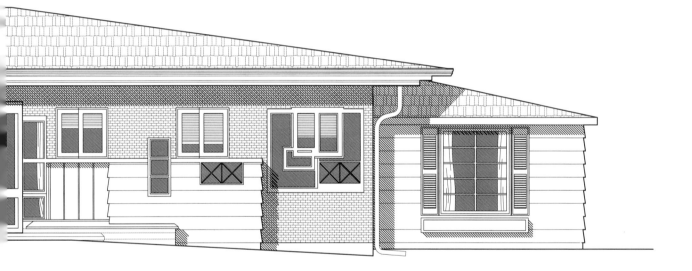

construction, the automobile, and a post-war culture influenced by technological advancements and modernization, alongside a social commitment of a return to family values, produced ubiquitous ranch-burbs across the Southern, Southwestern, and Western United States, especially in Dallas, Houston, Los Angeles, Atlanta, and Phoenix.[11] Because the ranch house was built in such quantities across such a large swath of the United States during the 1950s and '60s, it represents one of the most renovated, remodeled, and added-to residential types from the 1980s through today. Whereas the farmhouse expands in a telescoping or constellated manner and the Queen Anne expands by enclosing a front porch or by a rear addition, the ranch house is unique for its typically vertical expansion. Because of the ranch house's low-lying posture with an open plan, it is an ideal type for lifting the roof in order to introduce a second story, what is colloquially known as the "pop-top." If one were to read the pop-top through the lens of Le Brun's theory of eyebrows, it could lead to a reading of a raised brow—an inversion of the previous appearance of a knitted brow—suggesting surprise or attraction. Again, such physiognomic readings in architecture are slippery, even if uncomfortably provocative. Alternatively, considering corollaries between faces and façades through the composition and distribution of elements and features relating outward address and internal order, the pop-top tends to diminish idiosyncrasies of distributed elements through the cohering of independent planes and materials into a uniform whole.

The ranch house's political history cannot be easily divorced from its formal and spatial reading, which is what makes it a fascinating study in unresolved legibility. On the one hand, the composition of mass and the relationships between parts freely distributed across the front façade with a technologically advanced, family-centric interior that eschews Classically rigid compositions of axiality, symmetry, and hierarchy would seemingly imply that non-hierarchical architectural expressions correlate to (or reflect) social and economic equity and cultural tolerance. However, architectural order is no guarantee of these values—a discrepancy evidenced in the contrast between the non-hierarchical compositions of ranch houses' formal, spatial and material expressions and the post-war discriminatory lending practices that financed them. On the other hand, the ranch house still exemplifies an alternative space of Modernism that has endured as an evolving agent of reflection on (if not implementation of) broader social and cultural transformations. Thus it remains open to disciplinary and extra-disciplinary re-imaginations, ahistorical abstractions, and compositional alterations that shift perceptions, expressions, and policies.

1
Virginia Savage McAlester, *A Field Guide To American Houses* [1984] (New York City: Knopf Press,, 2013), 603.

2
Cliff May et. al., *Sunset Western Ranch Houses* (Los Angeles: Lane Publishing, 1946).

3
For a compete transcript of Le Brun's lecture, see Jennifer Montagu, *The Expression of the Passions: The Origin and Influence of Charles Le Brun's Conférence sur l'expression générale et particuliére* (New Haven: Yale University Press, 1994). See also René Descartes, *Les Passions de l'ame* (1649).

4
Vittoria Di Palma, "Architecture, Environment and Emotion: Quatremère de Quincy and the Concept of Character," *AA Files* 47 (2002), 52. See also Descartes's, *Les Passions de l'âme* (1649).

5
Vittoria Di Palma, "Architecture, Environment and Emotion: Quatremère de Quincy and the Concept of Character," *AA Files* 47 (2002), 52. See also Antoine-Chrysostome Quatremère de Quincy, "Caractére" in *Encyclopedia Méthodique: Architecture*, Vol. 2, (Madrid: Por Don Antonio de Sancha, 1788), 499.

6
Anthony Vidler, "Losing Face" in *The Architectural Uncanny: Essay's in the Modern Unhomely* (Boston: MIT Press, 1992).

7
Georg Simmel, "The Aesthetics of the Human Face" in *Georg Simmel, 1858-1918*, trans. Lore Ferguson, ed. Kurt H. Wolff (Columbus: Ohio State University Press, 1995) 275-281.

8

Colin Rowe, "James Stirling: A Highly Personal and Very Disjointed Memoir", in *James Stirling: Buildings and Projects*, ed. Peter Arnell and Ted Bickford (New York: Rizzoli, 1984), 22-23.

9

Francis Galton authored numerous articles in the late 1870s that explained both his techniques and theories, including "Composite Portraits" in *Nature* 18 (May 23, 1878), 97-100; "Generic Images" in *The Nineteenth Century* (July 1879), 157-169; and "Composite Portraiture" in *Photographic Journal 5* (1881) 140-146, ultimately finding no link between facial features and occupational or criminal tendencies. For more articles by Galton, see "Francis Galton and Composite Portraiture" *Gatlton.org*, http://galton.org/composite.htm (Accessed January 10, 2019).

10

Terry Gross, "Interview with Richard Rothstein, author of *The Color of Law: A Forgotten History of How Our Government Segregated America*, NPR, May 3, 2017, https://www.npr.org/templates/transcript/transcript.php?storyId=526655831. (accessed September 18, 2018).

11

McAlester, *A Field Guide To American Houses*, 602.

6.12
Massing for a ranch house pop-top renovation in Denver, Colorado.
Endemic Architecture, 2017–2019

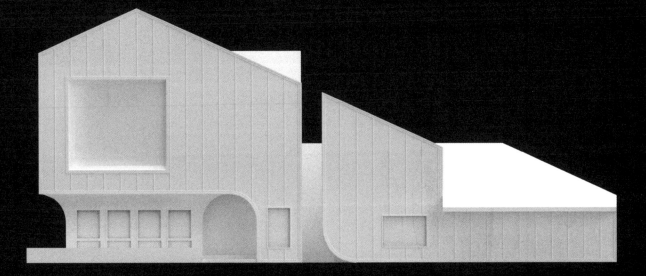

6.13
Elevations for a ranch
house pop-top renovation in
Denver, Colorado. Endemic
Architecture, 2017–2019

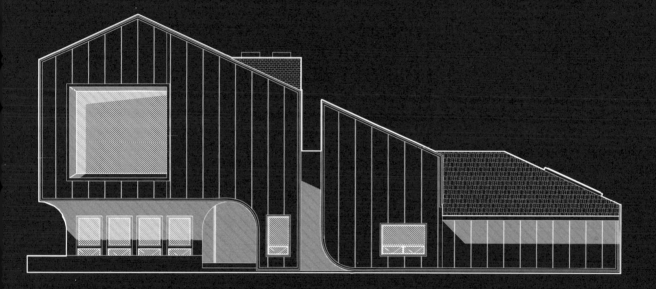

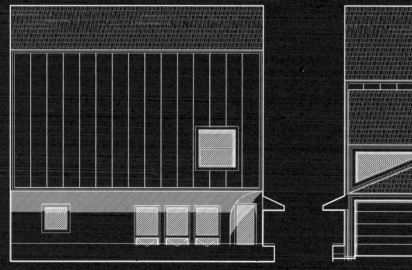

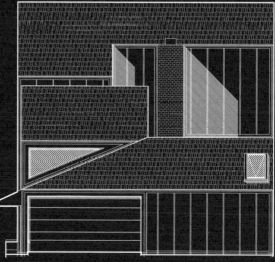

6.14
First (bottom) and second
(top) floor plans for a ranch
house pop-top renovation in
Denver, Colorado. Endemic
Architecture, 2017–2019

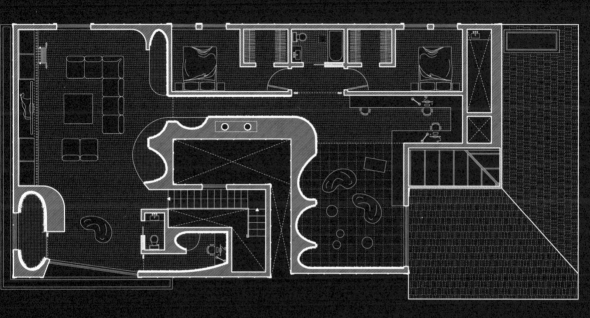

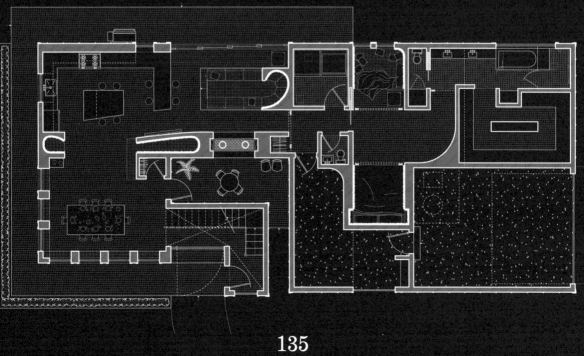

135

6.15
Rendering for a ranch
house pop-top renovation in
Denver, Colorado. Endemic
Architecture, 2017–2019

Parenthetical & Hyphenated Symmetry in the Federal-Style House

SYMMETRY

1

The quality of being composed of exactly similar parts, either reflected or rotated around an axis.

2

An architectural double entendre historically thought to connote harmony and beauty, but also used to invoke fear and anxiety.

The Federal-style house, named for the Federalist Party that dominated Boston politics after the British departure in 1776, is a Colonial sub-type that was dominant on the East Coast from around 1780 to 1820, a period during which the nation's population grew from three million to ten million. The Federal-style drew its primary architectural influences from English Neoclassicism—especially from the style developed by brothers Robert and James Adam. In Adam-style houses, notable for their delicate, uniquely ornamented interiors, "the components of buildings were symmetrically disposed on the exterior, but within the forms and spaces—the rectangle, the circle, and the oval—did not always correspond reciprocally around the central axis."[1] The Federal-style house evolved in New England as adaptations from pattern books and alterations were made to the earlier Georgian style. This new style was characterized by an overall symmetrical address and was significantly pared down compared to its English influences: ornament was flatter, plans were simplified, the palette of pastel colors was subtler, and the overall expression was more modest, matching the comparatively conservative tastes of 1770s New England. "The quoined corners, projecting pediments, and engaged pilasters of the colonial house disappeared, leaving a modest but delicately proportioned front porch. Windows were more generous and taller in proportion, with larger panes and thinner sashes."[2] The houses' ornamentation, as seen in their moldings, door frames, and fireplace surrounds, consisted of thin and delicate elements. The reduced exterior ornamentation highlighted the front door as a primary feature, typically capped by an elliptical fanlight and sidelights.

As the style spread across the country, its material expression varied by region: wood construction of Federal-style houses was typical in the North, while brick construction was prevalent in the South. The placement of fireplaces and chimneys also varies regionally: in the North, a central chimney was favored, whereas Southern Federal-style houses tended to have end-gable chimneys at either side of the house, though these regional distinctions were not universally true.

Rehearsing Symmetry in Architecture

Symmetry, or the disruption of it, often complicates legibility in architecture and adjacent fields. Symmetry of course has a long history in architecture, dating back to its disciplinary origins. Vitruvius and Alberti both associated symmetry with humanist proportioning and understood it in perceptual and metaphysical terms such as harmony, balance, order, and power. These sentiments have been reaffirmed time and time again in architectural writings since. A.J. Downing's book, *The Architecture of Country Houses* (1850), for example, dedicates a section to symmetry in the first chapter, titled "The Real Meaning of Architecture." Not one to shy away from bold proclamations, Downing stated that "symmetry is one of the greatest beauties in all architecture … for it is a beauty which can be bestowed on a cottage, a villa, or indeed any kind of building; as it is one which appeals intuitively to every mind, it is never neglected by artists who wish to impress the Beautiful upon their works. … [N]o object can be perfectly beautiful without it."[3] He went on to note the "superior effect" of a cube with two wings on either side over a plain cube, stating that the cube with wings "raises the character of the form from uniformity to symmetry."[4] In the book's preface, he included symmetry, along with proportion and order, as conditions for the production of beauty in architecture—qualities that refine the public's manners and distinguish a civilized society from a brutal one. Downing wrote with conviction, and though he noted differences between regular and irregular symmetry (what today we would call global and local symmetry), he concluded that proportion and regular symmetry are the prevailing qualities of beauty.

In the early 1980s, author on design technology, Philip Tabor, offered three supposedly updated effects of symmetrical compositions in architecture: empathy, efficiency, and hierarchy.[5] Empathy, for Tabor, builds on Vitruvian metaphysics—the idea that symmetry has an inherent humanist quality that we recognize as a likeness to our own bodies—whereas efficiency is concerned with the economies of organization and construction.

Notably, historical proclamations on symmetry in architecture have tended to assume that humanity equates to nobility, ignoring its other aspects. For example, symmetrical castles convey not only beauty, harmony, and balance, but also, in equal measure, exclusion and fortification. Castles connote *both* superiority *and* brutality over visual harmony; they are characterized by an unwelcoming, anticipatory affect, readied for inevitable attempts at disharmony. Indeed, even a cursory consideration of a symmetric castle—or a prison or a bunker—undermines proclamations of symmetry's generous perceptual or metaphysical effects in making the world universally harmonious. Instead, in these structures, symmetry is a tool for confronting a world experiencing disharmony, brutality, fear, insecurity, exclusion, and imbalance even if their intentions are that of social or moral reform.

Bounded and Unbounded Symmetry

Broadly speaking, two types of symmetry bookend a spectrum of symmetrical compositions: bounded and unbounded. Bounded symmetry relies on the discrete legibility of hierarchical elements and the symmetric continuity of a profile line. In bounded symmetry, hierarchical elements fix a terminal edge to the overall form that tends to convey the flatness of its own delineation on the picture plane. Symmetrical profiles are composed from familiar constituent elements that are both nameable and legible as geometric parts. Bounded symmetry is stable, nameable, and discrete. This type of symmetry has often been used in architecture to invoke notions of beauty, harmony, and so on.

Unbounded symmetry, by contrast, does not depend on the legibility of discrete elements, but rather on shifting hierarchies and densities of local symmetries that accrue to produce the perception of global symmetry. Unbounded symmetrical compositions pull the viewer's eye both across and into the competing hierarchies of shifting densities and material intensities. Such compositions tend to exhibit indeterminate edges, non-delineated receding depths, intensive materiality, and the appearance of global symmetry accrued through local symmetries with idiosyncrasies. Because symmetry of this kind is not contained by, nor legible through, the composition of a continuous profile, it does not disclose the flatness of a picture plane, but rather implies both

7.1 (right)
Five stages of unbound symmetry vertically arrayed by descending density. As the density decreases in unbound compositions, symmetry becomes less pronounced and local idiosyncrasies are more easily discerned.

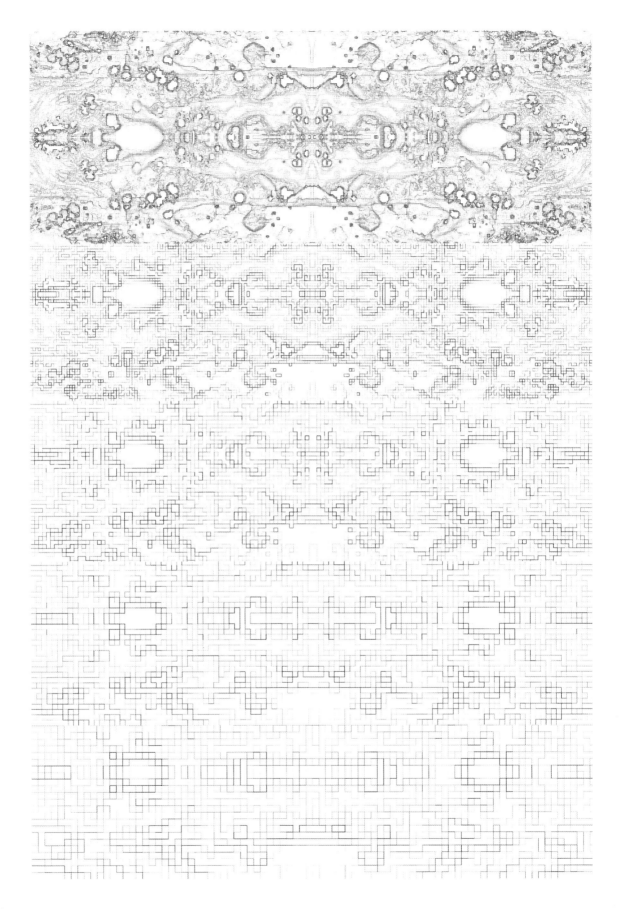

material and spatial viscosity. Unbounded symmetry moves visual and perceptual attention back and forth between subjective, associative qualities of the whole and fascination with local nuances.

The tension between the effects of the whole and the seamless transfer of local intricacies often provokes curiosity about relationships between form, space, order, and material.

7.2 (below)
AS BUILT_A Federal-style house with parenthetical symmetry near Boston, Massachusetts.

7.3 (right)
AS BUILT_A stone house in Kentucky with hyphenated symmetry. This house is not Federal-style, but is included here to demonstrate variations in kind that span across various types with regard to symmetry as conceptualized here.

Parenthetical and Hyphenated Symmetry in Bounded Compositions

Bounded symmetry in architecture often relies on the relationship between externally legible elements and internal programmatic correspondence. This relationship might be articulated in different ways—most commonly by means of bookending elements or of a centralizing element. To underscore the relationships these elements set up with other features in a symmetrical composition, two types of symmetry are prevalent in the Federal-style house: parenthetical and hyphenated.[6] Whether a Federal-style house exhibits parenthetical or hyphenated symmetry depends on the location of the fireplace(s) and chimney(s). Variations on the symmetrical composition of the house are

140

differentiated by these two primary elements and the secondary elements of windows and dormers.

In a parenthetically symmetric house, inward-facing fireplaces are located at either end, bracketing the interior as well as the exterior elevation with the corresponding chimneys. Specifically programmed rooms, such as the living room, dining room, kitchen, and bedrooms, are placed at the perimeter, but rather than a court or void at the center that might be found in other parenthetically symmetric buildings like a castle or prison, transitional spaces including the entry foyer and stair are found in place of a central open court in a Federal-style house. The perimeter rooms are typically arranged as an enfilade, creating a seemingly centrifugal movement that may appear to permit avoidance of the center altogether, although the perimeter enfilade is rarely complete. Instead, the enfilade is typically interrupted by a large bedroom, which can be entered only from the central space of the foyer and stair hall. Consequently, inhabitants cannot circulate from room to room around the entire perimeter of the house, introducing confusion as to whether the plan is centrifugal or centripetal. The centripetal plan creates tension between the asymmetric interior and the symmetric exterior which is bound together by bookending chimneys that create a hierarchically delineated profile with terminal edges as parentheses. Parenthetical symmetry is often encountered in fortifications, stadiums, prisons, or symmetrical buildings with central courtyards.

A Federal-style house with hyphenated symmetry has a single fireplace at its center, in the

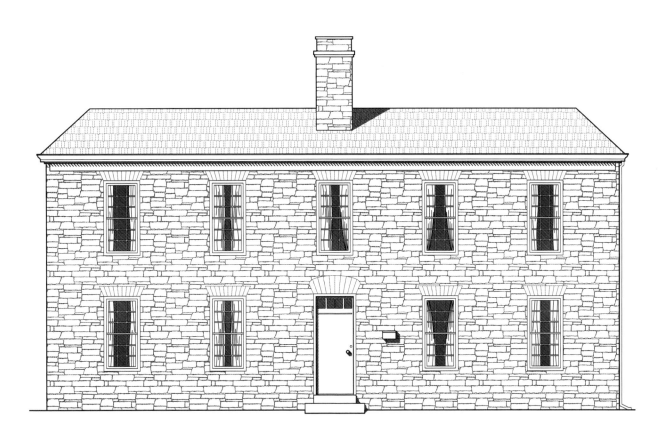

141

central living or family room. This centralized space for congregation and social engagement separates the two sides of the house, with kitchen and dining on one side and bedroom(s) on the other. The perimeter is lined with rooms as in parenthetical symmetry, though it is only on occasion enfilade. Instead, the central room is typically used as the primary means of access to all adjacent rooms at the perimeter, continuously reinforcing the center room as the hierarchical space of the house. Hyphenated symmetry unifies the collection of rooms into a common center, while in elevation hierarchy manifests at the center through the ascension of the chimney, drawing one's attention to the center rather than the perimeter. Hyphenated symmetry is often found in churches, university, civic, and government buildings.

A less common third condition also exists, something between parenthetical and hyphenated symmetry. In a Federal-style house this occurs when two fireplaces and chimneys are not located at each end or the center of the house but rather divide it into equal thirds. This type of symmetry functions similarly to hyphenation, but with a longer punctuation mark—more of an em-dash than a hyphen or an en-dash. Whereas a hyphen is used to conjoin two words and an en-dash indicates a range, often replacing the word 'to', longer em-dashes add emphasis and interruption. In the Federal-style house, em-dash symmetry often occurs in conjunction with a hip roof and tends to appear in plan inversely to parenthetical symmetry. Em-dash symmetry often features a complete enfilade permitting continuous circulation around

7.4
AS BUILT_A Federal-style house with em-dash symmetry in Boston, Massachusetts.

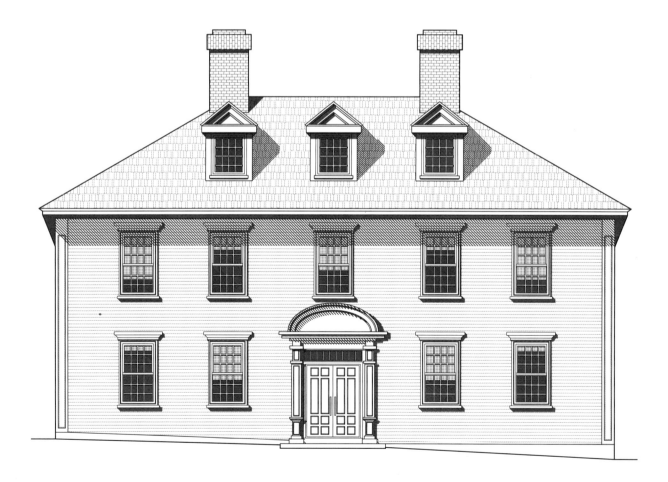

142

7.5A
Typical plan-to-front elevation relationships
for hyphenated (A1), parenthetical (A2), and
em-dash (A3) symmetry in Federal-style houses.

FIREPLACE(S) + PROFILES
*Altering the internal location and orientation of
the fireplace in Federal-style symmetry affects the
exterior profile, revealing a direct relationship
between internal and external coherence.*

7.5B1
Rotating the fireplace by 90 degrees in a house
with hyphenated symmetry rotates internal
order and creates a thinner chimney profile in
front elevation.

7.5B2
Rotating one of the two fireplaces by 90 degrees
in a house with parenthetical symmetry creates
an unbalanced symmetry. Altering the location
of the fireplaces affects internal order.

7.5B3
Mirroring one of the two fireplaces in em-dash
symmetry about the long axis changes interior
order but does not affect external symmetry.

7.5C1
Mirroring the fireplace in a house with
hyphenated symmetry about the short axis
alters interior order and doubles the thickness
of the chimney profile.

7.5C2
Rotating both of the fireplaces 90 degrees in
a house with parenthetical symmetry creates
wider brackets in profile. Changing their
location affects internal order.

7.5C3
Mirroring one fireplace about the long axis
and rotating and mirroring the other fireplace
in a house with em-dash symmetry creates
asymmetrical profiles in front and side elevations.

7.5D1
Mirroring the central fireplace and adding
two fireplaces to the short end of the original
fireplace in a house with hyphenated symmetry
creates internal polar symmetry and adds
thickness to the profile through the middle.

7.5D2
Rotating both of the fireplaces 45 degrees
and locating them in opposite corners in a
house with parenthetical symmetry creates an
asymmetrical profile with asymmetrical depth.

7.5D3
Rotating and double-mirroring the fireplaces in
a house with em-dash symmetry creates bilateral
internal symmetry with a symmetrical profile
having chimneys twice as wide as the original.

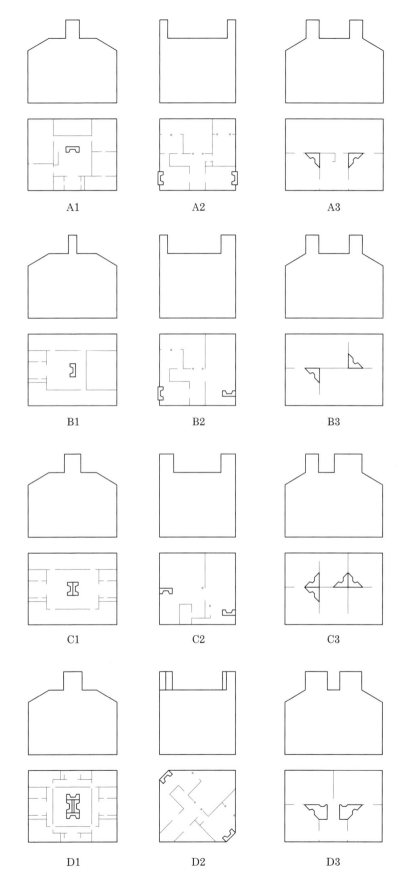

A1   A2   A3

B1   B2   B3

C1   C2   C3

D1   D2   D3

7.6A

AS BUILT_Elevation of parenthetical symmetry in a Federal-style house.

LOCAL MANIPULATIONS
Local manipulations by way of one-dimensionally scaling elements in the X or Y axis impacts the overall composition, producing competing legibilities with regard to local and global symmetry.

7.6B1

7.6B2

7.6B1
Using the center line of the left-hand dormer to scale the wall, roof, and chimney to the left by +10% in the Y-axis.

7.6B2
Using the center line of the left-hand dormer to scale the wall, roof, and chimney to the left by -10% in the X-axis.

7.6C1

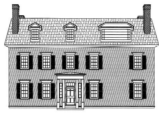

7.6C2

7.6C1
Using the center line of the right-hand dormer to scale the wall, roof, and chimney to the right by -10% in the Y-axis.

7.6C2
Using the center line of the right-hand dormer to scale the wall, roof, and dormer to the right by +10% in the X-axis.

7.6D1

7.6D2

7.6D1
Using the center line of the middle dormer to scale the dormer, window, and porch by +10% in the Y-axis.

7.6D2
Using the center line of the middle dormer to scale the dormer, window, and porch by +10% in the X-axis.

7.6E1
Y-axis scaling composite.

7.6E2
X-axis scaling composite.

7.6E2

7.6E1

the perimeter with the two fireplaces oriented facing outwards and located at the inside corners of the two front rooms, typically the family and dining or living room. The location and orientation of the fireplaces in this type of plan add emphasis to the circulation and rooms that encircle them, while also separating the foyer with stair hall as a discrete moment within the enfilade sequence.

7.7—Variations on parenthetical, hyphenated, and em-dash symmetry in houses are also often found in the duplex type. Especially in older duplexes, these three types of symmetry often further incorporate the two front doors and front porches or steps, as seen in this duplex in Berkeley, Colorado.

Mannered and Material Symmetry in Unbounded Compositions

In the 16th century, Mannerism refuted the ideal representations of Renaissance painting's perfect perspective and ideals of proportional beauty. Mannerist painters instead favored subtle elongations to bodily features, unnatural poses, competing perspectival depths, and odd symmetries. Their paintings tend to pull the eye across and into a scene where local idiosyncrasies develop into the perception of global symmetry. In Mannerist paintings, local symmetries, including odd twinning, acquire an almost material weight and texture, as the lack of a binding profile (save for the frame of the canvas) intensifies the interactions and perceptual coherence of the internal animations. For example, at first glance, Paolo Veronese's *The Wedding Feast at Cana* (1563) appears both symmetrically composed and asymmetrically populated. The painting is visually balanced, but it does not have global symmetry.

7.8—*Wedding Feast at Cana*. Paolo Veronese (1563). Overlaid with white lines indicating local symmetries.

7.9

Repetitive acts of mirroring or doubling while introducing
local idiosyncrasies at each repetition result in a compound
field of discrete parts where incremental alterations or
additions iteratively densify and shift the global arrangement.
Below, the *Wedding Feast at Cana* and the three types of
symmetry in the Federal-style house are used as input for
mirroring and doubling their organizations. At each iteration
an aberration (seen in heavier line-weight) is introduced
through the addition of a new segment, rotation, local
mirroring, or scaling.

Wedding Feast at Cana	Parenthetical Symmetry	Hyphenated Symmetry	Em-Dash Symmetry

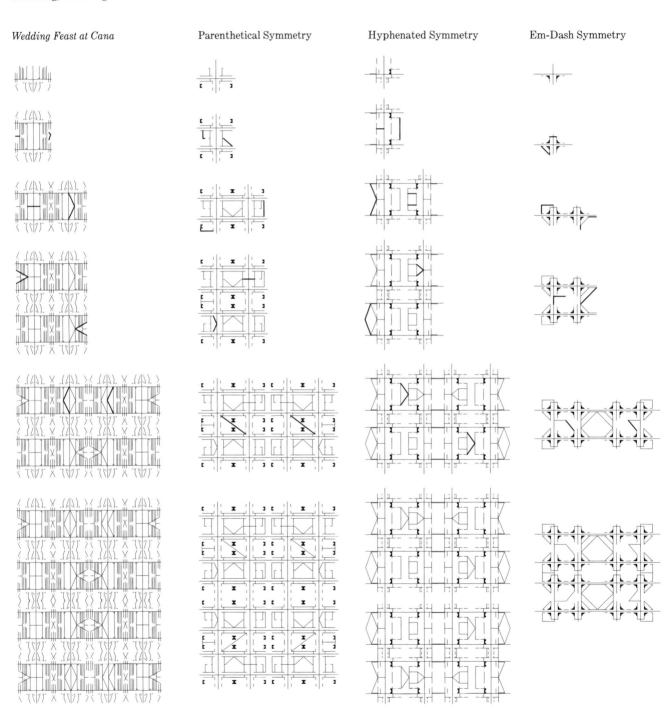

146

7.10
The subtraction of constituent parts in symmetrical compound fields de-densifies the composition, often creating disproportionate distribution and increasingly reading something like a scatter-plan as density decreases, as the perception of both local and global symmetry diminishes in relation to density.

Wedding Feast at Cana	Parenthetical Symmetry	Hyphenated Symmetry	Em-Dash Symmetry

147

However, multiple local symmetries—from the position of the musicians in the foreground to the postures of the wedding party participants to the direction of gazes to the columns around the court—shift the eye around and into the scene. Mannered symmetry is subtle and non-hierarchical and manifests through the layering of multiple local symmetries within an otherwise asymmetrical whole. Thus, local asymmetries are proliferated with idiosyncrasies via alterations to colors, materials, orientation, or profiles when mirrored or doubled; global symmetry is perceptually implied but literally denied. Taken a step further, the repetitive act of mirroring or doubling the whole while continuing to introduce local idiosyncrasies at each repetition results in a compound field of discrete parts where incremental alterations or additions iteratively densify and shift the global arrangement. Conversely, the subtraction of constituent parts de-densifies a compound symmetrical field.

Techniques of local symmetry with idiosyncrasies achieved through mirroring and doubling creates an effect common to Mannerist painting in which the slow enrollment of an audience's attention allows viewers to discover local nuances and shifting relationships within the whole. However, when addition or subtraction occurs disproportionately across the axis of symmetry, the presence of symmetry breaks down into an incomplete whole, or something like a scatter-plan, in which the perception of both local and global symmetry diminishes in relation to decreasing density.

Similarly, materially intensive symmetry is characterized by non-idealized, shifting hierarchies that emerge and recede through densities which have neither a delineated, continuous profile line nor discretely legible parts. In materially intensive optical symmetry, density is especially important both to the overall perception of global symmetry and to the local nuances. Increasing density strengthens the perception of symmetry and its spatial, textural, and associative qualities. At lower densities, symmetry begins to break down back into discrete elements and begins to lose the qualities of intensity and depth. Materially intensive symmetry tends to produce the strangest effects when it is encountered on asymmetrical forms. Whereas asymmetrical forms with asymmetrical material and symmetrical forms with symmetrical material can be visually comprehended quickly with little or no disruption to pattern recognition or conflicts between form and material,

asymmetrical forms with symmetrical material and symmetrical forms with asymmetrical material tend to cause visual oscillations *between* form and material. Competing hierarchies or disassociations between form and material result, as sometimes form and material align, say at a particular seam, and at other times their underlying qualities diverge or misalign.

Harmonious or Anxious: An Empirical Account on Symmetry's Double Entendre

While architects throughout history have tended to affiliate symmetry with optimistic ideas of balance, comfort, efficiency, and harmony, other creative practices, including poetry and cinema, use symmetry to entirely different ends. Symmetry is often used cinematically to illustrate and induce anxiety, suspicion, fear, or uncanny sensations. Consider the repeated use of interior visual symmetry in Stanley Kubrick's *The Shining* (1980), as emphasized by the indistinguishable symmetrical hallways, repeated use of twinning with mirrors or literal twins, or by Jack's writing room in The Overlook Hotel.

Alfred Hitchcock also used symmetrical architecture to provoke anxiety, including the farmhouse in *Psycho* (1960), the schoolhouse where the first major attack occurs in *The Birds* (1963), and the (nearly) symmetrical façade of the McKittrick Hotel in *Vertigo* (1958). Hitchcock once said that "there is no horror in the bang, it's all in the anticipation."[7] Accordingly, he often used symmetrical buildings in his films to build anticipation of the disparity between interior and exterior worlds, between the familiar and the uncanny.

Perhaps because of this tradition in horror films of exploiting the contrast between a *familiar* outward appearance and what lies within, symmetrical house façades eventually became icons of the haunted or abnormal. For example, the symmetric *Amityville Horror* (2005) house, as well as the house located in Burkittsville, Maryland, that inspired *The Blair Witch Project* (1999), itself becomes the source of anxiety and uncanniness. The plantation-like houses of the Colonial or Federal-style became particular favorites of horror film-makers. Examples include the Houmas House in *Hush...Hush Sweet Charlotte* (1964), Oak Alley Plantation in *Interview With The Vampire* (1994), the Brown Mansion in *Preacher* (2004), Felicity Plantation in *The Skeleton*

7.11A
Asymmetrical form with symmetrical material.

7.11B
Doubled asymmetrical form with symmetrical material per form.

7.11C
Mirrored asymmetrical form (globally symmetrical) with globally symmetric material.

7.11D, 7.11E
Symmetrical forms with asymmetrical material.

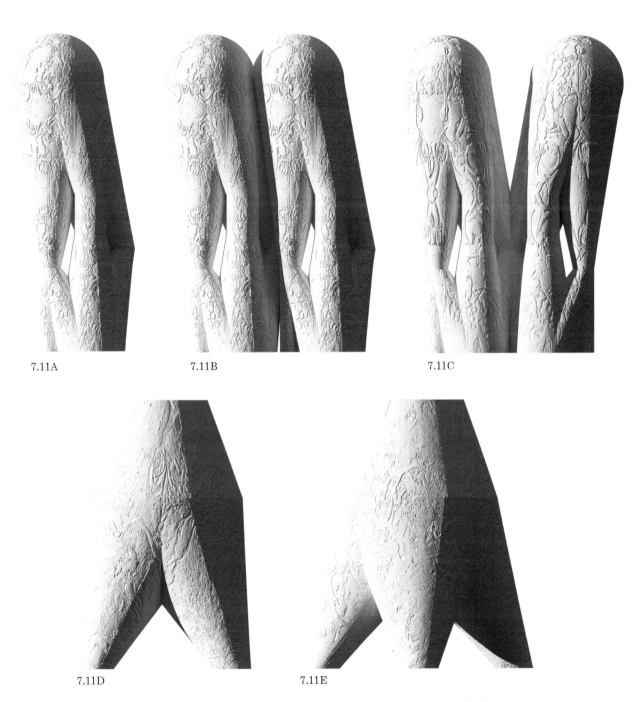

7.11A

7.11B

7.11C

7.11D

7.11E

149

Key (2005), the Creedmoor Plantation in *The Last Exorcism* (2010), The Evergreen Plantation in *Abraham Lincoln: Vampire Hunter* (2012), Buckner Mansion in *American Horror Story: Coven* (2014), and the list goes on.[8] There are of course cases of architectural symmetry used in film to connote delight, wealth, and power, as Vitruvius declared, but the prevalent use of symmetry to provoke anxiety and fear in horror films contradicts the historic traditions of architectural theory.

Symmetry is also used as a tool of cinematic composition, separate from the featured architecture. Horror films often use symmetry to parallel the introductory and concluding scenes by mirroring the same shot, camera movement, or thematic composition.[9] This technique concentrates feelings of fear and anxiety at the end of the film, reminding viewers of the beginning of the story when things appeared normal, encouraging them to relive the film after its conclusion, and suggesting a cyclical trap of unknown conditions found when looking both backward and forward.

For Vitruvius, da Vinci, and Alberti, among notable others, symmetry was understood as a humanist principle echoing the proportioning of the body and thus affirming rational order, humanism, and logic. Perhaps this is also what affords symmetry its double entendre of disorder, ghostliness, and horror: if symmetry appeals to humanist qualities, then it must also connote the dark side of humanity or its affiliated unknowns, such as the return of the dead, psychological rupture, and the uncanny. William Blake's 1794 poem "The Tyger" offers a theological underscore to this dichotomy in what Blake refers to as "fearful symmetry"—a warning against human creations that use the same technique, symmetry, as the divine creation of nature. Blake describes the tiger as both remarkably beautiful in appearance and horrific in its capacity for violence. Blake's poem unfolds a moral and physical corollary about the dual existence of beauty and destruction, noting that only a powerful being, such as a god, can create true symmetry.

The contrast between symmetry as historically championed in architecture and within adjacent fields such as film, painting, and poetry highlights its productive capacities for exposing alternative spatial, formal, organizational and perceptual or physiological effects. The central difference between these has to do with context—in other words, with 'worlds' and architecture's place within them. Historically in architecture the building held the capacity to affect its context—to construct the world through implied social and moral conduct linked to formal and spatial expressions—and therefore symmetry is most often understood in a humanist model as projecting harmony, economy, and beauty out from the building onto the operations of the outside world. In painting, poetry, and film, however, the world is often assumed to have been already constructed—with buildings as ancillary containers for the operations of social and moral behaviors learned elsewhere—and therefore symmetry inherits certain tendencies and psychologies that permeate from the outside world into the presumed comforts of its buildings, thus conjuring the effects of symmetry as dark, sinister, or frightening. In other words, the former posits the world as conditioned by the building; the latter posits the building as a condition of the world. Thus symmetry is an ultimate architectural double entendre caught between projecting and inheriting—between constructing identities and behaviors for the world and being subjected to existing social, cultural, and political constructs. This makes its use in residential architecture all the more provocative; is it intending to inscribe the world with a particular code of conduct, or is it receiving the effects of an outside world as a pre-authored domain?

1
Wendell Garrett, *Classic America: The Federal Style & Beyond* (New York: Rizzoli, 1992), 14.

2
Garrett, *Classic America*, 14.

3
A.J. Downing, "The Real Meaning of Architecture" in *The Architecture of Country Houses* (New York: D. Appleton & Co., 1850), 14.

4
Downing, *The Architecture of Country Houses*, 13.

5
Philip Tabor, "Fearful Symmetry: A Reassessment of Symmetry in Architectural Compositions." *Architectural Review*, 1023, (May 1982), 18-24.

6
Parenthetical symmetry in the Federal-style house is similar the I-house, which was common in 18th century rural America. However, the I-house type is only one room deep whereas Federal-style houses are typically two or more rooms deep. In addition, this observation on symmetry should not be misconstrued as any measure of affirmation of beauty, harmony, or superior composition as inherited from the history of architectural discourse.

7

This quote was attributed to Alfred Hitchcock in Halliwell's *Filmgoer's Companion* (1984).

8

For a longer list, see Chris Eggertsen's "New Orleans's Ultimate Horror Movie Filming Locations Map" *Curbed.com*, July 25, 2018, https://nola.curbed.com/maps/american-horror-story-originals-filming-locations (accessed February 3, 2019).

9

Rob Hardy lists several such films in his article "Startling Symmetry in the First and Last Frames of Famous Horror Films," including: *Black Sunday* (1960), *The Innocents* (1961), *Repulsion* (1965), *The Wicker Man* (1973), *Texas Chainsaw Massacre* (1974), *Halloween* (1978), *Invasion of the Body Snatchers* (1978), *The Evil Dead* (1981), *Poltergeist* (1982), *Christine* (1983), *Fright Night* (1985), *Henry: Portrait of a Serial Killer* (1986), *Hellraiser* (1987), *The Blair Witch Project* (1999), *May* (2002), *Open Water* (2003), *Bug* (2006), *Inside* (2007), *The House of the Devil* (2009), *I Saw The Devil* (2010), *The Woman In Black* (2012), *The Pact* (2012), *Lovely Molly* (2012), *The Conjuring* (2013), *It Follows* (2014), *Starry Eyes* (2014), and *Unfriended* (2014). Rob Hardy, "Startling Symmetry in the First and Last Frames of Famous Horror Films" *No Film School*, October 29, 2015, https://nofilmschool.com/2015/10/first-and-final-frames-horror-edition (accessed January 9, 2019).

7.12
Plan for a Federal-style house. Endemic Architecture, 2018–2019

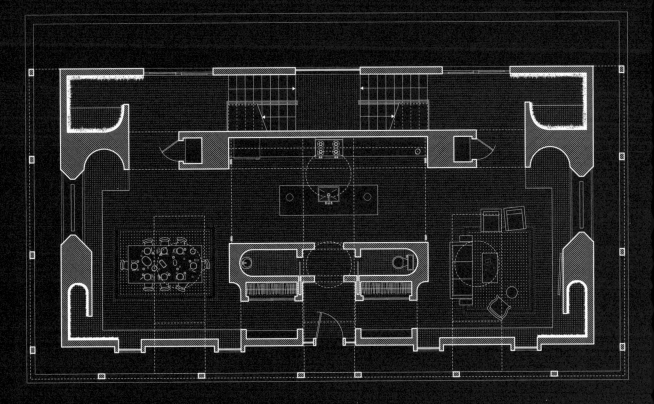

7.13
Rendering for a Federal-
style house. Endemic
Architecture, 2018–2019

8.1 (top left)
Diagrammatic comparison
of an American Foursquare
and a shotgun house.

8.2 (left)
AS BUILT_A shotgun house
in New Orleans, Louisiana.

8.3 (below)
AS BUILT_A shotgun house
in New Orleans, Louisiana.
Redrawn from an original
photograph by Brian
Vanden Brink.

155

8.4
AS BUILT_A camelback
shotgun house in New
Orleans, Louisiana.

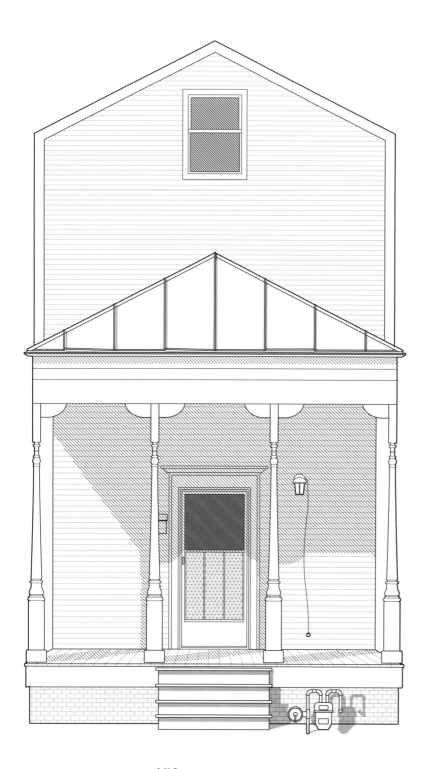

If the four rooms comprising each of these two residential types might be considered roughly the same by virtue of being square, the obvious difference lies in their spatial sequencing. Thus, the comparison between the American Foursquare and shotgun house challenges any sense of a strict binary between center and periphery in houses composed with square rooms. Whereas the collection of rooms in the American Foursqaure can be understood as an interrelated series of squares within a whole, the rooms of the shotgun house can be seen as individual, atomized cells that can be independently modified, shaped, shuffled, or programmed before being composed as a whole and unified by single hallway. Such spatial relationships emphasize the geometric properties of the parts. Thus points, partitions, and rooms can alternately be considered *primitives* to begin to modify the shotgun house to create new variations on the type without the constraint of strict geometric congruence.

Points – Partitions – Rooms

Alongside efficiency of construction and environmental sensitivity, the shotgun house can also be read geometrically as points, partitions, and rooms. This double reading is inherent to some degree in all the houses in this book and to architecture more broadly, but it is exemplified most clearly in this book by the shotgun house.

In order to illustrate the distinction and interplay between the two readings of the shotgun house, two assumptions are necessary: (1) that there are specific formal and spatial qualities that make the shotgun house legible as a type, which are linear circulation, rectangular massing, a three-to-five-square enfilade plan, and one-room width; and (2) that the previous assumption is dependent on elements and orders that can be reduced to points, partitions, and rooms for analysis, abstraction, and projection. This type of analysis raises questions about the relationship between procedure, abstraction, and type, which can be applied to architecture of nearly all scales.

Modifier 1: Points

Points are relational metrics used to locate and define a discrete boundary in a specific context. For example, points are the basic measurement used in surveying, as a first step in the division of land or to describe a boundary before pouring a foundation. In the shotgun house, the rectangular boundary of the house is typically conceived as an offset of the lot boundary. Thus, the points that define the lot line can be said to determine where exterior walls will be located, as well as interior partitions, which are determined by equal division. The shotgun house typically has few internal divisions, with the result that the only control points for simultaneously manipulating both the interior organization and exterior form of the house lay along its perimeter.

If points are considered to be the generative geometric units of the shotgun house, then the house's geometry could be altered primarily by shifting individual perimeter points in the X and Y axes (i.e., in plan) to alter exterior form while maintaining interior linear order. This reading prioritizes perimeter vertices as provisional metrics that simultaneously control exterior and interior alignments which can be understood as either individual cells or a topological network.

Modifier 2: Partitions

Another reading of the shotgun house might contend that the perimeter is strictly bound to a rectangular shape in plan and that the interior is open to spatial differentiation only through the seriality and dimensionality of partition walls independent of any relation to externally plotted points. In this reading, site context is irrelevant and the shape is neutral. It should be noted here that the term *partitions*, as opposed to *lines*, implies a three-dimensional physical quality. If the partition walls are the primary site of modification for the shotgun house, then the house's exterior form is fixed but the interior arrangements of rooms and circulation are editable and changeable. The unchallenged acceptance of an inherited boundary emphasizes spatial divisions as a virtue of interior partitions and allows them freedom to shift, re-orient, rotate, or change qualities like thickness, curvilinearity, etc. This is a common approach to renovation, especially when dividing a large house into smaller rentable units, or inversely, removing walls to create larger rooms.

This reading prioritizes inherent possibilities for the free location of partition walls to divide otherwise totalizing forms without challenging the proportional characteristics of the host form, in this case the shotgun house. Le Corbusier seemingly used a similar logic when designing Villa Le

8.6
When points are used as plan modifiers, the
vertices of tangential squares in a linear array are
used to push and pull interior and exterior form.

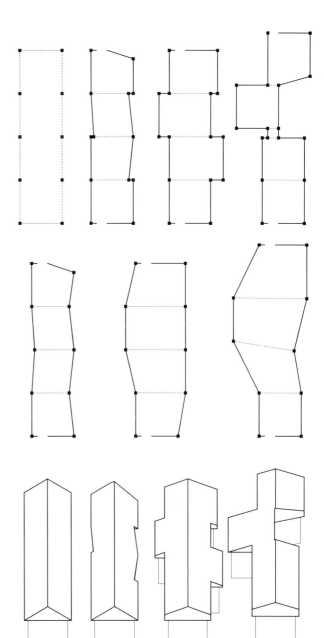

8.7
Corresponding massing for a shotgun house
modified by manipulated points.

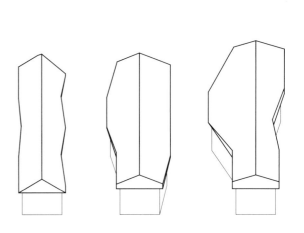

Lac for his parents in 1924. He designed the main house before a site was chosen, using proportions comparable to those of the shotgun house but with a flat roof for a garden rather than a gable roof. Villa Le Lac precedes Le Corbusier's prescription of the "five points," but they are all present to some degree, including the free plan. Despite similarities in their external proportions, the generic shotgun house and Villa Le Lac have notably different internal parti diagrams—one with equally spaced serial partitions and one with loosely arranged partitions mostly detached from the perimeter walls—and one might imagine Villa Le Lac as a genealogical modification of the shotgun. Though the shotgun house sometimes has a side entry, it opens directly into a room, just as the front entry does in a typical shotgun house. Villa Le Lac's side entry opens into a compressed entry hall in which one must turn an abrupt 90-degrees to progress into either the kitchen or the living space. The plan is still enfilade, but its partitions detach from the perimeter wall and assume variable shapes, thicknesses, and qualities. The telescoping one-point-perspective of linearly aligned doors in the shotgun house is usurped by

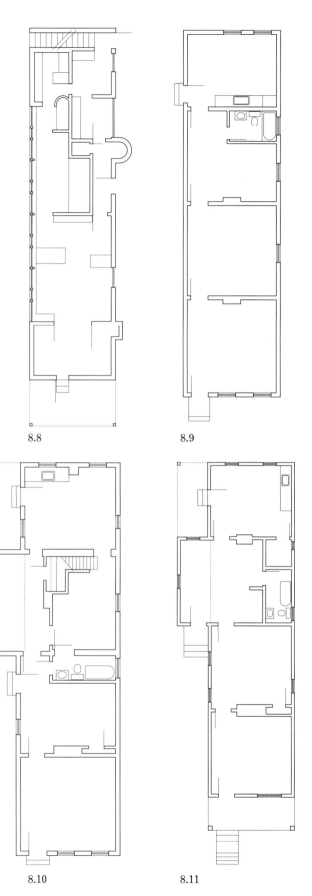

8.8

8.9

8.8
Plan of Villa Le Lac (detached oil storage with guest room omitted).

8.9
Typical shotgun house plan.

8.10
Typical camelback shotgun house plan.

8.11
Typical shotgun house plan with side entry.

8.10

8.11

160

8.12
When partitions are used as plan modifiers, interior spatial arrangements are altered without disturbing the exterior form.

8.13
Corresponding interior walls for a shotgun house modified by partitions.

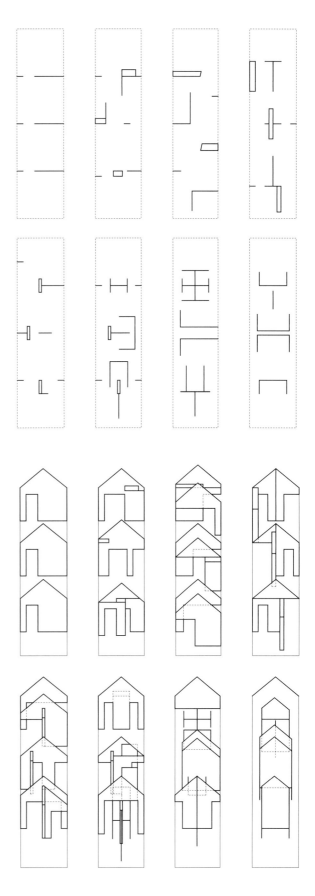

161

episodic near-thoroughfare views and movement in Villa Le Lac, demonstrating the influence of partitions to alter otherwise stable forms or volumes.

Modifier 3: Rooms

A third possible reading of the shotgun house defines its base unit as the room—an abstract unit of space typically tied to a desired use. With regard to the shotgun house, a re-reading through the logic of rooms suggests that discrete geometric entities—three or four serially arranged squares—are collectively pierced by a circulation path after the overall composition is achieved. If the room is the base unit, walls and vertices cannot be independently edited as they are indebted to the geometric description of the room as a spatial unit. In other words, if a "room" is a square, as is the case in the shotgun house and the American Foursquare, then only the square, not individual vertices or segments particular to it, can be rotated, scaled, or otherwise modified. However, a room can also be described in other terms—geometrically, materially, dimensionally, etc.—and all kinds of rooms can aggregate into a composition. Once a composition is achieved, the collection of rooms can be trimmed by a binding line, self-intersected, or assigned additional terms of specificity.

While the argument that the room is the base unit might seem to imply rigid programmatic specificity or precise order to the enfilade, as a functionalist might claim, the fact that all rooms are nearly identical squares in the shotgun house is a testament to appropriated use rather than determined function. Rooms, as abstract yet discrete spaces, have the capacity to construct (and not just contain) new expressions for known forms that impact both the inside and the outside of the house simultaneously. It follows that rooms need not be square in plan and cubic in volume, but can assume other formal and spatial qualities without disrupting the principal hierarchy of linear circulation—of both people and air—through linear array. This reading prioritizes the figure as a collection of rooms (articulated here as shapes) while maintaining the characteristic linear circulation and gable roof of the shotgun house.

The Perpetual Threshold

The alignment of doors in the shotgun house renders the interior as a constant state of transition, a perpetual threshold. Such is the nature of an enfilade in general, and in the shotgun house strict linearity amplifies the qualities of thoroughfare rooms. Historic debates surround this spatial arrangement, though it has generally been considered undesirable in residential architecture since the 1800s. Prior to that, however, the enfilade was regarded as a virtue, as people preferred to have more doors to and between intervening rooms. Alberti remarked about Roman architecture that "[i]t is also convenient to place the doors in such a manner that they lead to as many parts of the edifice as possible."[5] Robin Evans expanded on Alberti's position by explaining that in such houses "there was a door whenever there was an adjoining room, making a matrix of discrete but thoroughly interconnected chambers."[6] The shotgun house is decidedly simpler than a Roman villa, and its linear arrangement both confuses and clarifies the spatial idea of such a "matrix." Opposed to the enfilade organization of rooms with multiple doors, English residential architecture critic Robert Kerr wrote in 1865 of the "wretched inconvenience of thoroughfare rooms which made domesticity and retirement unattainable."[7] Kerr objected to the circulation of visitors and family members alike through each and every room and instead championed the need for spaces with varying degrees of privacy. Kerr argued instead for the terminal room, a room with one precisely located door that grants entry to the rest of the house.[8]

8.14 (opposite, top left)
When rooms are used as modifiers, interior and exterior order is constructed through the composition and relationship of defined shapes or figures placed in proximity to each other.

8.15 (opposite, bottom left)
Corresponding massing for a shotgun house modified by rooms.

8.16 (opposite, top right)
When rooms within rooms are used as modifiers, a fixed form is accepted within which the operations of room-as-modifier are carried out.

8.17 (opposite, bottom right)
Corresponding massing for a shotgun house modified by rooms within rooms.

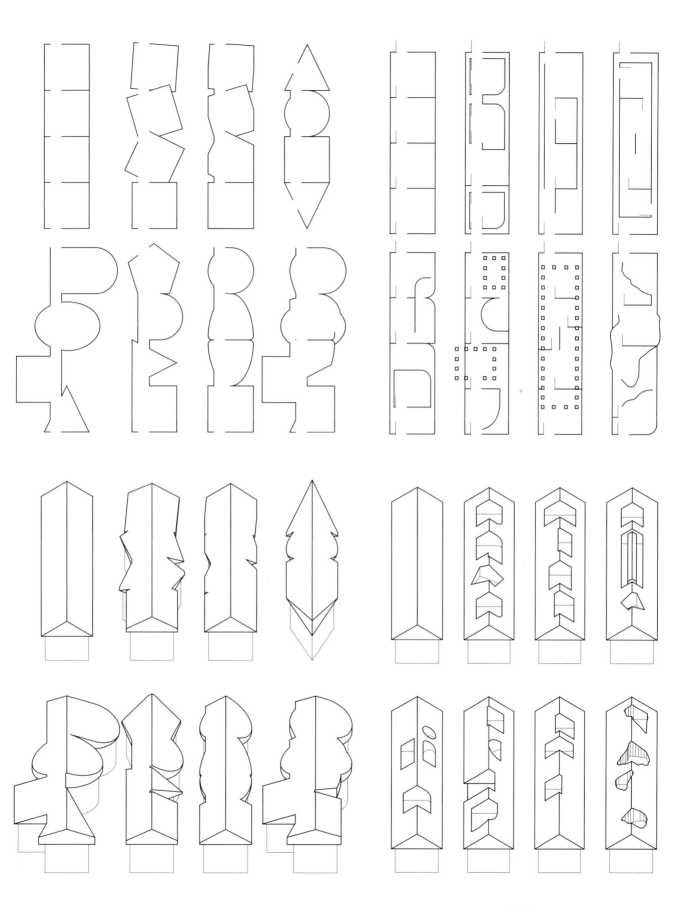

163

This leaves the shotgun house in a paradoxical state. Its linear enfilade, minimal as far as matrices go, is indeed composed with thoroughly interconnected thoroughfare rooms, yet each one also leads principally to the edifice of the house through a minimum of doors per room required to do so. The shotgun house could be said to have just one door, an elongated threshold. On the other hand, it can also be said to have many doors, as each thoroughfare room has at least two doors and therefore has at least twice as many doors as it does rooms.

We can infer from the distinctions among spatial preferences for the terminal room or the enfilade a contrast of values in the culture of residing. One prioritizes separation—the atomization of uses, privacy, activity, subjects, and encounters—while the other prioritizes perpetual, collective exchanges between program, privacy, activity, and occupants. This second set of priorities recalls the theory of the shotgun's origins as a space for gathering, rather than for separating, as found in the Yoruba word *togun*. Furthermore, returning to the other suggested origin word *shogun*, meaning *God's House*, the spatial logics of the shotgun house might be said to have an originating theological imperative of collectivity. Such speculations harken back to a time when the relationships between architecture—in particular, the spatial organization of the plan—and meaning were linked to spirituality or theological beliefs. This reading suggests that what is unresolved in the shotgun house's legibility, both in its origins and its spatial paradox, hinges on the nature of dwelling itself as the mediator between an individual and a collective.

1
Shotgun houses are most common in New Orleans, Louisville, Charleston, Charlotte, Houston, and the coastal regions of Florida.

2
Katy Coyle of R. Christopher Goodwin and Associates for the City of New Orleans Historic District Landmarks Commission, *Historic Mid-City Study Report* (June 2010), 15.

3
John H. Lienhard, "No. 820: Shotgun Homes and Porches" *Engines of Our Ingenuity*, http://www.uh.edu/engines/epi820.htm (accessed March 1, 2019).See also J.M. Vlach, "The Shotgun house: An African Architectural Legacy" in *Common Places: Readings in American Vernacular Architecture*, ed. D. Upton and J.M. Vlach.(Athens, GA: The University of Georgia Press, 1986), 58-78.

4
The Editors of Encyclopaedia Britannica, "Shotgun House" *Encyclopedia Britannica*, March 17, 2017, https://www.britannica.com/technology/shotgun-house (accessed March 1, 2019).

5
Leon Battista Alberti, *The Ten Books of Architecture* [1452], trans.James Leoni, ed. Joseph Rykwert (London: Tiranti, 1955), Book I, Chapter xii.

6
Robin Evans, "Figures, Doors and Passages" in *Translations from Drawings to Buildings and Other Essays* (London: Architectural Association Press, 1997), 64. Originally published in *Architectural Design* 48 (London: Academy Editions, 1978), 267-78.

7
This is Robin Evans's paraphrase of Kerr's visual and written analysis of 18th-century neo-Palladian Holkham Hall, designed by William Kent in Norfolk, England. Evans, *Figures*, 63. See also Plate XIII and its associated description in Robert Kerr's *The Gentleman's House: Or, How to Plan English Residences, from the Parsonage to the Palace* (England: Oxford University Press, 1865).

8
Evans, *Figures*, 64. See also Kerr, The *Gentleman's House*, Plate XII.

8.18
Plan for a shotgun house.
Endemic Architecture, 2018

Threshold

Room

Threshold

Room

Threshold

Room

Threshold

Room

Threshold

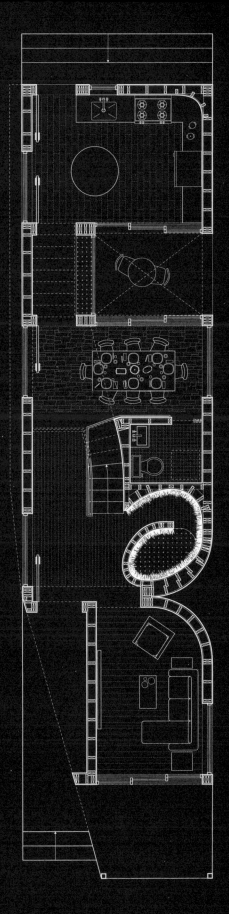

8.19
Proposal for a shotgun house.
Endemic Architecture, 2018

Party Walls & Other Interiors
in the Row House

PARTY WALL

1
A wall common to
two adjoining houses,
rooms, or buildings.

2
An urban interior
architectural element
that unifies and
divides contiguous
houses, sitting along
the property line.

Contiguous homes have been around since ancient times, but the type we know today as the row house originated in Europe. The oldest examples appeared in 16th-century Amsterdam, migrating to Paris by the turn of the 17th century. In America, the row house first appeared in Philadelphia when developer Thomas Carstairs designed one for William Sansom circa 1800. Other contiguous houses appeared in America as early as the 1690s, but unlike the row house, these houses had continuous brickwork on the front façade, rendering the building as one construction with multiple units within.[1] Carstairs's design is commonly considered the first American row house, as it was the first in which each house in the row expressed individuality through façade treatment, color, or discontinuous brickwork. In the row house, adjacent houses share side walls, also called party walls. Row houses soon appeared in New York City, Baltimore, Boston, and New Orleans, becoming one of the most prevalent urban residential types in America, particularly in the Northeast, where they were called Philadelphia Row Houses throughout the 1800s. In fact, before Philadelphia came to be known as the "City of Brotherly Love," it was called the "City of Homes" because it had such a high rate of home ownership due to the modest cost and efficient construction of row houses.[2] There is some ambiguity as to what can be considered a row house; for the purposes of this chapter a row house is broadly defined as a group of more than two narrow, contiguous, two- to five-story houses used only for residential purposes, with shared walls between houses and usually (but not always) non-continuous façade materials, forms, or colors.

The Double Entendre of Party Walls

Robin Evans once pointed out that when attention turns from the house to housing—from a place to an activity—"emphasis shifts from the nature of the place to the procedures of its assembly."[3] In the case of the row house, or row housing, this shift in attention introduces a double entendre of the party wall. As a shared wall—historically built of brick with two or more wythes—between two houses, the party wall both divides and unifies. It divides one house from its neighbor, while simultaneously asserting their mutual dependency for the purposes of structural support, efficiency of construction, fire safety, and house width-to-block size maximization as a procedure of assembly.

The seemingly simple duality of the party wall as an agent of both separation and connection is not without social and political drama, dating back at least to ancient Roman mythology. Book IV of Ovid's narrative poem *Metamorphoses* (8 CE) recounts the fate of Pyramus and Thisbe, a story of forbidden love in which the party wall is a central figure. The two young lovers live on opposite sides of a wall dividing one building into two houses. Their parents oppose their love because of a longstanding hatred, but the lovers manage to communicate by whispering to each other through a crack in the wall. They hatch a plan to flee their respective houses to be together, abandoning the wall that both divides and unites them. The tale ends in tragedy when a misunderstanding leads the protagonists each to commit suicide in a scenario which would later inspire *Romeo and Juliet*. The story of Pyramus and Thisbe has been adapted many times over, including as the play-within-a-play in Shakespeare's *A Midsummer Night's Dream*, in which an actor performs as the wall. The role of the wall which physically separates the lovers yet emotionally connects them reveals a lingering ambiguity in Evans's architectural dichotomy between the familial qualities (what he refers to as the "nature") of a singular house and the procedures of collective assembly in housing. The party wall introduces ambiguity to the otherwise clear differences between the house and housing—between the stand-alone construct for a single family and the collectivity of multiple families—because it is the principal element that can be said to belong simultaneously to both. The party wall defines both the singular house as a space and the procedures of assembly within the collective; therefore, neighbors who share a party wall have a fundamentally different relationship with walls and with their neighbors than those who do not.

In Philadelphia, where 70% of the housing stock today is row houses, the party wall was, and remains, a critical mechanism for housing the growing urban population; consequently, the party wall corresponded directly to the division of property and taxation.[4] In other single-family residential types, a property line establishes a boundary from which the exterior wall of a house must be offset, largely for the purposes of preventing the spread of fire from house to house. In the row house, however, the property line falls within the poché of the typically multi-wythe brick wall, introducing problems pertaining to ownership and structural assembly. Common logic would suggest that neighboring row houses would each have ownership of half the width of the wall. This logic was used, for example, in a Washington, D.C. building regulation from 1791, which stipulates that when neighboring houses are built with a party wall, the two parties must agree to the equal division of the foundation below and any portion of the wall above. However, this simple concept is complicated if each party hires a different builder and is compounded by the structural dependency each half has to the integrity of the whole—what's known in party wall law today as reciprocal rights. Reciprocal rights bind two or more parties to each other by mutual responsibilities, in this case for the purposes of safety and protection of property, to maintain the structural integrity of the party wall. Today, division is a challenging legal term, as evidenced in the Code of the District of Columbia, in which Title 1 of Government Organization, Chapter 13, of Surveyor Section 1-1325, dedicated to party walls, notes:

> Whenever, on such admeasurement, the wall of a house previously erected by any proprietor shall appear to stand on the adjoining lot of any other person in part less than 7 inches in width thereon, such wall shall be considered as standing altogether on the land of such proprietor, who shall pay to the owner of the lot on which the wall may stand a reasonable price for the ground so occupied, to be decided by arbitrators or a jury, as the parties interested may agree.[5]

170

9.2
AS BUILT_Row houses in
Philadelphia, Pennsylvania.
Redrawn from an original
photograph by Randy
Calderone.

9.3
AS BUILT_Row houses
in Brooklyn, New York.
Redrawn from an original
photograph by Rob
Stephenson.

The following section, S1-1326, further states that:

> If the wall of any house already erected cover 7 inches or more in width of the adjoining lot, it shall be deemed a party wall, according to the regulations for building in the District, and the ground so occupied more than 7 inches in width shall be paid for as provided in § 1-1325.[6]

aesthetics, but can determine who is responsible for thousands of dollars of repairs, and similarly effects renovations depending on where exactly the property line falls within the poché.

The traditional row house's floor-to-wall relationship also confuses any straightforward reading of individual units versus the whole. Unlike most of the houses in this book, which are framed predomi-

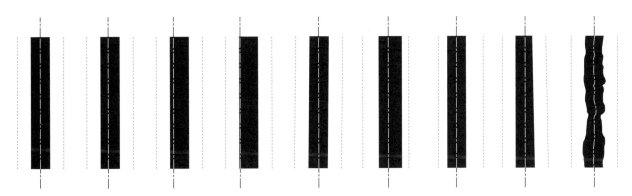

9.4—Diagram of possible relationships between the property line, the party wall, and the foundation.

In other words, if a wall is determined to be on Neighbor A's property then it must have been determined to cover less than 7 inches of Neighbor B's property, and Neighbor A must pay Neighbor B a fee for use of their land for the wall relative to its encroachment on Neighbor B's property. However, if the wall is 7 inches or more onto Neighbor B's property, it is a party wall.

While it may be possible to divide the party wall conceptually for the purposes of law and ownership, division is structurally impossible, as the wall is held together using incrementally perpendicular bricks or metal ties that link the two halves. Who owns the ties or cross-bricks? As an assembly, the wall is environmentally dependent on the two halves and on the air space between for the purposes of expelling moisture. If my "half" is determined to contain only 1/8" of the air space based on where the property line is and your "half" is 3/8" of the air space and there is a moisture problem in the wall, wouldn't you pay three times as much to fix it? What if the origin of the problem is found to be in the coping on the parapet where a little hole is found on my side of the wall? But what if it is also found that your side has clogged weep holes and is damming water inside? Such issues frequently land in courtrooms or an arbitrators office. Where the party wall is concerned, tolerance and precision are not simply measures of expertise and perfected

nantly with wood and thus have wood-to-wood connections, the row house does not typically have any vertical framing in the side walls, so there is no horizontal member to fasten the floor joist to. Instead, as the brick walls are laid, pockets are made to receive the wood joists. These joist pockets can hardly be considered a drawing detail as they typically consisted of crudely formed openings and copious amounts of mortar. One of the biggest concerns in this type of assembly is that if a joist fails in the middle of its span it results in a downward rotation that forces the side walls upward, sending it toppling over onto the neighboring property. This was known to happen when a fire in one house weakened its joists to a point of failure, potentially resulting in the collapse of the whole row. Therefore, as party walls proliferated in growing American cities, the ends of the floor joists were cut at a downward sloping angle, giving them the shape of a trapezoid so that if one joist failed the walls on either side would remain in place.

9.5 (next)
Compilation of seams between contrasting materials of neighboring row houses. Original photographs by Rob Stephenson.

9.6 (next, opposite)
Exposed party walls in Philadelphia due to the varying heights of neighboring buildings reveal various party wall profiles that incorporate chimneys, stairs, and interior changes in volume.

173

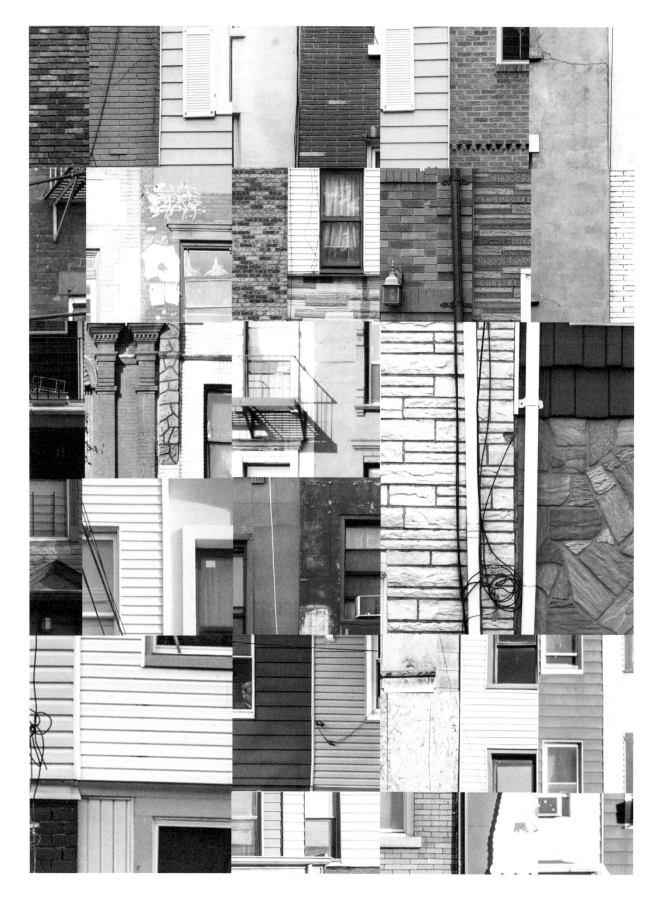

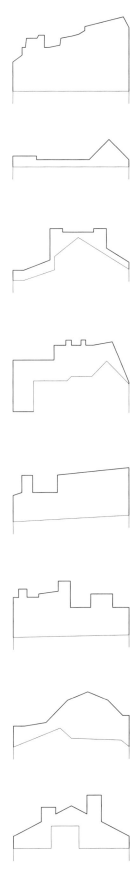

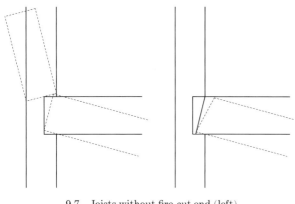

9.7—Joists without fire-cut end (left)
and joist with fire-cut end (right).

Lines of Tangency

The party wall is a distinctly urban architectural element that proliferates a quintessential urban type: the row house. Yet the party wall typically offers very little in terms of public address. If it is visible from the exterior, it is typically as the parapet running perpendicular to the front façade, which is useful for preventing the spread of fire, or as an exterior wall running perpendicular to the front façade that is only visible due to the varying heights of neighboring buildings. In these instances the party wall is often revealed to incorporate other elements, such as chimneys and stair towers, as well as discloses internal changes in volume through its own profile. Yet, given all the spatial and legal dramas associated with the party wall, it is perhaps surprising that it never pierces the front façade as an expressive element or manifests as an element that proposes alternative elevational figures or patterns of urban seriality. Instead, it is only through the different heights of neighboring buildings that the party wall is revealed as a series of urban profiles with expressive potential.

In row houses with uniform materiality it is not uncommon to find alternating slanted, half-round, or square bays that reveal internal divisions through exterior massing. However, the existence of the party wall in most row houses is typically legible on the front façade only through the contrasting adjacencies of brick sizes, coursing and bond patterns, joint contours, changes in color, variations in siding patterns, or contrasting materials—but the wall itself is almost never visible. It is often presumed that the line of material distinction equates to the location of the property line, and thus the division of the party wall into two halves, but this is rarely precisely true. Nevertheless, these material distinctions offer pluralistic expressions because the row house is primarily a generic box that easily adopts variations through the distribution of elements and materials, notably on the front façade. While brick was favored in Philadelphia, New York City favored brown stone quarried from New Jersey and Connecticut. In the 1950s Baltimore went all-in on covering brick row houses with Formstone—a stucco-based faux-stone invented in Baltimore in 1937—to such an extent that Formstone is banned today in many Baltimore neighborhoods because city officials deemed it to be ugly and associated with urban decay.[7] Variation and non-uniformity among neighboring façade materials is a hallmark of the row house. These material juxtapositions produce lines of material tangencies—horizontally discontinuous patterns broken by distinct vertical lines in regular increments. The vertical lines of material tangency—the façade seams—are the site of differentiation among aesthetic, economic, regulatory, and cultural influences that are particular to both the individuals and the collective of the row.

Outside, Like the Walls of a Room

The backside of the row house is also a site of unresolved legibility. While tangency and array do not necessarily breed any particular registration on the front façade, at the scale of a city block they create a new interior, an exterior interior where exterior walls become like those of a room.[8] The middle of the block, or the interior site of a row house block, contoured in plan by the various rear crenellations, is a trapped yet morphing figure constituted by the collection of individual maneuvers aimed at amplifying one house's (or even one floor's) view, exposure to light, yard space, deck area, or privacy. The resultant figure of the inner-block—the *other interior*—provokes its own urban qualities that juxtapose the underwriting logics of property division for legal purpose. This other interior reveals the possibility for other rows, other sources for social or political attention, or even alternative urban orders. The primary elements responsible for such crenellation are the slanted and the square bay window, though offsetting walls also contribute to the overall condition of the *other interior,* which can be described as:

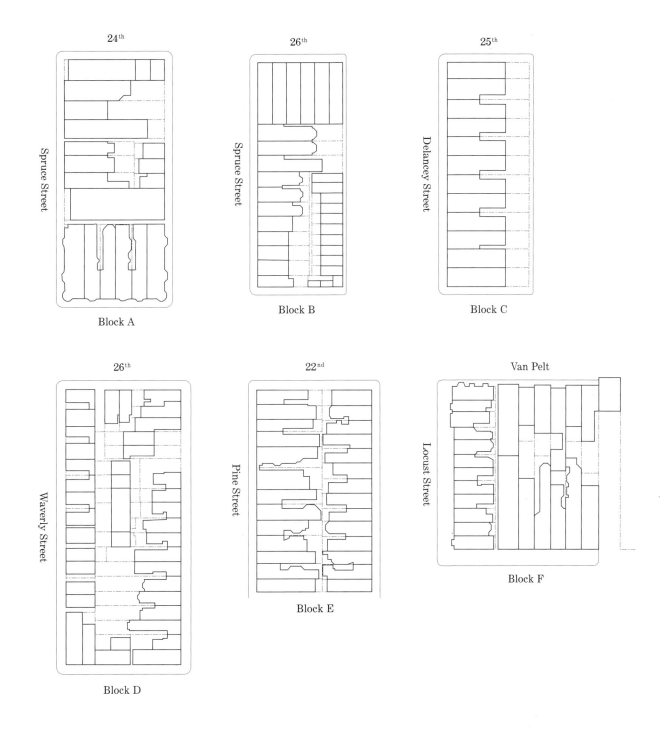

24ᵗʰ

Spruce Street

Block A

26ᵗʰ

Spruce Street

Block B

25ᵗʰ

Delancey Street

Block C

26ᵗʰ

Waverly Street

Block D

22ⁿᵈ

Pine Street

Block E

Van Pelt

Locust Street

Block F

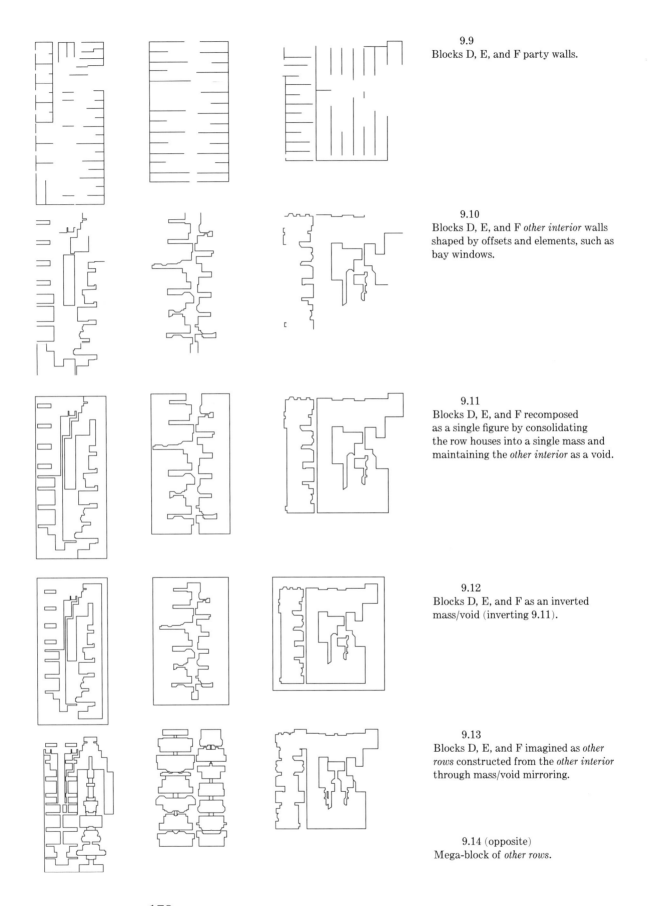

9.9
Blocks D, E, and F party walls.

9.10
Blocks D, E, and F *other interior* walls shaped by offsets and elements, such as bay windows.

9.11
Blocks D, E, and F recomposed as a single figure by consolidating the row houses into a single mass and maintaining the *other interior* as a void.

9.12
Blocks D, E, and F as an inverted mass/void (inverting 9.11).

9.13
Blocks D, E, and F imagined as *other rows* constructed from the *other interior* through mass/void mirroring.

9.14 (opposite)
Mega-block of *other rows*.

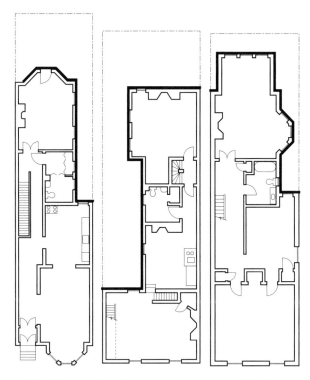

9.15—Plan drawings showing changing plan profiles due to offsets and bay windows in the rear of row houses.

1 Discretely Bound.

Each articulation within the plan profile is the result of discrete, nameable elements with measurable offsets from other architectural elements that have aggregated into an unpredictable figure, yet which are also easily modified, replaced, removed, or otherwise edited across multiple scales and time.

2 Accrued Subtleties.

Despite the overarching grid organization of the city and a certain degree of regulatory uniformity, the *other interior* exposes the potency of accrued subtleties to both re-construct and superimpose intervening preferences over the dominant form of order as an architectural ensemble. As Stan Allen has noted, "there can never be a perfect correspondence between the regulated geometrical structure of the planned city and the unruly practices it supports. ... This in turn suggests that the control exercised by any disciplinary regime can never be total."[9]

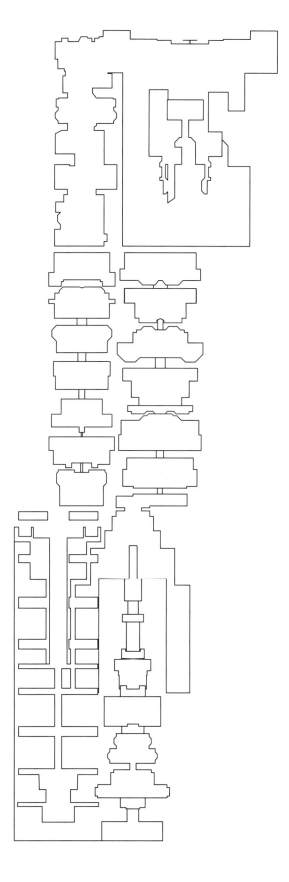

179

3   Calls for Other Others.

The *other interior* provokes. It implies the possibility for other types, other rows, other blocks, other cities, other parks, other parties, other communities, and other orders. The *other interior* is a shaped and bounded exterior. Momentarily forgiving the individuality of specific lots, the *other interior* is more like a courtyard than a backyard; it might even be likened to a front or side yard. It represents the qualities of both collective ambiguity and local specificity. It scales vague terms like "public" and "private" up and down until the distinction between them becomes increasingly blurred.

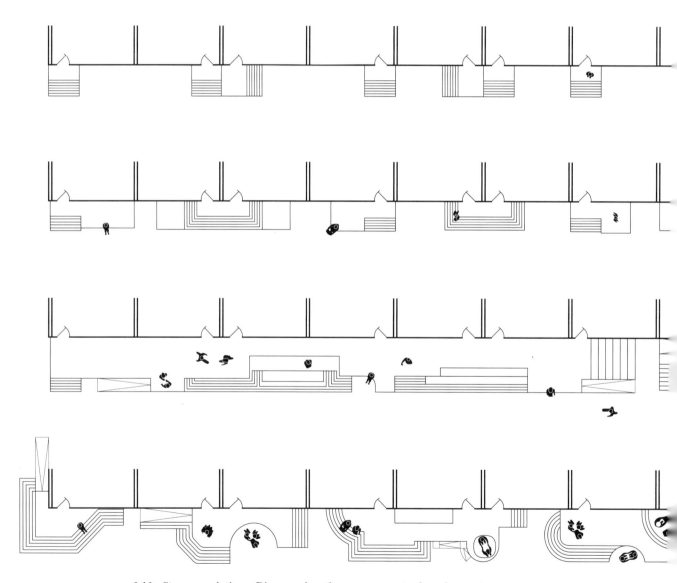

9.16—Stoop speculations_ Diagrams for other arrangements of row house stoops, ranging from a conventional order (top) to speculative ones (bottom three).

A Short but Necessary Comment
On the Stoop

Despite the compelling, multivalent allure of the *other interior*, the row house's frontispiece—the stoop—is already otherwise othered. The stoop is one of the row house's most visible and meaningful elements with regard to the social life of the building, the block, and even the neighborhood. The seemingly singularly purposed stair and its surrounds adjacent to the sidewalk are appropriated on full view of the city for socializing, leisure, tanning, gossiping, hanging out, smoking weed, playing games, playing music, letting the dog pee when it's snowing, first kisses, nervous "should I invite him up" moments, drunken wonderment after the bars close, tearful breakups a few short months later, light gardening, occasionally even laundry, unwanted cat-calling, dancing of all genres, cleaning, fixing, selling, buying, thinking, drinking, eating, and—usually sadly but sometimes blissfully—sleeping. Whereas the farmhouse porch discloses the frontality of an otherwise omni-oriented form and cleaves the house from its context, the row house's frontality as registered by the stoop is both contextually appropriate and socially

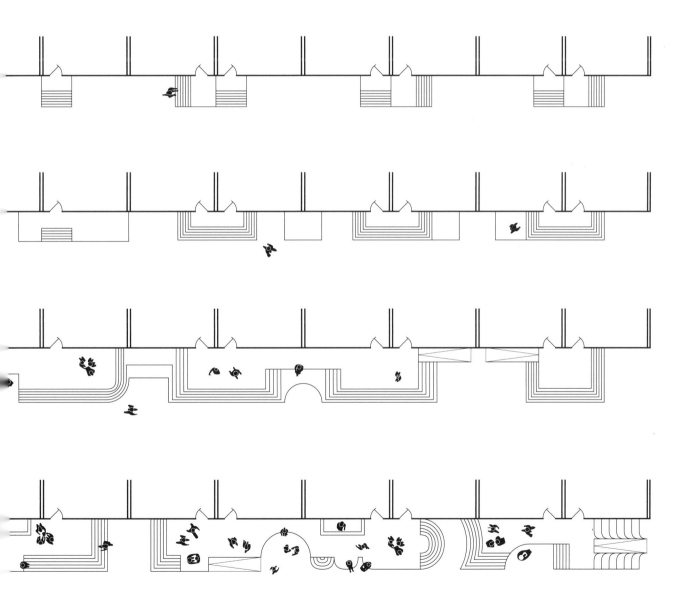

181

9.17
Other Party Walls_ Speculative diagrams for other forms of neighborliness suggesting that party walls could provide space for shared amenities between two neighbors, such as shared bathrooms, kitchens, a baby nursery, closets, or reading rooms.

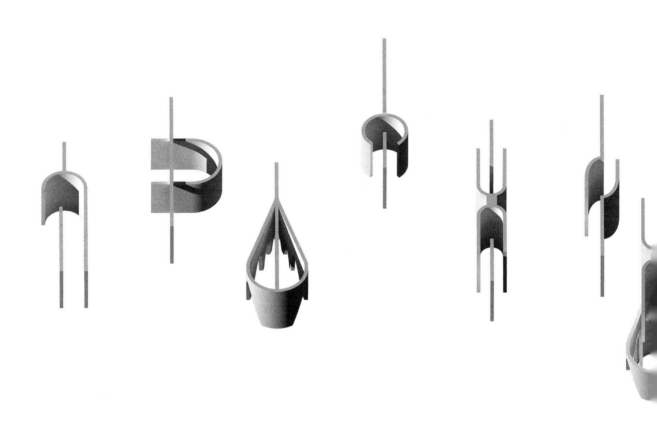

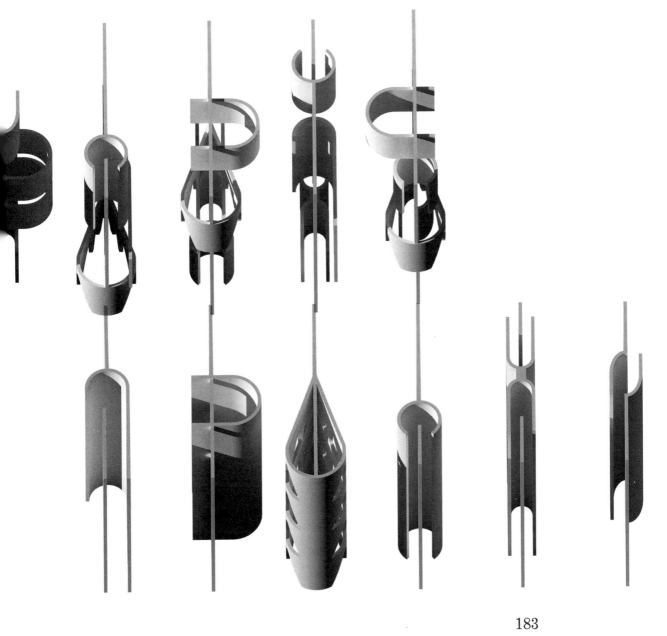

9.18 (left)
Four-floor stack of aligned
Other Party Walls.

9.19 (right)
Four-floor stack of mis-
aligned Other Party Walls.

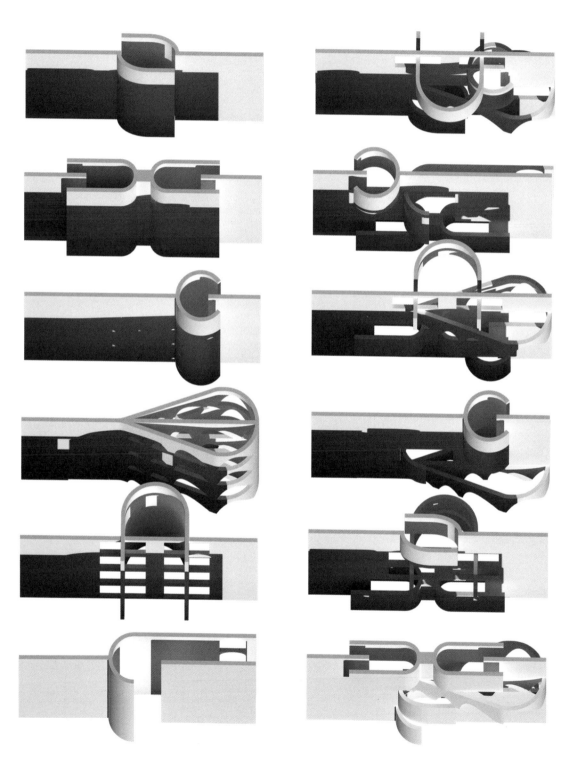

184

meaningful as it sutures the house to its context. The stoop is the first row of rows, a space that mediates between the social and political life of the city and the accrued tangency of residential interiors.

Other, Possible Dramas

Architects often foray into urban planning, most often using similar methods to those used by professional planners—large-scale plans with either broad-reaching infrastructural hierarchies or totalizing patterns of collective form tied to environmental or contextual imperatives. The party wall, however, is the fundamental element of urbanized residential architecture in many cities, registering at an architectural scale the personal desire for privacy, the social desire for collectivity, and the urban necessity of density. The organizational simplicity of linear array contrasts with the conceptual complexity of a singular wall serving two houses equally. The double entendre of the party wall holds the potential to open up possibilities for alternative expressions and experiences across multiple scales that might suggest other forms of neighborliness at the scale of the block and alternative urban orders at the scale of the city. Concentrating architectural attention on the party wall as a point of origin for the city might introduce spatial and social effects into other models of domesticity and urban planning that work from the party wall up, rather than from the ordered urban plan down. It might seem somewhat absurd to follow such a reductive thought to any logical conclusion—to reduce the possibilities for alternative urban orders all the way down to the qualities of a series of party walls—given the irreducibility of the city as a social, political, environmental, and physical construct. Yet it is no more absurd than conventional methods of urban planning which anticipate changes for the individual user based on broad strokes inscribed onto the city as a whole.

1
Amanda Casper, "Row Homes." *The Encyclopedia of Greater Philadelphia*, 2013, https://philadelphiaencyclopedia.org/archive/row-houses/ (accessed February 9, 2019).

2
Ibid.

3
Robin Evans, "Figures, Doors and Passages" in T*ranslations from Drawings to Buildings and Other Essays* (London: Architectural Association Press, 1997), 80. Originally published in *Architectural Design* 48 (London: Academy Editions, 1978), 267-78.

4
Design Advocacy Group, "The Housing Challenge," *The Healthy Row House Project*, http://healthyrowhouse.org/ (accessed February 9, 2019).

5
Code of the District of Columbia, Chapter 13, §1–1325, "Party Walls," current as of April 5, 2019. The code can be viewed at https://code.dccouncil.us/dc/council/code/sections/1-1325.html (accessed April 30, 2019).

6
Ibid., §1–1326.

7
Mark Byrnes, "Farewell Formstone: Requiem for a Baltimore Building Material," *City Lab*, December 14, 2012, https://www.citylab.com/design/2012/12/farewell-formstone-requiem-baltimore-building-material/4162/ (accessed February 10, 2019).

8
This wording was first used by Le Corbusier, who in *Towards A New Architecture* aptly claimed that "[t]he exterior is always an interioe. ... in architectural ensembles, the elements of site itself come into play by virtue of their cubic volume, their density and the quality of the material of which they are composed, bringing sensations which are very definite and very varied. ... The elements of the site rise up like walls panoplied in the power of their cubic co-efficient, stratification, material, etc., like the walls of a room." Le Corbusier. *Towards A New Architecture* [1923], trans. Frederick Etchells (London: Dover, 1986), 191-192.

9
Stan Allen, "Introduction" in *Practice: Architecture, Technique, and Representation* (London: Routledge, 2000), XXIII.

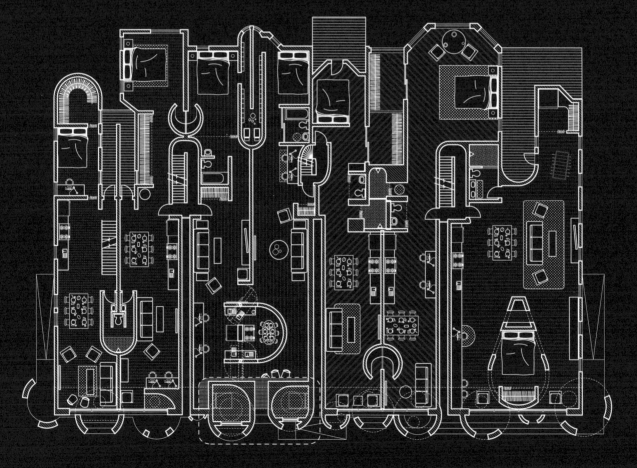

9.22
Proposal for row housing.
Endemic Architecture, 2019

Mixed-Up Stacks &
Cut Corners in Mixed-Use

STACK

1

A more or less orderly
pile or heap that
permits continued
expansion in the
vertical dimension by
adding more objects
on top of the previous
ones.

2

An architectural
condition in which
the internal uses and
external expressions of
a building accumulate
vertically and which
may or may not be
materially, formally,
and spatially coherent.

Mixed-use is a residential type that adjoins with commercial, cultural, institutional, or entertainment uses. The scale of mixed-use developments can vary from a single building to an entire neighborhood. Historically, mixed-use was the principal means of urban growth and development, often locating the many needs of town or city in immediate adjacencies. During the period of industrialization, and specifically after WWII, cities in the United States began implementing zoning policies for separate-use development that delineated specific zones for commercial, manufacturing, industrial, farming, and residential uses. The primary motive for the division of uses was to protect the health, welfare, and safety of the public, which most often resulted in horizontal segregation of use. However, cities expand vertically as well as horizontally, often stacking one use type over another, typically placing private residential use over some type of public use when housing is in the mix. The houses in the previous chapters of this book, except for the row house, are stand-alone, or detached, houses. From the cabin to the shotgun house, they are all physically detached from public uses such as restaurants, cafés, shops, cocktail bars, clothing stores, dispensaries, galleries, and so on. Residences in mixed-use buildings, on the other hand, combine residential use (houses, condos, or apartments) with public programs or amenities often located at the ground level. Mixed-use occupancy is today typically the result of zoning and building codes. Historically, zoning emerged through bureaucratic processes as a method for territorial codification and categorization that allocated acceptable uses in buildings to specifically defined areas within a city (or town), often with an explicit desire to separate housing and community uses from industry and commerce.

Mixing on Zoning

In no U.S. city is the zoning document more complex and layered than in New York City, where it consists of over 3,000 pages. New York City was the first city to implement a zoning code in 1916, but it was the 1961 zoning resolution that more overtly attempted to implement a Modernist belief in the rationally ordered city defined and divided by uses and adjacencies of buildings.[1] Yet, the eventual decline of industry and manufacturing left large buildings, often located along the waterfront, vacant. The imposed rational order of zoning began to conflict with shifting economies and the possibility for alternative uses. The new challenge became how best to facilitate *mixing* or *reuse*. Vacated warehouse or factory buildings, illegal for residential use under the 1961 (and 1916) codes, became some of the most desirable spaces in New York City—especially in Greenpoint and Williamsburg—for an emerging creative class of artists who illegally appropriated these vacant buildings as their residences and artist studios in the 1970s. As a result, the city authored the "Loft Law" in 1981, legalizing lofts in formerly otherwise zoned buildings. While the histories and nuances of New York City's zoning code are well documented and largely outside the scope of this book, what is important to note here is that the received histories of *mixed-use* center on the relationship between the house and the city. Since the 1960s, an era marked by urban renewal and increased gentrification, mixed-use development has occurred mostly through bureaucratic interventions that regulate architectural appropriations by marginalized populations or, alternately, as a predetermined condition of a municipality for new development that locates living, working, commerce, and play in direct tangencies or immediate proximities for economic or environmental benefit.

Brooklyn Short Stacks

The type of mixed-use of interest in this chapter is not the territorial, horizontal distribution of zones of uses, but rather an urban type that evolved out the imperatives of density and opportunistic urbanism that stacks one use atop another. Today, the term *mixed-use* is all too easily associated with large-scale, master-planned, developer-driven urban renewal. I use the term for the singular buildings of interest here for lack of a better term, but mixed-use—which has become almost synonymous with new zoning imperatives—feels like an awkward term for a context like Greenpoint or Williamsburg in Brooklyn where such conditions arose through people's inherent desire to live and work in close proximity during the mid-1800s, independent of zoning regulations.

> Greenpoint and Williamsburg developed more than 100 years ago during Brooklyn's great industrial age, when both sides of the East River were dominated by large factories, oil refineries, and shipyards. By the mid-19th century, the Eastern Districts waterfront had become heavily industrialized as ship builders, china and porcelain factories, glassmakers, oil refineries, sugar refineries, iron foundries, and other industrial establishments expanded. This transformation spurred the growth of a multi-ethnic residential community on nearby residential streets. The neighborhoods adjoin the waterfront that housed the workers, and within Greenpoint and Williamsburg, homes and factories intermingled, setting a pattern of mixed-use that sill shapes the neighborhoods today.[2]

At the scale of an individual building, uses can be said to be stacked more so than mixed. The term *stacked-use* draws attention to verticality, floors, and façades, while provoking curiosity about a building's overall form, public address, and urbanistic impressions beyond its intended use. *Use*, as a planning principle, is of course insufficient because it assumes that the totality of horizontal space in a city can be delineated by allocations of use, while the vertical distribution of use is unitized through spatial and social non-sequiturs within individual buildings. The vertical stacking of programs has been the subject of much 20th-century architectural speculation, including Rem Koolhaas's *Delirious New York* (1978). More recently, Preston Scott Cohen has written that "one of the most vexing questions for multistory buildings is the status of the ground floor because it belongs both to the horizontal seriality of the city and the vertical succession of the individual building."[3] From the exterior, a stacked building may appear as a coherent whole, or it might express its individuated levels depending on the façade composition, scale, sensitivity to the interior, and material expression.

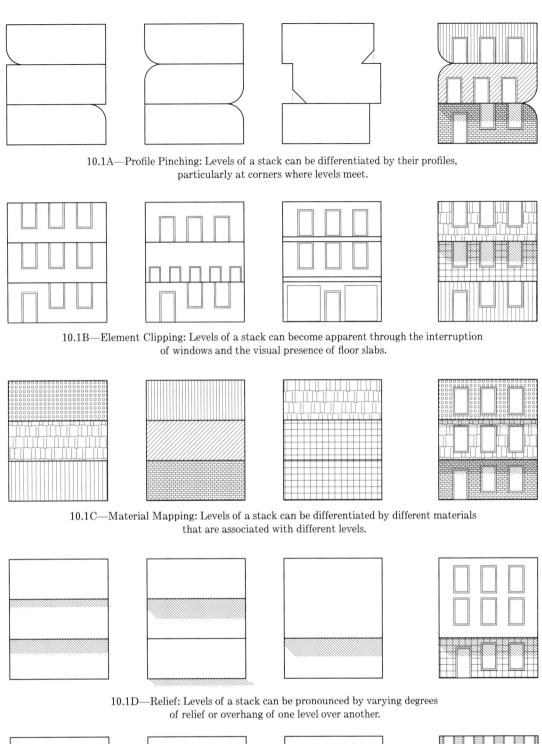

10.1A—Profile Pinching: Levels of a stack can be differentiated by their profiles, particularly at corners where levels meet.

10.1B—Element Clipping: Levels of a stack can become apparent through the interruption of windows and the visual presence of floor slabs.

10.1C—Material Mapping: Levels of a stack can be differentiated by different materials that are associated with different levels.

10.1D—Relief: Levels of a stack can be pronounced by varying degrees of relief or overhang of one level over another.

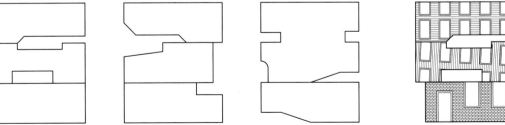

10.1E—Shaped Blocks: Levels of a stack can be differentiated by differently shaped profiles that permit different outdoor spaces at each level.

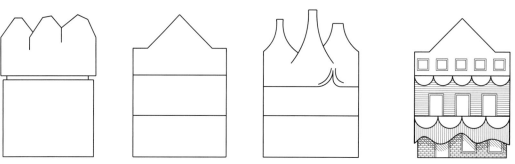

10.2A—Crown: A hierarchical top level of a stack that terminates
or makes difficult the addition of new levels.

10.2B—Gown: A systematized or patterned exterior that unifies
the levels while simultaneously acknowledging their vertical differentiation.

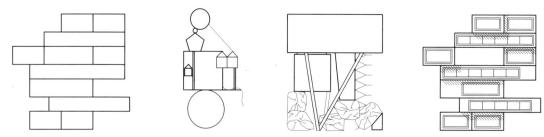

10.2C—Almost Piles: Loosely arranged, similar or dissimilar objects
that appear precarious in their vertical stability.

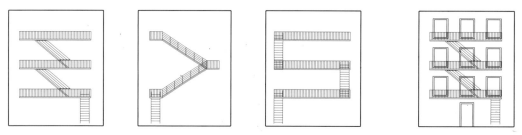

10.2D—Escape Routes: The functional use of egress that discloses internal levels.

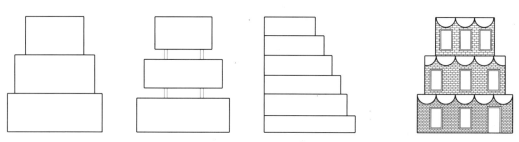

10.2E—Cakes: Stacked levels that have offsets, overhangs, or vertical relief on two or more sides.

Despite the architectural legacy of heroic imaginations for and about the high-rise tower, cities are also full of more modestly scaled two- to five-story "short stacks." The short stack tends to exhibit idiosyncrasies, inconsistencies, and ad hocism that registers the effects of time more expressly than totalizing tall stacks. In other words, short stacks are more reflective of urban qualities and the local cultures in which they reside. The short stack also tends to distinguish more clearly between its public use areas and the spaces of private residence by means of material expression, formal massing, and façade composition. As an example, the *Brooklyn Short Stacks* are a breed that can be categorized into three short stack situations as both an analytical reflection and a projection of alternative possibilities.

Situation 1: Discontinuous Diptychs
   & Triptychs
Brooklyn Short Stacks are often recognizable through the legible composition of two or three distinct layers, one atop another. Such discontinuous diptychs and triptychs are especially common in Greenpoint and Williamsburg, where there is typically little to no material and compositional uniformity among the stack layers. Whereas taller buildings often have building skins that lend a visual uniformity to the whole, the discontinuous diptych and triptych *Brooklyn Short Stack* is characterized by idiosyncratic elements, juxtaposed scales, and disjunctive material adjacencies. The stack explicitly expresses discontinuities among the individual layers, which are only unified by the fact that the massing of each layer in the stack aligns with the other layers at the front, sides, and back. This type of short stack often aggregates side by side, creating the overall effect along a street of variegation and shifting intensities of material, color, texture, and scale. Materiality, independently composed color palettes, asymmetries, elements, signage, lighting, scalar juxtapositions or elements, and myriad temporal uses—from restaurants to hardware stores, from produce markets to sex shops—with residential units stacked above reflect the multiple ownerships, rentals, and horizontally segmented expressions. These are precisely the urban qualities that today's pre-planned "mixed-use" development tends to mute through totalizing building skins and brand coherence or through material and formal self-similarity. Disjunction and discontinuity,

however, breed vibrancy by expressing diverse identities while easily accommodating changes through the addition, subtraction, or alteration of materials, forms, uses, and constituencies over time.

10.1 (previous) and 10.2 (left)
Diagrams for differentiating levels of stack. These are abstract diagrams; however, they are loosely based on common encounters with short-stack buildings so as to reveal generally familiar conditions of stack differentiation rather than case study examples or overly specific nuances. The far right drawings are combinations of two-to-three conditions within the set of diagrams.

For additional, recent considerations on stacks, see *Possible Mediums* (144-148) for descriptions and contemporary projects. I have tried here to avoid explicit overlapping conceptual content that is highlighted in the *Possible Mediums* stacks chapter as "Density" (loose or compact parts), "Color" (polychromatic or monochromatic), and "Material" (uniform or diverse), though it is impossible (and not entirely desirable) to avoid overlaps altogether. Perhaps the most obvious distinction is that the projects showcased in *Possible Mediums* are speculative explorations or examples of stand-alone buildings and proto-buildings, whereas the interest in stacks here has to do with evaluating and abstracting into a general set of circumstances the existing accumulation of short stack buildings that have been tangentially arrayed in the specific context of Brooklyn, New York.

Kelly Bair, Kristy Balliet, Adam Fure, and Kyle Miller, with Courtney Coffman, *Possible Mediums* (New York City: Actar, 2018).

10.3
AS BUILT_A discontinuous
triptych in Brooklyn,
New York.

Situation 2: Extrusion Confusion

A second manifestation of the *Brooklyn Short Stack* is a two- to three-story *extrusion* that sits atop a one- to two-story stack. Less common than discontinuous diptychs and triptychs, this type is also one of the most startling to encounter. In such stacks, the bottom and the top do not share formal logics or boundaries but appear instead as a collaged mass with an awkward merging between formal and spatial incongruities. While techniques of stacking and extruding can result in shared formal and spatial sensibilities, in the *Brooklyn Short Stack* they typically amplify legible differences. For example, the corner building at Union Avenue and N. 11th Street in Brooklyn currently consists of a bar and cocktail lounge on the ground level with massing that responds to the street grid of an oblique corner site. Above, however, a crenelated plan gives the appearance of extrusion into a two-story, vinyl-clad mass of residential units sitting awkwardly atop the layer below. The crenelated extrusion, evoking the form of bay windows, does not appear to respond to the site conditions and therefore appears unconcerned with the ground level's form, material, scale, and use. However, the legibility of vertical extrusion offers something that is not inherent in the stack alone: coherency. An extrusion has no beginning or end as a form; each segment is the same as the one before and the one after. Extrusion confusion in the *Brooklyn Short Stack* provides both the benefits of a stack's contextual sensitivities at the ground level and the economy, coherence, and abstract endlessness of an extrusion above.

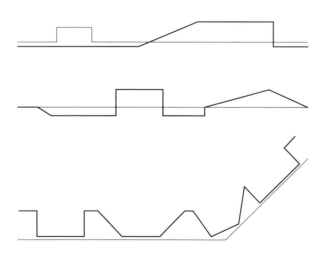

10.5 (below, left)
AS BUILT_Plan diagrams of extrusion confusion short stacks in Brooklyn, New York.

10.6 (below)
Hypothetical block shown as a plan diagram composed with only extrusion confusion short stacks.

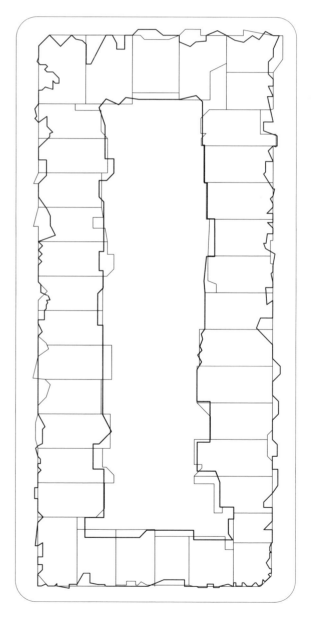

10.7
AS BUILT_Extrusion
confusion at Union Avenue
and N. 11th Street in
Brooklyn, New York.

Situation 3: Cutting Corners

In the nine-by-three block area between Manhattan Avenue., McGuinness Boulevard, the Brooklyn Queens Expressway, and Greenpoint Avenue in Brooklyn, each block has between ten and nineteen buildings along its long dimension and between seven and ten along its short dimension. Most of the 108 corner-lot buildings in this area are two- to four-story stacked-use buildings. This proportion remains relatively consistent throughout Williamsburg and Greenpoint. Taking as another example the area bounded by the Brooklyn Queens Expressway, the East River, 6th Street, and 9th Street, it becomes clear there is an element of corner doubt in Brooklyn. The orientation of a building located on the corner—whether its public address orients along the long dimension of the block or the short one—appears both discretionary and inconsistent.

The clearest manifestation of this indecision is seen in buildings whose corner is chamfered at the ground level, implying the desire for the building to appear as a member of both streets. Sociologists and urbanists will tell you that the chamfered or the filleted corner is better for safety and pedestrian movement. Architecturally, however, cutting corners provides the ground floor with an ambivalent orientation lingering between the perpendicularity of two streets that does not complete—but rather complicates—the legibility of the whole. In particular, the chamfered or filleted corner casts doubt on the value of window composition to make the "front" legible, as well as making the necessary incorporation of the door an awkward encounter with sidedness, perhaps akin to what you might feel if you could enter the front room of a house through its back door.

A wine bar at Wythe Avenue and 7th Street is one of many *Brooklyn Short Stacks* with a chamfered corner. Unified by its shingles pinned across its mass, the cut corner at street level draws into question the orientation and legibility of the whole. On the ground level, the building face along the short side of the block appears as the front, where the door to the apartments is located, covered by a small roof. It follows that the side of the building facing the long side of the block appears as the back on the ground level, showing just one window and a wall-mounted air conditioning unit. On the upper floors, however, this apparent orientation flips, as the window composition on the short side appears as the back and the long side appears as the front.

10.8
Plan diagrams of variations on the chamfered corner (top).

Hypothetical block shown as a plan diagram composed with only variations on the chamfered-corner short stacks (bottom).

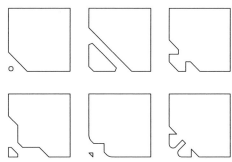

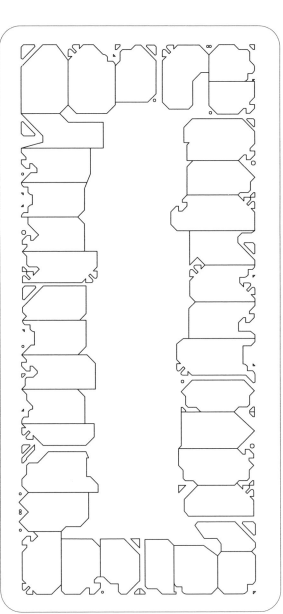

10.9 (left)

Nine-by-three block area between Manhattan Avenue, McGuinness Boulevard, the Brooklyn Queens Expressway, and Greenpoint Avenue in Brooklyn, New York, indicating buildings with a chamfered corner.

10.10 (right)

Nine-by-three block area bounded by the Brooklyn Queens Expressway, the East River, 6th Street, and 9th Street in Brooklyn, New York, indicating buildings with a chamfered corner.

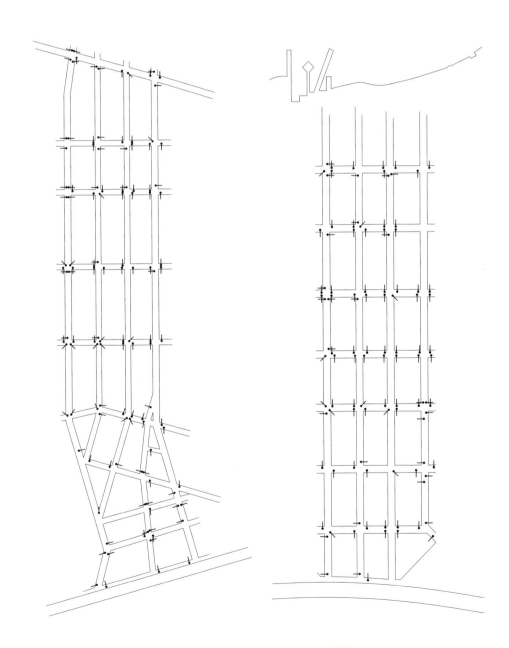

10.11
AS BUILT_A wine bar at Wythe Avenue and 7th Street in Brooklyn, New York, viewed from Wythe Avenue appears as the front at the ground floor, but as the side on the upper two floors.

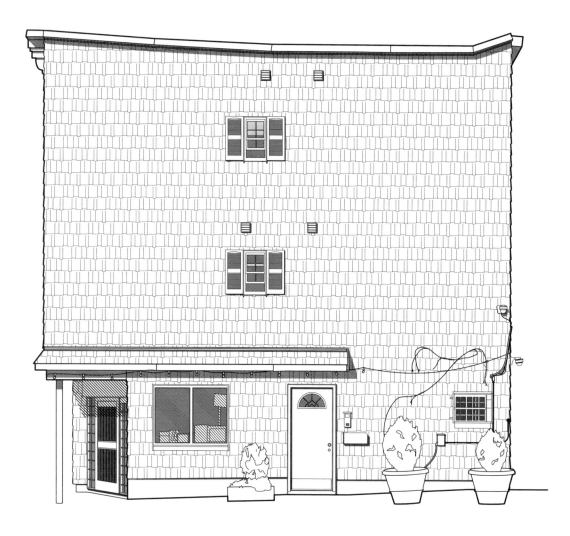

10.12
AS BUILT_The same wine bar at Wythe Avenue and
7th Street in Brooklyn, New York, viewed from 7th
Street appears as the front on the upper two floors,
but as the side on the ground floor.

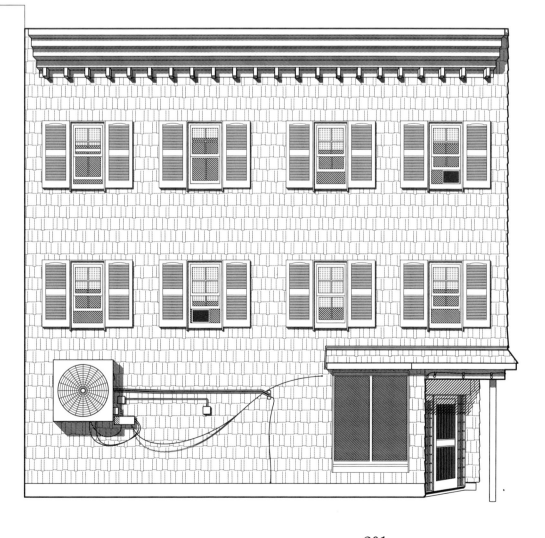

10.13
Hypothetical variations on short stack chamfered corners.
These variations on the chamfered corner suggest other
possibilities for the urban corner building that increase
opportunities for multiple entries, pedestrian movement,
and shared relationships to adjacent streets. They are
diagrammatic, and therefore use the same host form for all
variations while the screen shots of likely familiar software
programs are stand-ins for neighboring buildings. In some
cases the corner of the building remains intact, completing
the figure of the cube, as voids cut diagonally through the
mass to expose multiple entrances and public circulation. In
other cases the corner is cut away, diminishing the completed
figure of the cube, pushing entries away from the corner. In
yet other cases, a middle ground between these two is at play.

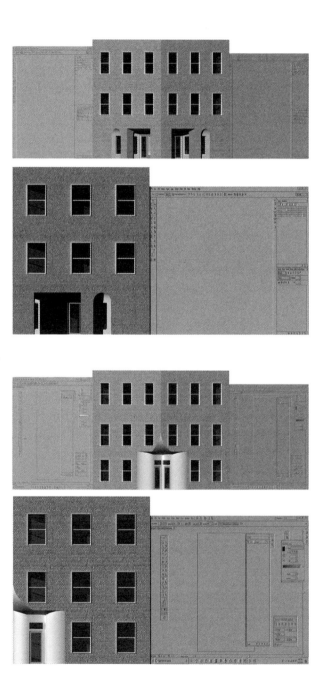

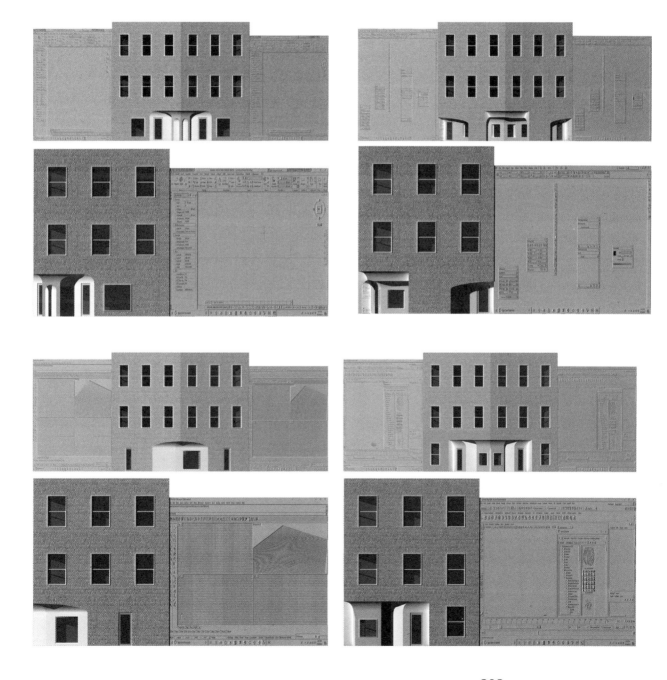

203

In a cut-corner short stack, public entry typically occurs through the chamfered plane, rather than through a principal façade. The chamfer disrupts the cubic form at its most vital point, where the corner meets the ground. Cutting corners in the short stack introduces doubt about the front and the side, yet introduces opportunities for omni-orientations in which the internal order of the stack manifests in varied ways at the ground floor and upper floors.

Stack Irony Through Uniformity

Historically, one of the hallmarks of mixed-use was the accumulation of diverse materials, colors, compositions, elements, expressions, and temporalities that accrued freely as an assemblage in varying degrees of correspondence with the variety of uses. This assemblage was not pre-composed as a unified whole with the possibility for different uses inside, but rather accrued through the multiplicity of desires and preferences among the constituents of the parts which manifest legibility as a stack. Accumulation and discontinuity were the primary characteristics of mixed-use assemblages fostering vibrancy, diversity, inclusion, density, idiosyncrasy, and contrast. Strangely, the implicit promise that mixed-use would inherently encourage mixed architectural and cultural compositions or expressions has today become mostly a developer's language for totalizing uniformity in the architecture of mixed-use. From Brooklyn, New York, to Aurora, Colorado, to Santa Clara, California, mixed-use development, when built anew, has increasingly become materially, compositionally, and formally about sameness rather than difference. Mixing has homogenized. Variegation, differentiation, and contrast among uses and constituent parts are usurped by the continuity of a whole that tends to smooth the temporalities of accumulation and assemblage into the presumed stability of continuity and synthesis. Alternatively, seeking new expressions for discontinuous diptychs and triptychs, extrusion confusion, and corner doubt in the short stack offers leverage for reimagining the mixed-use whole.

1
Julian Ferraldo, "Zoning for Exchange: Creative-Industrial Incubators in North Brooklyn and the Formalization of Innovation" (Master's Thesis, Columbia University, 2012).

2
The City of New York Department of City Planning (in association with the New York City Department of Parks and Recreation), "Chapter 7: Historic Resources" in *Greenpoint-Williamsburg Rezoning EIS* (2005), 9.

3
Preston Scott Cohen, "Successive Architecture" in *Log* 32 New York City: Anyone Corporation (Fall 2014), 156.

10.14
Proposal for a mixed-use
building in Brooklyn,
New York. Endemic
Architecture, 2018–2019

10.15
Proposal for a mixed-use
building in Brooklyn,
New York. Endemic
Architecture, 2018–2019

Recent trends in architectural production point toward an internally motivated compulsion for perverting known forms, exaggerating the qualities of the banal, reconceiving expressions through post-digital representation, critical mess-making, or subverting conventions in order to encourage new outcomes that break with the architectural canon. All these trends sponsor alternative forms of experience intended to construct new social and political arrangements.

It is simultaneously true that recent trends in architectural production point toward a deferral to external influences such as municipal codes, typological legacy, environmental imperatives, or social justice. Social, environmental, and political circumstances thus inform working methods and concepts within the discipline. While these two schools, ripened by a plurality of their own sub-genres, may at first appear to be at odds with each other, this book is an attempt to bridge between them—bridging between architecture's internal and external motivations by probing sites of unresolved (and unresolvable) legibility in common house types. This productive open-endedness is the basis for a model of practice I refer to as *disciplinary whimsy*.

Disciplinary whimsy is a means of reorienting the familiar by accepting the non-autonomy of architectural forms, compositions, and elements and perverting them through the lenses of political and cultural protocols, historical contexts, and formal, spatial, and material manipulations.

Whimsy, however, does not mean free play, nor carelessness, and it carries the prerequisite of disciplinary knowledge. When used most productively, whimsy may be only vaguely perceptible, but its effects put pressure on entrenched conventions, codes, assumptions, and socio-political cues through careful reflections on—and manipulations to—otherwise familiar forms and cultural norms. In so doing, whimsy dovetails internal disciplinary interests with external circumstances. Disciplinary whimsy has the capacity to stir deeply rooted histories, resurrect past discussions, and reveal scholarship internal to the field and it can shift the arc of cultural, social, and political attention by carefully trading the familiar for the *almost familiar*. The *almost familiar* does not necessarily break with conventions or rules. The binary of following versus breaking the rules is tired and unproductive. The power of disciplinary whimsy lies in the command of nuance and subtlety. This type of whimsy is not the result of accidents or glitches within the architectural process. Instead, deviations and transgressions arise from disciplined intentionality with careful execution in order to substantiate the breach of typological contract. As a condition of unresolved legibility, disciplinary whimsy activates cultural histories, inherited forms, and current pre-authored external constraints and returns new sources for future (re)imaginations, techniques, and methods. As Alan Colquhoun has stated, "this 'present' includes much of what was previously thought to belong to a superseded past, and it may be that the power of architecture to communicate at all relies on its ability to understand and transform its own language."[1]

Darlings

Whereas disciplinary whimsy casts a broad umbrella as an approach to architecture, the familiarity of elements and vernacular forms occurs at locally defined scales that continues to hold and acquire new architectural value in changing cultural, social, and political, spheres. Critics from Nikolaus Pevsner to Peter Eisenman, however, have staunchly differentiated between *buildings* and *architecture*. For Pevsner the bicycle shed is not architecture, just as for Eisenman architectural elements alone are not sufficient to distinguish architecture from building.[2] Yet, many architectural elements and small-form types that exist as parts within a whole are beloved by both architects and broader cultures alike. I call these *darlings*, due to their dual status of cultural and architectural endearment. Darlings are culturally dear, as evidenced by their widespread association with the comforts of residential architecture and their inscription into municipal codes. They are also architecturally dear, as evidenced by successive generations of architects revisiting them as sources for disciplinary imagination, theorization, and architectural expression. Some of the most notable darlings are columns, walls, gable roofs, dormers, vaults, arches, domes, corner turrets, doors, windows, porches, stoops, and chimneys. Darlings are ideal sites for manipulating architectural expressions, and they serve as ongoing sources of unresolved legibility in architecture. Through manipulation, darlings sponsor myriad expressions ranging from amusement to oddity, eccentricity, banality, humor, exaggeration, critique and so on. The history of distortion among the darlings within the discipline transcends generations and styles, offering insights into methods of constructing internal forms of knowledge by manipulating external constraints. The tenets of disciplinary whimsy—manipulation of references, the disturbance of famil-iar forms, the overturning of received histories, perverting external constraints through architectural form—can perhaps be seen most clearly in the darlings.

Darlings are distinct from programmatically obligated typologies such as schools, hospitals, theaters, transportation centers, and so on.[3] In fact, darlings are rarely whole buildings, but rather are most often encountered as distinguishable parts within a larger whole. Their status as parts enables darlings to be character-defining features of a larger whole while also sustaining their own lineage of architectural study. As sources for cul-tural and political comforts tied to architectural legibility, and for their disciplinary re-imaginations tied to formal and intellectual manipulation, darlings are productive fodder for exploiting relationships between culture and architecture.

Darlings are ideal sources of unresolved legibility in architecture. In this book, darlings, as I have defined them, serve as primary sources for analytical retrospec-tion and open projections that sit within more broadly defined residential types and extra-disciplinary circumstances. Roofs, walls, floors, stairs, porches, stoops, doors, win-dow, fireplaces, chimneys, and the corner turret are biopsied while recognizing their own cultural, political, contextual, and social histories that reveal terms for formal, spatial, and material manipulations in architecture. Thus, darlings enable analysis, alternative conceptualizations, and terms for revivified expressions in everyday architecture.

1
Alan Colquhoun, "Typology and Design Method" in *Essays in Architectural Criticism: Modern Architecture and Historical Change* (Cambridge: MIT Press, 1981), 43.

2
When considering the difference between architecture and building, Pevsner claims that "a bicycle shed is a building; Lincoln Cathedral is a piece of architecture." For Pevsner, architecture is differentiated from mere building if it is designed to have a specific aesthetic appeal. Nikolaus Pevsner, *An Outline of European Architecture* (Harmondsworth: Penguin, [1942] 1957), 23.

Similarly, in Peter Eisenman's book *Inside Out*--and in particular in the chapter "In My Father's House Are Many Mansions"--elements in architecture are drawn into corollary with words and poetry. Eisenman claims that, although all poetry has words, words alone do not guarantee poetry, just as all buildings have elements but their presence alone does not constitute architecture, as distinct from building. Peter Eisenman, "In My Father's House Are Many Mansions" in *Inside Out* (New Haven: Yale University Press, 2004), 8.

3
This is based on a wide variety of resources outlining program and typology that collectively shape, catalog, theorize, and codify the field's understanding of typology, including Nikolaus Pevsner's book *A History of Building Types* (1902) and Rafael Moneo's text "On Typology" in *Oppositions* 13 (1978), as well as building occupancy, zoning, and fire codes.

Acknowledgments

This book would not have been possible without the clarity, criticism, and concision brought to it by Ryan Roark. This book is undeniably better because of her dedication to it through her editing and insights. Likewise, Sean Yendrys's graphic design perfectly parallels the attitude of the book and helps bring tension to the drawings and emphasis to the content. The support of the California College of the Arts Architecture Division staff and faculty and Dean Keith Krumwiede are deeply appreciated and helped make this book possible. Gordon Goff and Jake Anderson of AR+D Publishing provided continued support and careful attention to this book over the course of its conception and production, without which this book would not have become a reality.

Architecture is better with friends, mentors, heroes, and heroines—and sometimes an architectural nemesis too. There are too many to list here properly, but I am grateful for the personal friendships, spirited discussions, compelling projects, thoughtful pedagogies, and shared experiences that permeate our field from generation to generation.

Most of the work and ideas in this book did not directly involve the dedicated individuals who have worked with me in my office; however, without their contributions over the past few years this book would not have been possible. Thank you Nate Wesseldyk, Sofia Anastasi, Brian McKinney, Mitchell Price, Maya Annotti, Rajah Bose, Trenton Jewett, Sarah Herlugson, Taylor Metcalf, Gina Bugiada, Nate Oppenheim, Tyler Smith, Alexandra Bernetich, Ryan Doidge, Samantha Okolita, Danielle Tellez, Adam Steinbach, Paul Mitchell, and Katie Donahue.

Most of all, thank you Mom, Dad, Nikki, Olive, Brian, Allison, and Reagan for your unconditional support that extends well beyond books and buildings.

Clark Thenhaus is founding director of Endemic Architecture. Thenhaus is an assistant professor of architecture at the California College of the Arts.

Bibliography

BOOKS

Alberti, Leon Battista. *The Ten Books of Architecture*. Translated by Leoni. Edited by Rykwert. (Book I, chapter xii. London, reprinted 1955).

Allen, Stan. *Points + Lines: Diagrams and Projects for the City*. New York: Princeton Architectural Press, 1999.

Allen, Stan. *Practice –Architecture, Technique, and Representation*. London: Routledge, 2000.

Allen, Stan and McQuade, Marc. *Landform Buildings*. Baden, Switzerland: Lars Müller Publishers ; [Princeton, N.J.] : Princeton University School of Architecture, 2011.

Bair, Kelly; Balliet, Kristy; Fure, Adam; Miller, Kyle. *Possible Mediums*. New York City: Actar, 2018.

Boullée, Etienne-Louis. *Architecture: Essai sur l'art* (1789-99) ed. Jean-Marie Perouse de Montclos, Paris, 1968.

Cohen, Katherine Powell. *Images of America: San Francisco's Haight-Ashbury*. San Francisco: Arcadia Publishing, 2008.

Colquhoun, Alan. *Essays in Architectural Criticism: Modern Architecture and Historical Change*. Chicago: Graham Foundation for Advanced Studies in the Fine Arts; New York: The Institute for Architecture and Urban Studies; Cambridge: MIT Press, 1981.

Debord, Guy. *Society of the Spectacle*, translated by Ken Knabb. Canberra: Hobglobin Press, 2002.

Downing, A.J. *The Architecture of Country Houses*. New York: D. Appleton & Co., 1850.

Duchscherer, Paul and Svendsen, Linda. *Beyond the Bungalow: Grand Homes in the Arts & Crafts Tradition*. Salt Lake City: Gibbs Smith, 2005.

Eisenman, Peter. *Inside Out*. New Haven: Yale University Press, 2004.

Evans, Robin. *Translations From Drawings to Buildings and Other Essays*. "Figures, Doors, and Passages." London: Architectural Association Press. 1997. Pg.54-91. Originally published in Robin Evans, "Figures, Doors, and Passages." Architectural Design No. 48, Academy Editions (London), 1978. Pg. 267-78.

Foucault, Michel. *The Order of Things: An Archeology of the Human Sciences*. New York: Vintage Books, 1994. Originally published in the United States by Pantheon Books, a division of Random House Inc., in 1971.

Garrett, Wendell. *Classic America: The Federal Style & Beyond*. New York: Rizzoli, 1992.

Greenberg, Clement. *Art and Culture: Critical Essays*. Boston: Beacon Press, 1961.

Hefner, Gretchen. *The Missile Next Door*. Cambridge: Harvard University Press, 2012.

Hejduk, John. *7 Houses*. New York: The Institute for Architecture and Urban Studies, 1980.

Hess, Alan. *The Ranch House*. New York: Harry Abrams Inc, 2004.

Holl, Steven. *Pamphlet Architecture 9: Rural & Urban House Types in North America*. New York City: Princeton Architectural Press, 1982.

Kerr, Robert. *The Gentleman's House: Or, How to Plan English Residences, from the Parsonage to the Palace*. England: Oxford University Press, 1865.

Larkin, David. *The Farmhouse Book: Tradition, Style, Experience*. New York: Universe Publishing, 2005.

Larsen, Michael and Pomada, Elizabeth. *Painted Ladies: San Francisco's Resplendent Victorians*. New York: E.P. Dutton, 1978.

Marx, Leo. *The Machine in the Garden: Technology and the Pastoral Ideal in America*. New York City: Oxford University Press, 1964.

McAlester, Virginia Savage. *A Field Guide to American Houses*. New York: Alfred Knopf, 1984, 2013.

Miller, Donald. *Lewis Mumford: A Life*. New York: Grove Press, 1989.

Quatremère de Quincy, Antoine-Chrysostome. "Caractére" in *Encyclopedia Méthodique: Architecture*, Vol. 2, 1801.

Rowe, Colin. *The Mathematics of the Ideal Villa and Other Essays*. Cambridge: MIT Press, 1976.

Rybczynski, Witold. *A Short History of an Idea: Home*. New York: Viking Press, 1986.

Toy, Sidney. *Castles: Their Construction and History*. New York: Dover Publications, 1984.

Venturi, Robert. *Complexity and Contradiction in Architecture*. New York: Museum of Modern Art in association with the Graham Foundation for Advanced Studies in the Fine Arts, Chicago, 1966.

Vidler, Anthoy. *The Architectural Uncanny: Essay's in the Modern Unhomely*. Boston: MIT Press, 1992.

Vidler, Anthony. *Claude-Nicolas Ledoux: Architecture and Social Reform at the End of the Ancien Régime*. Cambridge: MIT Press, 1990.

ESSAY'S

Cohen, Preston Scott. "Successive Architecture," *Log 32*, New York City: Anyone Corporation (Fall 2014) 153-163.

Di Palma, Vittoria. "Architecture, Environment and Emotion: Quatremère de Quincy and the Concept of Character," *AA Files*, London: Architectural Association, No.47 (Summer 2002): 45-56.

Edna Scofield. "The Evolution and Development of Tennessee Houses," *Journal of the Tennessee Academy of Science no. 11* (1936): 229-240.

Frampton, Kenneth. "Towards a Critical Regionalism: Six Points for an Architecture of Resistance" in *Postmodern Culture*, Ed. Hal Foster. (London: Pluto Press, 1983).

Galton, Francis. "Composite Portraits Made by Combining Those of Many Different Persons into a Single Figure,"*Nature* (1878): 97-100.

Galton, Francis. "Generic Images." *Proceedings of the Royal Institution* no. 9 (1879): 157-169.

Koolhaas, Rem. "Cronocaos," *Log 21*, New York City: Anyone Corporation (Winter, 2011) 119-121.

Lynn, Greg. "New Variations on the Rowe Complex," First published in *Any Magazine*, New York: ANY no. 7/8 (1994): 38-43.

Moneo, Rafael. "On Typology," *Oppositions 13*, Boston: MIT Press (Summer 1978): 23-44.

Rowe, Colin. "James Stirling: A Highly Personal and Very Disjointed Memoir," in *James Stirling: Buildings and Projects* compiled and edited by Peter Arnell and Ted Bickford. New York: Rizzoli Publications (1984): 22-23.

Simmel, Georg. "The Aesthetics of the Human Face," translated by Lore Ferguson in Georg Simmel, (1858-1918), edited by Kurt H. Wolff. Columbus: Ohio State University Press, (1995): 276-281.

Tabor, Philip. "Fearful Symmetry: A Reassessment of Symmetry in Architectural Compositions," in *Architectural Review*, 1023, (May 1982) 18-24.

GOVERNMENT DOCUMENT

City of New York. *Greenpoint-Williamsburg Re-zoning EIS, Chapter 7: Historic Resources*. New York City: The City of New York Department of City Planning in association with The New York City Department of Parks and Recreation, 2005. Last modified March 4, 2005. Accessed March 12, 2019.

MAGAZINES

May, Cliff with editorial staff of Sunset Magazine. "Western Ranch Houses," *Sunset Magazine*, Los Angeles: Lane Publishing, 1946. (Reprinted by Hennessey+Ingalls, 1999).

ONLINE BOOKS

Fellows, Will. *A Passion to Preserve: Gay Men as Keepers of Culture*. Madison: University of Wisconsin Press, 2004. Google Books. Web. 28 September, 2018. https://books.google.com/books?id=0wf_zMk3D8AC&pg=PA132&dq=colorist+movement+gay&hl=en&sa=X&ved=0ahUKEwjRg5_J99bdAhXNMt4KHaRHD_QQ6AEIJzAA#v=onepage&q=colorist%20movement%20gay&f=false

Lavin, Sylvia. *Quatremere de Quincy and the Invention of a Modern Language of Archteicture* Cambridge: MIT Press, 1992. Google Books. Web. 16 June, 2018. https://books.google.combooks?id=oQTYfRtWbioC&pg=PA138&lpg=PA138&dq=de+quincy+essential+character&source=bl&ots=4syU9eWw_u&sig=msXjBtvUdrj6ACZqo_zX8fPbnKs&hl=en&sa=X&ved=2ahUKEwjeifvZppDeAhUCHzQIHd_mBpMQ6AEwA3oECAkQAQ#v=onepage&q=de%20quincy%20essential%20character&f=false

Lewis Manufactoring Company. *Houses of Character*. Bay City Michigan, 1920. Google Books. Web. 12 November 2018. https://books.google.com/books?id=aZ8aAAAAYAAJ&pg=PA9#v=onepage&q&f=false

Mallgrave, Harry Francis. *Modern Architectural Theory: A Historical Survey, 1673–1968*. Cambridge: Cambridge University Press, 2005. Google Books. Web. 03 October, 2018. https://books.google.com/books?id=iK7ld8-oYswC&printsec=frontcover&dq=harry+francis+mallgrave&hl=en&sa=X&ved=0ahUKEwiS0LDSnZjeAhUjTt8KHe6PC0EQ6AEIPDAD#v=onepage&q=harry%20francis%20mallgrave&f=false

Schlereth, Thomas. *Material Culture Studies in America*. "America, 1876-1976, The Structuralist View." Landham, MD. AltaMira Press, 1999. Google Books. Web. 21, September 2018. https://books.google.com/books?id=CjfQVHKzZHkC&pg=PA56&lpg=PA56&dq=edna+scofield++tennessee&source=bl&ots=2jxgUwstq4&sig=ACfU3U2ONURcVqUZGqGOPVeE4_dX3ReSAg&hl=en&sa=X&ved=2ahUKEwi4t9iW_frgAhXL64MKHYFWAL0Q6AEwAXoECAgQAQ#v=onepage&q=edna%20scofield%20%20tennessee&f=false

Wittkower, Rudolf. *Architectural Principals in the Age of Humanism*. London & New York: W.W. Norton & Company. 1971. Google Books. Web. 2 February 2019. https://books.google.com/books?id=c7JP6iqyu9kC&printsec=frontcover&source=gbs_ge_summary_r&cad=0#v=onepage&q&f=false

ONLINE ENCYCLOPEDIA

Chapter 1:
Cabin

Encyclopedia Editors, "Log Cabin," *Dictionary of American History*. Accessed October 2, 2018. https://www.encyclopedia.com/literature-and-arts/art-and-architecture/architecture/log-cabin

Chapter 2:
Mountain House

Wikipedia contributors, "Wyntoon," *Wikipedia, The Free Encyclopedia*. Accessed September 4, 2018. https://en.wikipedia.org/w/index.php?title=Wyntoon&oldid=872740159

Chapter 8:
Shotgun House

Editors of The Encyclopedia Britannica. "Shotgun House," *Encyclopedia Britannica*. Last modified March 17, 2017. Accessed March 1, 2019. https://www.britannica.com/technology/shotgun-house

Editors of Wikiarquitectura. "Villa Le Lac," *Wikiarquitectura*, Accessed March 19, 2019. https://en.wikiarquitectura.com/building/villa-le-lac/

PHOTOGRAPHY / IMAGES

Chapter 1:
Cabin

1.1, AS BUILT drawing based on: Historic American Buildings Survey, Creator, and Abraham Lincoln, Jones, Lester, photographer. *Abraham Lincoln Birthplace, Hodgenville, Larue County, KY*. Hodgenville Kentucky Larue County, 1933. Documentation Compiled After. Photograph. Library of Congress, https://www.loc.gov/item/ky0095/.

1.14, 1.15, Photos courtesy of Dylan Krueger.

1.17, *Federal-Abolition-Whig trap, to catch voters in*. New Orleans, Lousiana, 1840. [New Orleans: s.n] Photograph. Accessed September 27, 2018. Library of Congress, https://www.loc.gov/item/2008661363/.

1.18, "Harrison & Tyler" *campaign emblem*. United States, 1840. Photograph. Accessed September 27, 2018. Library of Congress, https://www.loc.gov/item/2008661359/.

Chapter 2:
Mountain House

2.4, Heart's Wyntoon Estate. Photo courtesy of California State University, Chico, Meriam Library Special Collections.

2.5, Sculptured House. Photo by Charles Deaton, courtesy of The Charles Deaton Archive.

2.6, Bradford Residence. Photo courtesy of Bart Prince, Architect.

2.7, Whiting Residence. Photo courtesy of Bart Prince, Architect.

2.8, Prairie House. Photo courtesy of Herb Greene, Architect. Photograph by Robert Alan Bowlby.

Chapter 3

3.5, 3.6, Aerial Images. Map data: GoogleEarth, Landsat / Copernicus.

Chapter 4

4.1, The Cockettes. Photo courtesy of Bud Lee Picture Maker, 1971.

Chapter 8

8.2, 8.3, Shotgun Houses Photo courtesy of Brian Vanden Brink. http://www.brianvandenbrink.com/index.html

Chapter 9

9.2, Row houses in Philadelphia, Pennsylvania. Photo courtesy of Randy Calderone for AS BUILT. http://www.randycalderonephotography.com/

9.3, Row houses in Brooklyn, New York. Photo courtesy of Rob Stephenson for AS BUILT. http://www.robstephenson.com/

9.5, Façade Compilation. Photos courtesy of Rob Stephenson. http://www.robstephenson.com/

THESES

Ferraldo, Julian. "Zoning For Exchange: Creative-Industrial Incubation in North Brooklyn and the Formalization of Innovation." (Columbia University, Graduate School of Architecture, Planning, and Preservation. New York City. Requirement for Master's Degree of Science in Urban Planning, 2012).

Lilian McRae, "The American Shotgun House: A Study of its Evolution and the Enduring Presence of the Vernacular in American Architecture," (University of Arkansas, Fayetteville. Architecture Undergraduate Honors Thesis, 2012).

WEBPAGE

Chapter 1:
Cabin

Chestnut, Lauren. "William Henry Harrison: He Didn't Die of Hypothermia." *Blonder and Thinner*. Last modified May 26, 2010. Accessed October 5, 2018. https://blonderandthinner.blogspot.com/search?q=William+Henry+Harrison

Flanders, Judith. "Log Cabin History: The Secrets of Making a Home." *The History Reader: Dispatches in History From St. Martins Press*. Last modified September 9, 2015. Accessed October 12, 2018. http://www.thehistoryreader.com/modern-history/the-making-of-home-secrets-of-log-cabin-history/
HGTV. "Shows A-Z." HGTV. *Shows A-Z*. Accessed October 20, 2018. https://www.hgtv.com/shows/shows-a-z

Hill, Michael and Kohane, Peter. "The Signature of Architecture: Compositional Ideas in the Theory of Profiles." *Architectural Histories: The Open Access Journal of the EAHN, 3(1), Part 18*. European Architectural History Network (2015). Accessed October 11, 2018. https://journal.eahn.org/articles/10.5334/ah.cu/#

History.com Editors. "William Henry Harrison." *History*. Last modified August 21, 2018. Accessed April 12, 2019. https://www.history.com/topics/us-presidents/william-henry-harrison

Klien, Christopher. "The Birth of Lincoln Logs." *History*. Last modified in 2019. Accessed August 23, 2018. https://www.history.com/news/the-birth-of-lincoln-logs

"Determining the Facts: The Log Cabin Tradition." *National Park Service*. Accessed October 2, 2018. https://www.nps.gov/nr/twhp/wwwlps/lessons/4logcabins/4facts1.htm

"Visual Evidence: The Detail of Corner Notching." *National Park Service*. Accessed October 2, 2018. https://www.nps.gov/nr/twhp/wwwlps/lessons/4logcabins/4visual1.htm

Schwartz Foster, Feather. "William Henry Harrison: The Big Lie." *Presidential History Blog*. Last modified April 10, 2017. Accessed October 8, 2018 https://featherfoster.wordpress.com/2017/04/10/william-henry-harrison-the-big-lie/

"William Henry Harrison." *The White House. William Henry Harrison*. Last modified in 2006. Accessed August 20, 2018. https://www.whitehouse.gov/about-the-white-house/presidents/william-henry-harrison/

Chapter 2:
Mountain House

Atkinson, Jack. "The Deaton Sculpture House." *Arts & Food*. Last modified September 1, 2017. Accessed March 15, 2019. https://artsandfood.com/2018/09/the-deaton-sculptured-house-aka-the-sleeper-house-in-colorado.html/

"Hearst's Wyntoon Estate." *Calisphere: University of California*. Owning institution: University of California, Chico campus. Accessed March 3, 2019. https://calisphere.org/item/778013799b8037a721cf3d63cf3e73de/

Giovannini, Joseph. "Bart Prince Creates a Light-Filled Residence in New Mexico," *Architectural Digest*. Last modified August 1, 2017. Accessed February 24, 2018. https://www.architecturaldigest.com/story/prince-article-102008

"Why the International Orange Color?" *Golden Gate Bridge Highway & Transportation District*. Accessed September 20, 2018. http://goldengatebridge.org/research/factsGGBIntOrngColor.php

"Wyntoon." *Great Buildings Online*. Last modified 2013. Accessed September 13, 2018. http://www.greatbuildings.com/buildings/Wyntoon.html

"Contrasting Concepts of Harmony in Architecture: The 1982 Debated between Christopher Alexander and Peter Eisenman." *Kataraxis 3*. Accessed December 4, 2018.http://www.katarxis3.com/Alexander_Eisenman_Debate.htm

Prince, Bart. "Projects." *Bart Prince, Architect*. Accessed February 16, 2019. http://www.bartprince.com/default.html

U.C. Berkeley CED Archive Editors. "6. Projects for the Hearst Family: Wyntoon." *U.C. Berkeley Environmental Design Archives*. Accessed September 28, 2018. http://exhibits.ced.berkeley.edu/exhibits/show/juliamorgan/wyntoon

Chapter 3:
Farmhouse

Jones, Jennifer. "The American Farmhouse and its History." *House Plans and More*. Accessed August 14, 2018. http://houseplansandmore.com/resource_center/farmhouse-history.aspx

Leigh Mattern, Jessica. "The Very Practical Reasons Farmhouses are Usually White." *Country Living*. Last modified July 27, 2016. Accessed August 12, 2018. https://www.countryliving.com/life/a39301/whitewashing-history-farmhouse/

Chapter 4: Queen Anne
"Cockettes: Historical Essay." *FoundSF*. Accessed September 9, 2018. http://www.foundsf.org/index.php?title=Cockettes

Lennon, Grace. "Victorian Architecture Past and Present." *Dunn Edwards Paints*. Last modified October 2, 2014. Accessed September 5, 2018. https://www.dunnedwards.com/colors/specs/posts/victorian-architecture-past-and-present

San Francisco Planning and Preservation Department. *Preservation*. San Francisco: City and County of San Francisco, 2019. Accessed January 15, 2019. https://sfplanning.org/preservation

San Francisco Planning and Preservation Department. *Historic Preservation Commission*. San Francisco: City and County of San Francisco, 2019. Accessed January 15, 2019. https://sfplanning.org/commission/historic-preservation-commission

SF Heritage. "A History of Heritage." *SF Heritage*. Accessed August 28, 2018. https://www.sfheritage.org/about/

Chapter 5:
American Foursquare

"Foursquare Style 1895-1930." *Antique Home Style*. Last modified 2015. Accessed November 5, 2018. http://www.antiquehomestyle.com/styles/foursquare.htm

Poore, Patricia. "American Foursquare Architecture and Interiors." *Old House Online*. Last modified September 7, 2010. Accessed November 4, 2018. https://www.oldhouseonline.com/articles/american-foursquare

Jackson, Angela. "The Main Elements of the American Foursquare." *Arrow Hill Cottage*. Last modified April 28, 2018. Accessed November 4, 2018. https://www.arrowhillcottage.com/the-main-elements-of-the-american-foursquare-home-style/

Massey, James and Maxwell, Shirley. "The Story on Sears Houses." *Old House Online*. Last modified January 29, 2013. Accessed November 10, 2018. https://www.oldhouseonline.com/house-tours/story-sears-houses

"Sears Archives Homepage." *Sears Archives*. Accessed November 10, 2019. http://www.searsarchives.com/

"Sears Homes 1908-1914." *Sears Archives*. Accessed November 10, 2019. http://www.searsarchives.com/homes/1908-1914.htm

"Sometimes, It Takes a Village of Historians to Document a Hillrose." *Sears Homes*. Last modified February 5, 2016. Accessed November 4, 2018. http://www.searshomes.org/index.php/tag/sears-hillrose/

"The Wardway Warrington in West Virginia." *Sears Homes*. Last modified May 27, 2013. Accessed November 4, 2018. http://www.searshomes.org/index.php/tag/foursquare-kit/

"The Fullerton: Meets the Needs of So Many People." *Sears Homes*. Last modified May 9, 2012. Accessed November 4, 2018. http://www.searshomes.org/index.php/2012/05/09/the-sears-fullerton-meets-the-needs-of-so-many-people/

Thorton, Rosemary. "American Foursquare 1890-1930." *Old House Web*. Accessed November 10, 2018. http://www.oldhouseweb.com/architecture-and-design/american-foursquare-1890-1930.shtml

Chapter 6:
Ranch

Craven, Jackie. "Ranch Style House Plans from the 1950s." *Thought Co.* Last modified January 15, 2019. Accessed February 3, 2019. https://www.thoughtco.com/ranch-house-plans-for-america-177540

Gross, Terry. "A Forgotten History of the U.S. Government Segregated America." *NPR*. Last modified May 3, 2017. Accessed September 18, 2018. https://www.npr.org/templates/transcript/transcript.php?storyId=526655831

Hill, Michael and Kohane, Peter. "The Signature of Architecture: Compositional Ideas in the Theory of Profiles." *Architectural Histories: The Open Access Journal of the EAHN, 3(1), Part 18.* European Architectural History Network (2015). Accessed October 11, 2018. https://journal.eahn.org/articles/10.5334/ah.cu/

"Ranch Style." *Cliff May Library*. Last modified 2017. Accessed September 27, 2018. http://ranchostyle.com/clifflibrary.html

"Sir Francis Galton F.R.S." *Francis Galton and Composite Portraiture*. Accessed January 10, 2019. http://galton.org/composite.htm

Chapter 7:
Federal-Style

De Vries, Hendrik. "Symmetry and Mirroring in The Shining." *Frameland*. Last modified 2017. Accessed January 10, 2019. http://frame.land/symmetry-and-mirroring-in-the-shining/

Eggertsen, Chris. "New Orleans Ultimate Horror Movie Filming Locations Map." *Curbed New Orleans*. Last modified July 25, 2018. Accessed February 3, 2019. https://nola.curbed.com/maps/american-horror-story-originals-filming-locations

Hardy, Rob. "Startling Symmetry in the First and Final Frames of Famous Horror Films." *No Film School*. Last modified October 29, 2015. Accessed January 9, 2019. https://nofilmschool.com/2015/10/first-and-final-frames-horror-edition

Marshall, Howard Wright. "Vernacular Architecture in Rural and Small Towns." *Missouri Folklore Society*. Copyright 1994, Curators of the University of Missouri. Accessed February 1, 2019. http://missourifolkloresociety.truman.edu/marshall.html

"Symmetry in Architecture." *Study*. Accessed January 23, 2019. https://study.com/academy/lesson/symmetry-in-architecture.html

"Songs of Innocence and Experience: The Tyger by William Blake." *Spark Notes*. Accessed January 17, 2019. https://www.sparknotes.com/poetry/blake/section6/

Wentworth, Bruce. "Historic Styles: Federal / Adams (1780-1840)." *Wentworth Studio*. Accessed January 22, 2019. https://www.wentworthstudio.com/historic-styles/federal/

Wentworth, Bruce. "Federal." *Ask the Architect*. Accessed January 22, 2019. http://www.askthearchitect.org/architectural-styles/federal-style-architecture

Chapter 8:
Shotgun House

"History of the Shotgun House." *Cajun Grocer*. Last modified May 5, 2017. Accessed March 3, 2019. https://www.cajungrocer.com/blog/history-shotgun-house

Campanella, Richard. "Shotgun Geography: The History Behind the Famous New Orleans Elongated House." *NOLA*. Last modified February 12, 2014. Accessed March 7, 2019. https://www.nola.com/homegarden/index.ssf/2014/02/shotgun_geography_new_orleans.html

Cangelosi Jr., Robert. "Did a Property Tax on Street Frontage Bring About the Shotgun House? New Orleans: Truth vs. Tales." *Preservation Resource Center of New Orleans*. Last modified June 29, 2018. Accessed April 2, 2019. https://prcno.org/property-tax-street-frontage-lead-shotgun-houses-built-new-orleans-truths-vs-tales/

City of New Orleans. *City Planning Commission*. New Orleans: The City of New Orleans, 2019. Accessed February 17, 2019. https://nola.gov/city-planning/master-plan/

City of New Orleans. *City of New Orleans Property Viewer*. New Orleans: The City of New Orleans, 2019. Accessed February 17, 2019. http://property.nola.gov/

"Villa Le Lac." *Collection Morel*. Last modified 2010. Accessed March 2, 2019. http://villa-morel.com/villa-le-lac/

"Shotgun Houses." *Data Research Center*. Last modified 2019. Accessed March 8, 2019. http://www.datacenterresearch.org/pre-katrina/tertiary/shotgun.html

"Louisville Shotguns 1." *Daytonology*. Last modified December 7, 2011. Accessed March 5, 2019. http://daytonology.blogspot.com/2007/12/louisville-shotguns-i-28-year-old-book.html

Gay, Patricia. "The Shotgun House: New Orleans' Ubiquitous Building Type." *Youtube*. Video file posted February 2, 2016. Accessed March 29, 2019. https://www.youtube.com/watch?v=YM2QxwB8FGA

Linehard, John. "Shotgun Homes and Porches, No. 820." *Engines of Our Ingenuity.* Last modified 1997. Accessed March 1, 2019. http://www.uh.edu/engines/epi820.htm

Chapter 9:
Row House

Bernardy, Sebastian and Madaus, Vincent Meyer. "Typecast: Front of House." *Urban Omnibus.* Last modified May 17, 2017. Accessed February 9, 2019. https://urbanomnibus.net/2017/05/front-of-house/

Byrnes, Mark. "Farewell Formstone: Requiem for a Baltimore Building Material?" *CityLab.* Last modified December 14, 2012. Accessed February 10, 2019. https://www.citylab.com/design/2012/12/farewell-formstone-requiem-baltimore-building-material/4162/

City of Philadelphia. *City of Philadelphia Atlas.* Philadelphia: The City of Philadelphia, 2019. Accessed February 8, 2019. https://atlas.phila.gov/#/2413%20SPRUCE%20ST/deeds

Code of District of Columbia. *Party Walls.* District of Columbia: D.C. Law Library. Last modified April 5, 2019. Accessed February 10, 2019. https://code.dccouncil.us/dc/council/code/sections/1-1325.html

Code of District of Columbia. *Party Walls.* District of Columbia: D.C. Law Library. Last modified April 5, 2019. Accessed February 10, 2019. https://code.dccouncil.us/dc/council/code/sections/1-1326.html

Design Advocacy Group. "The Housing Challenge." *The Healthy Row House Project.* Accessed February 9, 2019. http://healthyrowhouse.org/
Schmidt, Emily. "Typecast: The Row House." *Urban Omnibus.* Last modified April 13, 2016. Accessed February 9, 2019. https://urbanomnibus.net/2016/04/201604typecast-the-row-house/

Reilly, Pamela. "Rethinking the Row House." *Pennsylvania Historic Preservation.* Last modified 2017. Accessed February 11, 2019. https://pahistoricpreservation.com/rethinking-the-row-house/amp/

"The Philadelphia Row House: America's First Row House." *Row House Living.* Last modified February 4, 2009. Accessed February 10, 2019. https://row-house-living.com/2009/02/04/the-philadelphia-row-house-americas-first-row-house/

Stephenson, Rob. "Commissions: At Face Value." *Rob Stephenson.* Accessed February 10, 2019. http://www.robstephenson.com/

Stephenson, Rob. "Typecast: At Face Value." *Urban Omnibus.* Last modified February 1, 2017. Accessed February 10, 2019. https://urbanomnibus.net/2017/02/at-face-value/

University of Pennsylvania. "PennDesign Archives." *University of Pennsylvania Archives.* Accessed February 5, 2019. https://www.design.upenn.edu/architectural-archives

Chapter 10:
Mixed Use

Brooklyn Public Library. "Williamsburg." *Our Brooklyn.* Last modified 2005. Accessed January 3, 2019. https://www.bklynlibrary.org/ourbrooklyn/williamsburg/

Crunkleton Commercial Real Estate. "If Someone Says 'Live, Work, Play,' Just One More Time." *The History of Mixed-Use Developments.* Last modified July 14, 2015. Accessed December 28, 2018. https://crunkletonblog.wordpress.com/tag/the-history-of-mixed-use-developments/

Dunlap, David. "Zoning Arrive 100 Years Ago: It Changed New York Forever." *New York Times.* Last modified July 25, 2016. Accessed, January 26, 2019. https://www.nytimes.com/2016/07/26/nyregion/new-yorks-first-zoning-resolution-which-brought-order-to-a-chaotic-building-boom-turns-100.html

Erickson, Amanda. "The Birth of Zoning Codes: A History." *CityLab.* Last modified June 19, 2012. Accessed January 21, 2019. https://www.citylab.com/equity/2012/06/birth-zoning-codes-history/2275/